$15⁰⁰

GAY MEN'S FRIENDSHIPS

D1564994

WORLDS Of DESIRE
THE CHICAGO SERIES ON SEXUALITY, GENDER, AND CULTURE
A Series Edited by Gilbert Herdt

GAY MEN'S FRIENDSHIPS

....

INVINCIBLE COMMUNITIES

....

PETER M. NARDI

The University of Chicago Press
Chicago and London

PETER M. NARDI is professor of sociology at Pitzer College of the Claremont Colleges. He is coeditor of *Social Perspectives in Lesbian and Gay Studies: A Reader, In Changing Times: Gay Men and Lesbians Encounter HIV/AIDS,* and *Growing Up before Stonewall: Life Stories of Some Gay Men* and editor of *Men's Friendships.* He is also special features coeditor of *Sexualities* and a member of the editorial boards of five other academic journals.

The University of Chicago Press, Chicago 60637
The University of Chicago Press, Ltd., London
© 1999 by The University of Chicago
All rights reserved. Published 1999
08 07 06 05 04 03 02 01 00 99   1 2 3 4 5

ISBN: 0-226-56843-1 (cloth)
ISBN: 0-226-56849-0 (paper)

Library of Congress Cataloging-in-Publication Data

Nardi, Peter M.
    Gay men's friendships : invincible communities / Peter M. Nardi.
        p.   cm. — (Worlds of desire)
    Includes bibliographical references and index.
    ISBN 0-226-56843-1 (cloth: alk. paper). — ISBN 0-226-56849-0
(pbk. : alk. paper)
    1. Gay men—Social networks—United States.   2. Gay men—United
States—Social conditions.   3. Gay men—United States—Psychology.
4. Male friendship—United States.   I. Title.
II. Series.
HQ76.2.U5N37   1999
302.3'4'086642—DC21   98-49657
                                                                        CIP

I hear it was charged against me that I sought to destroy insti-
    tutions;
But really I am neither for nor against institutions;
(What indeed have I in common with them?—Or what with
    the destruction of them?)
Only I will establish in the Mannahatta, and in every city of
    These states, inland and seaboard,
And in the fields and woods, and above every keel, little or
    large, that dents the water,
Without edifices, or rules, or trustees, or any argument,
The institution of the dear love of comrades.

— *Walt Whitman, 1860*

Contents

Acknowledgments

This book would not have come into being without the explicit contributions of friends, although they are not, of course, responsible for how I may have reworked their suggestions and advice:

Drury Sherrod, whose research on men's friendships grabbed my attention many years ago, collaborated with me in developing the questionnaire, collecting the survey data used in this book, and writing up the results in an earlier publication. His ideas, influence, and friendship have helped immensely in my own work. If his career had not taken a different turn, this book would rightfully be coauthored with him.

Barry Adam, Allan Bérubé, Ralph Bolton, John D'Emilio, Barry Glassner, Michael Messner, Stephen Murray, Ken Plummer, and Wayne Wooden talked to me about the manuscript, read drafts, and offered encouragement. Their involvement helped enormously. As friends and colleagues they contribute to and support my life and work in many ways.

My terrific editors Matthew Howard, who initiated the idea of my doing a book on gay men's friendships, and Doug Mitchell, who gracefully steered the project through all its channels, persuaded me—over food and wine at Patina in Los Angeles and at many other wonderful dinners, through conversations, and via E-mails—that I was the one to do it. I cannot thank Matt and Doug enough; they have indeed become more than editors and have been welcomed enthusiastically into the web of my friendship network.

Ruth Barzel, Steven Cain, Erik Carlson, Charles Kern, Michael McLeod, and Waugh (Wally) Smith made various important contributions (including coding data, offering editing suggestions, and finding respondents). Without them, and without the many anonymous others in the Los Angeles area gay/lesbian organizations who made their meetings and members available for the study and allowed me to present my preliminary ideas at their events, this project could not have been undertaken.

Funding for various stages of this study came from the John Randolph Haynes and Dora Haynes Foundation, the Pitzer College Faculty Research Awards Committee, and, most significantly, the Rockefeller Foundation, which provided me in November 1997 with an incredible month of uninterrupted time, experiences, conversation, food, and new friends at its conference and study center in Bellagio, Italy.

I cannot overlook my life-sustaining network of friends who really made this all possible, even if they were not directly involved in reading the drafts and debating the rational side of our emotional friendships. In so many ways, this work exists because of them; their friendships have provided me with the experiences that form the ideas and subtext of this book. Thanks for being my support and my identity.

I also want to acknowledge my sister Donna and her family (Tom, Emily, and Maggie) who contribute in many other important ways to my identity and history, and my late parents, Jeanne M. and Peter J. Nardi, who taught my sister and me the value and importance of friendships. They regularly filled our house with their friends, who were always there to provide many happy times and social support.

While it would be risky to start listing all of my friends by name (out of fear of inadvertently leaving someone out), I do, however, want to single out my longest friendship, the one I share with John Bartolomeo. Our friendship began almost forty years ago in the Bronx, drifted away on a raft, was renewed in graduate school, and has been sustained by our weekly calls ever since. This book is about us, and about all our friends.

Maybe it's because I grew up in an Italian-American family in the Bronx, and extroversion was one of the requirements for membership, but I seem to know a lot of people. Many of them I would call friends, most are probably acquaintances, and some are part of my regular "family of friends." Or maybe it's because I'm gay, and we gay people have a different way of doing friendship, or so the story goes. Listen to what Dennis Altman, an Australian political scientist, reports about his visits to America in the late 1970s and early 1980s, and consider how some fifteen years later many of his observations about friendship continue to ring true:

> Both lack of marriage and exclusion from the heterosexual world of conventional families tend to make friendship all the more important for homosexuals; while sociologists in recent years have shown some interest in gay coupling, they have tended to completely miss the significance of friendship among both gay women and gay men. Over the years numbers of people have said to me that they place more importance on their friends than on their lovers, and what many gay lives miss in terms of permanent relationships is more than compensated for by friendship networks, which often become de facto families . . . . Former lovers often are drawn into such networks, so that many gays are surrounded by a rich network of friends (often originally sexual partners) and past and present lovers, which can be far more supportive than are most nuclear families.[1]

Although he does not pursue the topic explicitly in his book, Altman does capture the key ideas that are regularly invoked   1 today when gay people speak about friendship. Altman is also correct in stating that sociologists have generally ignored the subject; this too is still true today, not only of sociologists but also of many other behavioral scientists who study friendship and overlook the experiences of gays and lesbians.[2]

What follows, then, is partly an attempt to make sense of my own experiences with friends and partly an effort to bring the discussion of friendship and its meaning in gay men's lives to the sociological forefront. Doing these things reveals layers of conceptual problems. Since friendship is often an emotional process, the act of discussing and measuring it risks modifying what friendship is and thereby transforming it into a more rational process than it really is on a lived daily basis. But, as will be seen, it is reductionist to relegate friendship to the realm of the emotional and psychological. For friendship is also a social process, embedded in a society's institutions, cultural norms, and structural opportunities. It is a rational decision-making process and not solely an uncontrollable act or desire.

At the same time, given its elusive nature, friendship is a difficult concept to grasp. Our language conspires to make it hard to understand; the word "friend" is thrown around quite loosely and requires layers of explanation for coherent communication. Poets, novelists, musicians, filmmakers, and philosophers have been more successful in their creative works at signaling its depth and multiple meanings than have academics in our attempts to study it. But heroic poems, song lyrics, novels, and buddy movies tend to focus on the individual and the emotional. Maybe friendship is a topic better suited to those who deal in artistic and abstract images. Then again, its central role in the lives of gay men, gay communities, and social movements begs for a more rational and sociological understanding. I say this because I am not a poet; I am a sociologist who lives within networks of friends, trying to make logical sense of the emotional and political world around me.

My quotidian routine requires contact with a variety of people, including colleagues at the college, students in classes, neighbors on my city block, friends on the phone or over a meal, E-mail correspondents, a relative or two, strangers in shops and at the gym, gay strangers in city streets and cafés, many recognizable faces who often remain unknown. Clearly, a range of familiarity, along with a diversity of disclosing and sharing, exists among my network of daily interactions. Even so, for me, there is comfort in being among my gay and lesbian friends and even in being among the gay strangers in my neighborhood and on city streets. This comfort comes from more than just a psychological sense of who I am; to participate in spaces also occupied by others who have grown up with a stigmatized identity and who may have experienced—despite other significant differences—at least some similar forms of personal and social marginalization is a sociopolitical connection, perhaps one of brotherhood and sisterhood.

In my life friendships appear to take on a significance and power that they do not seem to do for most of my heterosexual male friends. This is not to say that these friends do not experience important and strong friendships. What is relevant is that it seems to me that my friendships are more central in my life, for my identity, and for my community membership, compared to heterosexual men's friendships as I see and read about them. And I am not the only one who believes this. Over and over again, I hear and continue to be told what Altman has expressed: a central narrative of gay men's lives is that of how important their friends are to them, how this "rich network of friends" is like a family, how sex has been a dimension of their earlier friendships with some of their friends, and how, for some, their friends mean more and last longer than do their romantic relationships.

This book is an exploration of that narrative, with its goal being to contribute to the understanding of the meanings gay men in the contemporary urban United States attach to their friendships, and to uncover the sociology of these interpersonal relationships. While looking at the psychological joys and sorrows of friendship development and maintenance I also want to look at its structure and its location in the organization of everyday life. What are the cultural constraints and options limiting gay men in American society—especially those that deal directly with hegemonic masculinity and heterosexuality—and how do these connect with friendship formation and maintenance? I want to understand how interpersonal friendships contribute to a political or civic friendship and to the emergence of social movements, gay identities, gay communities, and gay neighborhoods.

Aristotle, the Other Self, and Civic Friendship

The connections between interpersonal and civic friendship that I seek to understand can be traced to the writings of Aristotle, one of the key figures in the development of ideas in Western culture about friendship, and about men's friendship in particular. In the fourth century B.C.E. he presented his ideas on friendship in Book VIII and Book IX of *Nichomachean Ethics,* in which he distinguishes among three kinds of friendships: those based on what is good, those based on what is pleasant, and those based on what is useful. In useful friendships "the partners do not feel affection for one another per se but in terms of the good accruing to each from the other."[3] These friendships are easily dissolved, are impermanent, and are typical of the elderly and of young men in the prime of their lives. Pleasurable friendships similarly exist for the pleasure given, not necessarily for who the people are. These are friendships guided by emotion, and they often exist among young people: "They become friends quickly and just as quickly cease to be friends. For as another thing becomes pleasant, the friendship, too, changes, and the pleasure of a young man changes quickly."[4]

Friendships based on goodness, however, are the ideal, since "The perfect form of friendship is that between good men who are alike in excellence or virtue."[5] Good friends act toward their friends because of those friends' good qualities and virtues. The friendship is altruistic in that it advances the happiness of another, and this is an end in itself because "each partner receives in all matters what he gives the other, in the same or in a similar form."[6]

Aristotle's work on friendship has yielded numerous articles and books debating his ideas and how applicable they are today.

Some argue that there are "significant discrepancies between ancient and modern intuitions on friendship" yet agree that Aristotle's ideas on primary friendship form the foundation upon which many modern concepts stand.[7] Without getting into what could be a book in itself, I want to highlight two important elements of Aristotle's friendship ideas: the concept of the "other self" and that of "civic friendship." Of Aristotle's ideas, these relate most directly to some arguments I make throughout this book about gay men's friendship.

Other Selves

Virtuous or primary friends, for Aristotle, are "other selves" to each other: "all friendly feelings toward others are an extension of the friendly feelings a person has for himself."[8] Virtuous friendships benefit both the self and the good of another through the interpersonal aspects of their goals and values. These friendships are a "joint becoming, by the partners, of one another's selves."[9] Reason, emotion, and appetite must live in harmony within a person's life to justify a claim that he has a self. And achieving this moral goal of selfhood (virtuous rationality) makes possible these primary friendships.[10]

Therefore, when Aristotle writes that a good man "has the same attitude toward his friend as he does toward himself, for his friend really is another self,"[11] he is setting forth an idea that goes beyond egoism. Cicero, in his essay *On Friendship,* expresses the similar belief that "The man who keeps his eye on a true friend, keeps it, so to speak, on a model of himself." These beliefs could be enlisted to serve as a guide to understanding how the role of friendship contributes to a sense of self in terms of gay identity development and maintenance. As I show throughout the following chapters, for most gay men, friends are other selves with whom they can be truly themselves. It is through friends that gay men verify and expand upon their sense of self as gay; family members rarely provide this information or identity in the way family provides racial minorities, for example, with their identities as they grow up.

Civic Friendship

Friendship is not only important for identity development and maintenance; it also contributes to the strengthening of community and to subculture identity. If good friendship can serve as a way of linking two moral and virtuous selves, how might this translate into a form of political or civic friendship? Again, articles and book-length exegeses have been written on Aristotle's notion of civic friendship and what he means when he writes that "Friendship also seems to hold states together."[12] Rather than getting sidetracked by a lengthy discussion of this issue, I want to highlight just a few key points that are used in the book for a more detailed analysis of gay community. For Aristotle, when tyranny exists, there is the smallest amount of friendship: "Friendship is present to the extent that men share something in common, for that is also the extent to which they share a view of what is just. And the proverb 'friends hold in common what they have' is correct, for friendship consists in community."[13]

Philosopher Sibyl Schwarzenbach argues that a constant theme in Aristotle's works is that of how "in a just society citizens experience a form of friendship or *philia* for each other—they wish each other well for their own sake, do things for fellow citizens both individually and as a citizen body, and share in values, goals, and a sense of justice."[14] The good kind of political friendships are similar to virtuous personal friendships; that is, they are altruistic, as Paul Schollmeier has written, since "good citizens wish and do what is good for the sake of each other. These citizens would also be likely to reciprocate and to recognize their good wishes and actions, for they take turns at ruling, and they would recognize that they do."[15]

Friendship, thus, is the binding force of communities because "in contributing to the utmost actualization of individual citizens, primary friendship also generates and sustains the highest good of all, i.e., that of the city."[16] As scholars have interpreted Aristotle, political friendship of the good kind includes a polity of brotherhood, a shared agreement, a community's "scheme of cooperation."[17] In modern societies, sharing values of tolerance, being law-abiding, acknowledging principles of respect, discerning the rights and interests of each individual, and recognizing a value of caring, all coexist with a doctrine of individual rights that "might even be considered one of the highest expressions of political friendship ever."[18]

Aristotle's conceptions of civic friendship and virtuous friendship are linked by a shared notion of reproduction, an idea promoted by Schwarzenbach. She writes that "Philia is the legitimate self-related interest of reproduction or of bringing another into being."[19] Reproduction is a process that expresses all things' yearning to live eternally. In raising a child, one raises another self—a friend, in Aristotle's terms: "A friend is thus not numerically the same as me; he or she need not be my biological offspring, but a friend is, in an important sense, the moral continuance in existence of another like myself."[20] Gay men's development of friendships in contemporary society might be seen as a type of reproductive act through which they create others that are politically and socially like themselves.

Viewing gay men's friendship as mechanisms of social reproduction in which gay masculinities, gay identities, gay cultures, and gay communities get created, transformed, maintained, and passed on (and not just produced for consumption), is a central idea in this book. One of my respondents, Ed,[21] spoke about his much older close friend as a "role model, a mentor" and another respondent, Aaron, told of how his newly made friend introduced him around: "I was new in town . . . and he made a real effort to get me into his network of friends." I want to argue that for gay men friendship has the potential in this postmodern society of providing multiple narratives for the social reproduction—and not simply the social construction—of gay selves and of political communities in which hegemonic masculinity and gay masculinity blend to produce a new gendered order characterized by new relations of masculinities. Friendship is a personal process as well as a social one, and it's at this intersection, where self and community are reproduced among gay men, that the power of friendship can be palpably experienced. As philosopher John Cooper has written, "According to Aristotle we value, and are right to value, friendship so highly because it is only in and through intimate friendship that we can come to know ourselves and to regard our lives constantly worth living."[22]

Organization of the Book

The chapters that follow include overviews of the key research that has been done on friendship (in historical documents and in contemporary social sciences), summaries of the ways friendships are depicted in books and articles written about and by gay men and lesbians, and results from a questionnaire survey of 161 gay men and from interviews with 30 other gay men. Although data were collected from 122 lesbians, I have chosen to focus on gay men in order to raise specific questions about the ways masculinity is organized in today's society.[23]

In addition to considering the data collected through the interviews and questionnaires, I make an effort to include in the book many quotations from and summaries of other research, for several reasons. I want to embed the findings from my study in the context of work done on friendships and, in particular, on men's friendships. It is important for the reader to understand what other research has uncovered in order to assess the findings I present about gay men and their friendships. Without knowing how heterosexual men, for example, structure their interpersonal relationships with other men and women, it would be difficult to support some of the arguments I make about how gay men's friendships both contest and reproduce hegemonic masculinity. The studies dealing with friendship to which I refer are part of the narrative that contributes cultural myths and facts to what we know about men's friendships and that often influences how both gay and nongay men act as a result.

I want, also, to quote directly from works by gay and nongay writers who have spoken about gay men's friendships, usually from personal experiences rather than in response to survey research. What these writers say is part of the cultural narrative that shapes not only the way people view gay men but also the way gay men view themselves and their friendships. Although I was tempted to include fictional works, films, plays, songs, and poetry as part of this cultural narrative, I soon realized that to do so would mean writing another book. I hope someone else with the necessary skills and desire will extend this research in those directions. Throughout the chapters, then, I interweave data from the questionnaire, excerpts from the interview narratives, findings from academic research studies, and quotations from popular gay writings. I hope that, as a result of my doing this, the reader will get a fairly full picture of the meanings of friendship in the lives of some gay men today.

Since my objective is to provide a context for rather than a comprehensive summary of the major research that has been done on men's friendships—others have done the latter already, and their discoveries comprise book-length works[24]—in the first two chapters I set the stage by highlighting some of the major historical and contemporary findings. Chapter 1 makes a case for a study of gay men's friendships and for their importance in understanding the complexities of sexuality, gender, and identity. It considers the key points made by observers of gay lives and the limited research that has been done on the subject, and contextualizes these points by offering some historic examples of heroic friendships and men's friendships. The chapter highlights the central themes developed throughout the book, including the notion that gay men's friendships have the potential for challenging the dominant structures of masculinity while providing important sites for gay men's development, for the maintenance of personal identity, and for the reproduction of gay community and political identity.

Chapter 2 begins at the end of the nineteenth century, when a period of rising hegemonic masculinity emerged, just as concepts about homosexuality were becoming pathologized and heterosexual masculinity was becoming reified. It looks at how these changes created limits to the way men structured their friendships. The chapter briefly summarizes the contemporary behavioral sciences literature about men's friendships in the twentieth century, in Western culture and in other selected societies. The chapter sets the stage for the findings from my research on gay men's friendships today.

Arguably, two of the most frequently discussed topics related to friendship, and to gay men's friendships in particular, center around the role of friends as surrogate family members and around issues of sexual behavior and attraction. Before presenting specific details about the meaning and characteristics of gay men's friendships, I decided to jump right into the two controversial areas of family and sexuality. Chapter 3 discusses the prevalent "friends as family" metaphor and questions how widespread its use actually is among gay men. What does it really mean, and how do gay men employ it?

Chapter 4 explores the world of sex and friendship—a virtually unstudied area in friendship research, but one that is a central dynamic among men whose friends could also be their sexual and romantic partners. I develop a schematic map to guide us through the numerous variations in the relationship between sex and friendship that gay men describe in talking about their friendships with other men. Some men, I learned, adhere to firm rules of no sex with friends, whereas others talk about "fuck buddies"—acquaintances or casual friends whose main role is to provide sexual gratification. The map also sets out the ways gay men distinguish between those who are friends and those who are potential lovers.

After raising the issues of sex and friendship and friends as family, I describe in chapter 5 who gay men's friends are and where they meet. Although an overwhelming majority of gay men's best and closest friends are other gay men, many have women friends and straight male friends. Gay men construct a network of friendships—ranging from those with "fag hags" to those with college roommates—of varying degrees of intensity, but no matter the type of friendship, friends are often similar in terms of their values and their social status.

Many gay writers talk about how important friendships are to gays and lesbians. Chapter 6 presents the numerous ways that gay men talk about and define friendship—what it means to them and what its constitutive elements are. After looking at this topic I then turn to a discussion of the process of friendship—how friendships are formed and how they are maintained. In addition to talking about the research on the factors that facilitate the early stages of making friends, keeping a friendship going, and turning it into a closer and more committed friendship, I discuss how gay men do and talk friendship. It's in this chapter that the divergence from heterosexual masculinity becomes evident and the unique combination of hegemonic and gay masculinities is highlighted.

The last two chapters focus on the personal and social importance of friendship. Chapter 7 considers the role friendship plays in developing social support and in maintaining gay identity, and it discusses what happens when friends fail to provide support. Not all friendships work out, and while most just fade away, sometimes specific incidents and betrayals create tensions that can only be resolved by dissolving the friendship. Finally, in an attempt to develop a theoretical nexus between the psychological and the sociological, chapter 8 takes the discussion from the micro to the macro level, moving from an analysis of the benefits of social support and personal identity development to one of the political and social importance of gay men's friendships. Not only do friendships have the potential to unite and mobilize gay men into new social movements, but gay men's friendship might challenge the gender order of American society. By questioning how masculinity is constructed in our contemporary culture, gay men's friendships serve as a model for a newer, more integrative model of gay masculinity and heterosexual masculinity. The possible changes that can be effected by gay men's friendships illustrate the politics of friendship, the power of invincible communities of friends, and "the institution of the dear love of comrades."[25]

"FRIENDS TAKE YOU PLACES
YOU'VE NEVER BEEN"

Gay Men, New Modes of Relations,
and Heroic Friendships

The development toward which the problem of homosexuality tends is the
one of friendship. . . . But two men . . . face each other without terms or
convenient words, with nothing to assure them about the meaning of the
movement that carries them toward each other. They have to invent, from
A to Z, a relationship that is still formless, which is friendship.

— *Michel Foucault, "Friendship as a Way of Life," in* Ethics: Subjectivity and
Truth

Friendship networks are the avenues through which gay social
worlds are constructed, the sites upon which gay men's identities and communities are formed and where the quotidian dimensions of our lives are carried out. It is through the grounded
relationships with friends that the personal and the political, the
micro and the macro, the individual and the collective, all come
together. Friendship may be the central organizing element of
gay men's lives—the mechanism through which gay masculinities, gay identities, gay cultures, and gay neighborhoods get
created, transformed, maintained, and reproduced. Friendship
appears, as forcefully as any human behavior, at the intersection
of self and society where the individual and the community re-
side. There friendship raises salient questions—especially for
gay men—about how a culture organizes, contests, and reproduces sexuality, about concepts of family, and about the gender
order. Yet friendship among gay men is a poorly understood
relationship that has been studied very little and is not easily
explained.

Friendship is an ineffable concept that philosophers, writers, poets, and artists have nonetheless been attempting to describe for centuries. It has been called "the least contested, most enduring, and most satisfying of all close personal affiliations."[1] Friendship is a soulful experience, raised to the highest levels of affection and intimacy. In his essay *On Friendship* written during the first century B.C.E. Cicero says, "For the essence of friendship consists in the fact that many souls, so to speak, become one," and in the sixteenth century Michel de Montaigne declared: "In the friendship I speak of, our souls mingle and blend with each other so completely that they efface the seam that joined them, and cannot find it again."[2]

From Aristotle's important writings in the fourth century B.C.E. on friendship in the *Nicomachean Ethics,* to the poems from ninth-century China (like those of Po Chu-I, who told of his dream about briefly visiting an old friend who "seemed to be regretting that joy will not stay; / That our souls had met only for a little while, / To part again with hardly time for greeting"), to descriptions of friendship in the *Mahabharata* that portray Krisna and Arjuna's friendship as "one self that has been made twofold,"[3] the intensity of and depth of feeling about a best friendship have historically been expressed in many cultures in terms of a mingling and blending of essences between two people. Such a friendship is often depicted as more important than love, as is illustrated by sociologist Georg Simmel's belief when he writes that friendship may be "more apt than love to connect a whole person with another person in its entirety; it may melt reserves more easily than love does."[4] Maybe Cole Porter captures it the most succinctly in his lyric, written in 1939: "It's friendship, friendship, / Just a perfect blendship."

Not all friendships, however, reflect this intense fusing of souls. Some friends are less intimately involved with our lives; they float past, float on, sometimes float back again, to paraphrase the novelist John Barth.[5] Some are profoundly close, while others remain important for only portions of our lives. And a few are mere acquaintances whose friendship lasts the duration of the work day and whose souls never quite blend with our own. Still, we call them all "friends." Our language is limited in the ways it can describe the types of friendships we have: we use the word "friend" much too loosely, relying on it to describe everyone from an acquaintance to a romantic partner. There's an adjectival obligation when talking about friendship and the multiple circles of people we encounter throughout our lives; when used alone, the word "friend" doesn't tell us enough.

Consider the words of Eugene[6], a thirty-one-year-old respondent who said that "friendship is a word which I have to apply adjectives to make its meaning clear—'he's my best friend' as opposed to a 'close friend' or an 'occasional friend' or a 'convenient, fair-weather, or opportunistic friend.'" Or, to put it much more elaborately and rationally, here are the five types of friendship Kevin described when I asked him what friendship meant to him:

> Casual friendships are those built on the common enjoyment of similar recreational experiences. . . . Situational friendships are those built on a substantial accumulation of shared good experiences . . . such as working together, rooming together. . . . Emotional friendships [involve] shared confidences and advice, particularly in matters of the heart. . . . Enterprise friendships build on common participation in some project of significant scope and importance, such as community, religious, or charitable work. Hard work together in pursuit of a common dream can forge some of the strongest bonds of friendship. Inspirational friendships entail an exchange of new ideas, new experiences, and new perspectives which are continually broadening. These friends take you places you've never been nor ever thought you wanted to go, and make you love it.

But such attempts to quantify, measure, assess, categorize, rationalize, or simply speak of friendship ironically contradict its very appeal—that it is an emotional connection with another person and not something to talk about out loud. As Dan said to me: "Your questions are disturbing. I hadn't thought of these things. . . . In some way I've just taken my friendships for granted and haven't analyzed them. It even bothers me a little to think of them in terms of evaluating them." Perhaps friendship is really the thing that dares not speak its name or that, at least, should be left to the aesthetic talents of poets, songwriters, filmmakers, and novelists who can create literary and emotional images of friendship more elegantly than is possible when describing it scientifically.

Jim's words, on the other hand, forcefully challenge us to assess how important friendships are in gay men's lives and to observe how powerfully friends connect and socialize gay men to core concepts of identity, community, and political activism. "Friends reinforce identity," he says. "It's a huge thrill the first time you're in a gay crowd, so it becomes meaningful to be with gay friends. Because we are oppressed, it's important to have networks of friends."

Research on Gay Men's Friendships

Despite the intensity with which they discuss friends, gay men remain overlooked in most research on friendship, even though sexual orientation may illustrate important variations within gender and may uncover the ways men (and women) differ in terms of how they enact friendship in everyday life. In Beverley Fehr's otherwise extensive book reviewing mostly psychological studies on friendship, not one mention is made of gay men's or lesbians' friendships.[7] Lillian Rubin's important book on friendship includes a little on the role sexual orientation plays in friendship, but the focus is more on homophobia in heterosexual men and on the barriers to their achievement of intimate friendship that it creates.[8]

If gay men should be included in a study, they are typically discussed in terms of their friendships with straight women. Cross-sex friendships between gay men and heterosexual women "are the friendships across the gender line that seem to afford the greatest equality and the fewest tensions."[9] While this may be so, data are rarely presented, and gay men's friendships with other gay men—the relationship that is more likely to exist in contemporary gay lives and that is more likely to demonstrate more potential equality—is seldom discussed. Letty Cottin Pogrebin's popular book on friendship similarly discusses mainly gays' and lesbians' friendships with heterosexuals, not gay-gay friendships, thereby perpetuating an isolated view of gay people as unconnected to larger communities of other gays.[10] This dimension—the fascination with which no doubt arises in part out of a stereotypical association made between being a gay man and femininity—surpasses any similar discussions of gay men's friendships with each other.[11]

We know from anecdotal findings, literature, plays, movies, and personal narratives that gay men consider their friendships unique, special, and necessary for survival. Some have argued that their friendships may be even more intense than heterosexuals' friendships, especially when the affection and mutual support that come from friendship "enables the cultural survival of people who deviate from social norms and who suffer hostility and ostracism from others."[12] Within the material and symbolic cultures of gay communities, there is demonstrably an emphasis on the relationship between friendship and the values and norms of gay life. Gay writers are particularly explicit in their conceptualization of gay men's friendships as integral to a feeling of community. For example, Ethan Mordden writes, "What unites us, all of us, surely, is brotherhood, a sense that our friendships are historic, designed to hold Stonewall together. . . . It is friendship that sustained us, supported our survival."[13]

During the 1970s attention to the connection between gay community and friendship increased. Edmund White, in his description of his tour of America, says this about New York's gay life: "Its greatest offering to gays is friendship. . . . [F]or many people it has taken the place of love. Sex is casual, romance short-lived; the real continuity in many people's lives comes from their friends. Some advocates of friendship would argue that to receive sustenance from a dozen men and women is better than to pair off with just one other person, from whom one expects too much and receives too little."[14] White also argues that the division among sex, romance, and friendship is not unlike the Freudian trilogy in which sex is the id, ego the friendship, and romance the superego. And by separating them rather than conflating them into marriage, as heterosexuals do, "passionate, durable friendships" are promoted.[15] This duality of emotion and strength, feminine and masculine, feelings and solidity, is at the core of what I want to argue is a uniqueness about gay men's friendships. In their enactment, gay friendships both contest and reproduce the elements of hegemonic masculinity and exhibit dimensions of expressiveness and instrumentality, of passion and durability.

Dennis Altman was also traversing America in the late 1970s and, as I mention in the introduction, he similarly extols the saliency of friendship for gay men as "de facto families . . . which can be far more supportive than are most nuclear families."[16] These images—especially ones of friends as family—have pretty much set the standard for most discussions on gay friendship, even in the academic literature.[17] Based on data collected in 1970 Alan Bell and Martin Weinberg conclude that gay men's friendship cliques "often took the place of the extended family, particularly for those whose homosexuality had brought about alienation or estrangement from their own families. . . . In the cliques of longer standing and larger membership, different individuals tended to take on roles analogous to those of different family members."[18]

Another study conducted in the late 1960s by Martin Weinberg and Colin Williams demonstrates the valuable socialization process of friends, especially for the predominantly urban white sample of men, most of whom were not openly gay during that era.[19] Those with low social involvement with gay friends reported less self-acceptance and more depression, guilt, loneliness, anxiety, and shame about their homosexuality. Those who were most socially involved with other homosexuals learned to deal with the heterosexual world with "a more subtle, less generalized, and more realistic appreciation of the situation" while also coming into contact with homosexual role models who successfully managed their publicly perceived deviant identity and provided a retreat from oppression.[20]

On the other hand, a study that questions the commitment of friends is Carol Warren's ethnography of a gay community in southern California in the early 1970s. One of her respondents said his friendships with gay men were "very instantaneous" but not as lasting as the ones with heterosexual friends because "gay people notoriously move around a lot so that you know people for brief periods of time. . . . [T]hey're much more chummy about their relationships with each other. . . . [W]hen they run into each other if they haven't seen each other for a while you'd think they were running into their long-lost best friend in the world."[21] Friendships are characterized by a superficial intimacy, Warren suggests; they are easily made and easily ended: "When they do move, [gay men] can easily meet and become integrated into a ready-made circle of gays, in a way the nonstigmatized may not, and thus not depend for friendship or fun on 'keeping up with' old friends."[22]

Other studies from the post-Stonewall years, however, demonstrate that friendships of varying degrees of intensity play an important role in the development and maintenance of gay identity and community, a topic I return to in the last chapters. Based on data collected in 1978 from 112 white gay men over the age of forty, Raymond Berger finds that those who had more gay friends "showed higher levels of self-acceptance, lower levels of depression, greater life satisfaction, less anxiety about their homosexuality, and less fear of aging and death."[23] He also concludes that, for older gay men, friendships are more important to psychological adjustment than is participation in gay organizations.

In his research on the so-called "gay clone" of the late 1970s in New York, Martin Levine reported that friendship cliques socialized new members by providing emotional support, economic cooperation in the form of loans and job leads, social control, and sexual regulation.[24] Through the use of approval and praise, compliance was rewarded; criticism and "dishing" punished transgressions of the clique's norms, one of which was not to have sex with other clique members. Cliques themselves were often a part of "crowds" that were larger social groupings in which people knew men in other cliques, sometimes sexually, usually just by sight through attendance at the same "circuit" of gathering places (baths, bars, gyms, restaurants, etc.). Their crowd, with the exception of their particular clique, was a source of "tricks," fuck buddies, and casual acquaintances.

Then the appearance of AIDS and the burdens imposed by continuous caregiving, illness, and the subsequent deaths within the clone circles created emotional stresses and pressures resulting in the dissolution of many friendship groups.[25] Some of these men then joined other circles that were organized around AIDS, including HIV-positive support groups, volunteer committees, and activist organizations. Such organized groups typically became a source of friendship for many gay men in the larger urban areas.[26]

Contemporary research on gay men reinforces many of these earlier findings and the role of friendship in identity development. Gilbert Herdt and Andrew Boxer's study of adolescents in a Chicago social support services center in the early 1990s found that "Friendship contexts were the most common relational setting for the first same-sex relationship following puberty."[27] Seventy-three percent of the boys reported that their first sexual partner was a friend or peer (no more than three years older or younger than they were). Also, two-thirds of the boys in the study came out first to a friend who was usually of the same age and gender. Their best friends typically came from the youth group. Outside the group, the young people—especially the youth of color, who felt the pressure of ethnic identity and traditions—were much more reluctant to reveal their sexual orientation.[28]

In discussing her interviews with San Francisco Bay Area gay men and lesbians, anthropologist Kath Weston notes that "People from diverse backgrounds depicted themselves as the beneficiaries of better friendships than heterosexuals, or made a case for the greater significance and respect they believed gay people accord to friendship."[29] While some of this may be due to "self-congratulation," Weston observes that gay and lesbian people see kinship as an extension of friendship rather than as an exclusive, sometimes antagonistic, relationship, as heterosexuals were thought by the respondents to view it.[30]

One explanation that might account for urban gay men's friendship being intense is the historical migration of single men to large cities in response to changing work arrangements.[31] For example, in the early part of the twentieth century, the large presence of single men in New York, especially in the absence of many women who remained at home until the men had earned money, increased the possibility of same-sex sexual relations occurring and created groups of men who shared similar experiences.[32] More recently, the migration of many gay men to large cities in the 1970s once again set up the conditions of density and critical mass necessary for the emergence of gay groups, gay identity, and gay community.[33] Of course, gay men in rural and suburban areas were also able to develop networks of friends, but theirs took on different components because of the absence of institutional structures typically found in larger urban centers and because it was necessary to depend more on nongay neighbors and kin.[34]

Urban arrangements typically lead to specific structural conditions conducive to a particular style of friendship formation, especially if migration away from consanguine family has occurred. According to research conducted in the late 1970s by Claude Fischer on city life, urbanism slightly increases the number of friends one has; for those "with more time, mobility, and resources, urbanism more clearly promoted friendships" whereas "[k]in in the vicinity apparently limit individuals' opportunities—or needs—to have nonkin ties."[35] Among the people he surveyed, those with many friends tended to be young, educated, affluent, never married, childless, white, and without many relatives in the area, and the friends were more likely than were coworkers and kin to be similar to one another, to spend free time together, and to feel close to one another.[36] These findings line up remarkably well with descriptions and findings I will report about gay men and their friends.

Traditional networks are typically composed of relatives, neighbors, and members of religious organizations, while modern networks are formed with coworkers, members of secular organizations, and acquaintances. In short, as urbanism increases, fewer traditional relations are maintained, and people become more willing to label others, including doctors, friends of friends, schoolmates, and ex-neighbors, more freely as friends.[37] Because there are concentrations of people who are similar (a result perhaps of self-selection, since some move to the city to seek particular social worlds), urbanism tends to promote friendships and other relations at the expense of the more traditional networks. And, contrary to popular representa-

tions, city dwellers' relations are "at least as involving and intimate, if not more so, than small-town residents' relations with
theirs."[38]

Hence, the combined power of urban dwelling (most of the
gay men in my study resided in cities) and self-selection to seek
like-minded others may result in an increased intensity sur-
rounding the meaning of friendship in gay men's lives. If kin
are far away, and if ties with work and (nongay) neighborhood
are weaker, it is reasonable to hypothesize that urban gay men
have a stronger commitment to networks of friends than heterosexual men might have, resulting in a difference in the ways gay
men organize, maintain, and conceptualize friendships.

New Modes of Relations

In a series of interviews published in the early 1980s in several
gay publications, Michel Foucault begins to articulate ideas
about gay men's friendships. Foucault argues that what most
disturbs people about gays is the potential to "develop relationships that are intense and satisfying even though they do not at
all conform to the ideas of relationship held by others. It is the
prospect that gays will create as yet unforeseen kinds of relationships that many people cannot tolerate."[39] He goes on to discuss
the intense connection between men in such institutions as the
military, and how gay men can learn new lifestyles to express
their feelings for each other in ways that do not resemble those
that have existed in these institutions.

By developing a culture that encourages pleasure in interpersonal relationships, gays acknowledge that "with our desires,
through our desires, go new forms of relationships, new forms
of love, new forms of creation."[40] And for Foucault, friendship
is the relationship that needs development, not the normaliza-
tion of homosexuality. He believed that gay rights should go
beyond arguing about individual identity and should begin to
invent new modes of relationship, new modes of being together,
and that they should create new relational possibilities: "try to
imagine and create a new relational right that permits all possible types of relations to exist and not be prevented, blocked, or

annulled by impoverished relational institutions."[41] This would include developing a "system of obligations, tasks, reciprocal duties . . . a system of supple and relatively codified relations" that support long-term and stable relations, just like (but different from) the system that supported the relations of friendship in Hellenistic and Roman worlds.[42]

Foucault argues that the history of friendship is a "very, very important" subject, since the classical friendship was "a very important kind of social relation: a social relation within which people had a certain freedom, certain kind of choice (limited of course), as well as very intense emotional relations."[43] Up until the sixteenth and seventeenth centuries friendship was not seen as dangerous, Foucault says. Then many institutions (such as the military, schools, and universities) started to minimize and control affectional relations between males. By the eighteenth century sex between men became problematized, since "friendship had disappeared. As long as friendship was something important, was socially accepted, nobody realized men had sex together. . . . [T]he disappearance of friendship as a social relation and the declaration of homosexuality as a social/political/medical problem are the same process."[44]

How gay men develop new modes of relations through their friendships is one of the underlying themes of this book. Gay men's friendships, in various forms and among diverse gay men, both replicate the way men in American society are expected to act toward other men, and contest the gendered norms of masculine relations. In taking part in such friendships, and especially in incorporating the intensity and pleasures of sexuality into these friendships, gay men create and reproduce relationships of a different order and with the potential for developing political communities of identity.

Men's Heroic and Romantic Friendships

Although Foucault's provocative ideas have yet to be researched in a comprehensive history of men's friendship, there is some evidence supporting his arguments about the connection between the emergence of homosexuality as a social issue and the changes in the way men relate to one another in friendship. For a good deal of premodern society, men's friendships were a mode of relations that differed from contemporary friendships; they were intense, erotic, romantic, chivalric, and sometimes sexual. Consider some of the earliest literature on men's heroic friendships in Western culture, which can provide some context for understanding the power of contemporary gay men's friendships (without implying in any way that these classic friendships were equivalent to modern concepts of homosexuality).

Loyalty, bravery, duty, heroism, and intimacy characterized many premodern images of friendship, as the following selected examples from classical Greece, the Middle Ages and the Renaissance, and the nineteenth century, illustrate.[45] There is no more perfect depiction of heroic loyal friendship than that of Achilleus and Patroklos from Homer's *The Iliad*. Upon hearing about Patroklos' death, Achilleus pours black ashes over his head and face, tears at his hair, and sighs heavily. He laments that recent accomplishments bring little pleasure, "since my dear companion has perished, Patroklos, whom I loved beyond all other companions, as well as my own life."[46] Similarly, in chapter 1, verse 26 of the book of 2 Samuel from the Old Testament, David describes his profound friendship with Jonathan as "exceedingly beautiful and amiable to me above the love of women."

These two classic stories of male friendship, along with the Babylonian or Assyrian epic of Gilgamesh and Enkidu, are described by David Halperin as examples of heroic friendships—friendships that only males can have and that occur only in couples relatively isolated from a third person, another couple, or women.[47] The friendships have an "outward focus" within a political or military public space to accomplish some social action. However, these friendships exhibit "a structural asymmetry"; they are hierarchical—"the hero with his side-kick, his faithful retainer, his pal"—and not an egalitarian relationship.[48]

Perhaps these heroic friendships are indeed a good model for one type of erotic male friendship that was also prominent in the late nineteenth century and that exists in various forms today. Not all friendships are egalitarian, despite Aristotle's emphasis on equality as the defining element of friendship and the admonition of Confucius to "have no friends not equal to yourself."[49] Some gay men's friendships, while reciprocal, are between people who are not exactly similar or who engage the world in different ways; they demonstrate "a structural asymmetry." Fred, one of my respondents, illustrated this eloquently: "My closest friends have been people who feel the world and experience it as I do, who can at least understand how and why I react to it as I do, but who perceive and interpret it somewhat differently, who grab it by different handles and can explain it to me in terms that heighten my enjoyment and understanding of it and help to reconcile me to parts that I find disturbing or puzzling."

Friendships in the classic narratives also revolve around elements of sexuality and family that today are central to our understanding of modern gay men's friendships. According to Halperin, the storytellers appropriate sexual relations and kinship relations when defining heroic friendships in order to make them into significant paradigmatic images of human solidarity. But in privileging sexual and familial relations as the epitome of importance, they simultaneously imbue friendship with a salience not previously present: "They invoke kinship and conjugality, in other words, only to displace them, to reduce them to mere *images* of friendship."[50]

This narrative tradition of heroic buddies introduces us, then, to an alternative interpretation of classic male friendship, one that depends more on the asymmetrical but reciprocal nature of their kinship-like and conjugal-like relationship, rather than one that views the eroticism of these male couples in the context of the sexual categories developed in later ages. Whether the erotic and romantic dimensions of traditional male heroic friendships were sexually consummated or not has been debated for centuries. Certainly this is a trope of modern writings about ancient friendships that suggests more about today's evolving sexual and relationship taxonomies than it does about the historic societies that produced these stories. Using such couples as Achilleus and Patroklos or Jonathan and David as paradigmatic models of gay male romantic/sexual couples probably says more about contemporary categories of relationships than it does about the way friendships were likely constructed in classic ages.

Stories of heroic male friendships generate debates about how men's subjectivity concerning their interpersonal relationships has been constructed over time. This subjectivity may be as interesting as any objective analysis of such relationships would be. What it tells us is that uncovering the meanings of people's narratives concerning their friendships and sexual relationships is not a simple task of description. A multiplicity of meanings and subjective identities are confronting complex social structural arrangements in the reproduction of relationships that give self a significance and coherence.

These heroic friendships provoked an intensity of intimacy between men that often resulted in a high degree of emotional overlap with love relationships, as historian John Boswell's work on same-sex unions in Europe during the Middle Ages suggests. He writes, " 'Just friends' would have been a paradox to Aristotle or Cicero: no relationship was more emotional, more intimate, and more intense than friendship. . . . Friendship was also passionate and indissoluble."[51] Because friendships and romantic relationships shared so many similar characteristics, it has, however, been very difficult to clarify exactly what the ceremonies Boswell uncovered in his research were. He discovered at least eight versions of a ceremony of union between two people of the same sex from before the twelfth century and "a virtual explosion of copies of the ceremony, with at least seventeen surviving" from the twelfth century.[52] Few were found from later centuries, but because of a resurgence of such ceremonies in the fifteenth and sixteenth centuries, many others were identified.

From the time Boswell's book was published in 1994, debates have proliferated about whether these ceremonies were a same-sex version of a heterosexual marriage ceremony or whether they simply represented a commitment between "soul mates" "to become brothers"(as Boswell translates it), that is, an agreement between friends.[53] The kinds of intimate friendships men experienced with each other (typically in pairs rather than in networks of acquaintances) took on many of the trappings of heterosexual romantic relationships.

What role sexuality played in these heroic friendships is, as mentioned above, difficult to determine, especially since such descriptions were rarely written down. However, in a revealing analysis of court records in late medieval Florence, Michael Rocke concludes that "homosexual relations were part of the experience of many, if not most, males, to varying degrees" and that sodomy was "a dynamic factor in male social inter-action and cohesiveness."[54] Many networks of male friends and acquaintances in neighborhoods and workplaces were united through erotic ties to boys. In fifteenth-century Florence same-sex activity was so extensive that the word *florenzen,* meaning "to sodomize," entered the German language, and a sodomite was a *Florenzer.* The collective character of homosexual activity "provided crucial sources of complicity, comradeship, and soli-darity" while also validating masculinity and solidifying friend-ships.[55]

This is not meant to suggest that underlying all the romantic and heroic friendships of the past was a fulfilled sexual desire. Erotic attachments were not always consummated nor do they necessarily fit the categories of sexual and social relationships that have been established in modern times to describe such relationships. But in Renaissance Florence, as Rocke concludes, "Sodomy was intimately connected to the intense bonding and camaraderie so characteristic of male sociability in this culture. The links between homosexual activity and broader male social relations were so dense and intertwined that there was no truly autonomous and distinctive 'sodomitical subculture,' much less one based on a modern sense of essential diversity or 'devi-ance.'"[56]

Nineteenth-century writings from the United States also offer evidence of the dominance of intimate and romanti-cized male friendships.[57] Other than familial ties, Jonathan Ned Katz writes, "'friendship' has been the only legitimate model for same-sex intimacies. . . . At the turn of the century, the European literature on same-sex 'friendship' verged on the explicitly homosexual."[58] Katz says that such works as Edward

Carpenter's 1902 book *Ioläus: An Anthology of Friendship* contains historical documents on same-sex intimacy; Henry Clay Trumbull's 1892 *Friendship the Master-Passion or The Nature and History of Friendship, and Its Place as a Force in the World* focuses on same-sex relationships in the Bible, in ancient Greece, and among Native American Indians; and Elisàr von Kupffer's 1900 German anthology *Chivalric Affection and Comrade Love in World Literature* presents homosexual literature that many saw as an important contribution to a rising German gay liberation movement.[59] In fact, the German word for friend, *Freund,* often referred to a lover and *Freundschaft* to an "erotic-affectional relation, either hetero- or homosexual."[60]

But in many of the writings of this period, passages about friends and friendship replace explicit descriptions of same-sex sexuality and contain euphemisms for sex, romantic-emotional relationships, or "just" friendship. It was a literary time for the praise of intimate male friendships in American society, perhaps indicating that public acceptance of male friendships had increased. For Walt Whitman, in the Calamus section of *Leaves of Grass,* friendship among men is a "high-towering love" and "a manly love," something central to the formation and maintenance of society, or an invincible "city of friends." Further depictions of intense men's friendships exist in Herman Melville's characters, Ishmael and Queequeg, in *Moby Dick,* (and in the book's dedication to his close friend Nathaniel Hawthorne); Ralph Waldo Emerson's essay on friendship with its central element of tenderness; and Theodore Winthrop's forgotten novels of the 1860s, which illustrate that "a range of possibilities [for male friendship] existed that could run from boyhood 'chums' to an idealized comradeship of 'knights-errant' to an anguished and guilt-ridden projection of the self onto figures of Gothic evil."[61]

Whether the images of male friendship are Whitman's more egalitarian romantic ones or the more unequal ones reinforcing hierarchical male power in Winthrop's novels, they remind us that the boundaries used today to demarcate permissible heterosexual behaviors are not the same as those that were used in the mid- to late nineteenth century. And, as actual letters and diaries written by many middle-class young men show, the intimate friendships of this era were not limited to fictional accounts.[62]

Anthony Rotundo talks about the close relationship between Daniel Webster and James Hervey Bingham in the early 1800s as being similar to a marriage: "The two young men shared the joys and sorrows of life, offered each other emotional support, revealed their deepest secrets, and even spoke to one another in terms of endearment."[63] The diary of James Blake contains entries about his friendship with fellow engineer Wyck Vanderheof in the mid-1880s and describes how they exchanged "a kiss of purity," pledged "ever to love, ever to cherish and assist each other," and "laid our head upon each other's bosom and wept" as they spent their last night together in bed.[64]

Despite accounts of touching, kissing, and caressing, scant evidence exists in the diaries and letters about sexual relationships between the men in these romantic friendships, although there are some stories of men engaging in same-sex sexual acts in other historic documents.[65] It is likely, then, that some of these intimate friendships might also have had sexual components. To rephrase Lillian Faderman's assessment of romantic friendship between women, had the romantic male friends of other eras lived today, many of them would have been openly gay; and had the gay men of our day lived in other eras, most of them would have been romantic friends.[66]

In an age before people and identities were viewed as homosexual, "The nineteenth-century culture did not force a mutually exclusive choice between intimate friendship and sociability. . . . [It] allowed for more varied interpretations of manhood than the late twentieth century," Karen Hansen concludes in her analysis of romantic friendship between working-class men.[67] However, intimate friendships between nineteenth-century middle-class men appeared to be confined to youth and, in some ways, were seen as rehearsals for marriage and as tests for manhood, when men were expected to make a lifelong commitment to a woman, to pledge loyalty, share secrets, lend emotional support, and be physically affectionate—just the kinds of behaviors they engaged in with their male friends.[68] The letters and diaries written by middle-class youth in the northeast

United States often include entries about their pursuit of wives and love of women.

Romantic friendships between nineteenth-century men enjoyed considerable cultural support, especially among the bourgeoisie in the Victorian era, who invoked the classical antiquity works of Aristotle and Cicero and the biblical story of Jonathan and David to uphold the moral virtue of male friendships.[69] It is important to remember that friendship has historically been viewed as something that could only exist among men and from which women were excluded. As Montaigne says, "The ordinary capacity of women is inadequate for that communication and fellowship which is the nurse of his sacred bond; nor does their soul seem firm enough to endure the strain of so tight and durable a knot."[70] How ironic, then, that some of the emotional and intimate descriptors of classic male friendship are the ones used today to extol friendship among women and to illustrate what's missing from the friendships of those who embrace hegemonic masculinity.

But, as I argue throughout the book, gay men's friendships may be one arena in which the elements of normative masculinity are challenged, yet in which they are also combined in complex ways with newer, more intimate forms of gay masculinity, thereby fulfilling Foucault's desire to see the creation of new modes of relations. Friendship among gay men can be passionate and indissoluble, intimate and durable; it can both contest and reproduce heteronormative masculinity. It is a "formless" relationship, Foucault says, that is "the sum of everything through which [gay men] can give each other pleasure."[71]

When the word "homosexuality" became more commonly used in medical and scientific discourse to describe sexual "inversion" and "perversion," and as "heterosexuality" itself became named as a category demarcated by a rejection of intimacy between men, the meaning of romantic friendships between men gradually changed.[72] The inference of a sexual component became a reality that could be interpreted as pathological and that affected the way men engaged in relations of friendship.

It was not too long before psychiatry started to view too close an emotional attachment between men as evidence of a homosexual inclination and, therefore, of an illness in need of treatment. John D'Emilio and Estelle Freedman write, "The medical labeling of same-sex intimacy as perverse conflated an entire range of relationships and stigmatized all of them as a single, sexually deviant personal identity. Same-sex relationships thus lost the innocence they had enjoyed during most of the nineteenth century."[73] In the early twentieth century the concept of friendship included a range of erotic, sexual, and platonic possibilities. But as issues of homosexuality, masculinity, and sexuality in the post-Freudian era entered the public discourse, men's friendships in particular grew more limited in scope.

Along with significant organizational changes in the workplace, especially among the middle class, a cult of masculinity developed that required clear-cut distinctions between the genders—and between heterosexuals and homosexuals. As George Chauncey phrases it, noneffeminate middle-class men became heterosexuals "only when they defined themselves and organized their affective and physical relations to exclude any sentiments or behavior that might be marked as homosexual."[74]

Hence, today we find traditionally all-male social institutions (such as the military, sports clubs, college fraternities, religious organizations) grappling with ways of maintaining the homosociality of male bonding and friendship without the appearance of homosexuality. R. W. Connell says, "in the last two centuries of European and American culture . . . erotic contact between men was expelled from the legitimate repertoire of dominant groups of men, and hegemonic masculinity was thus redefined as explicitly and exclusively heterosexual."[75]

The boundaries between hegemonic masculinity (heterosexuality) and homosexuality have to be guarded. In an era of distinct categories, the introduction of gay men into the confined spaces of these institutions threatens the very meaning of masculinity and limits men's ability to link arms in friendship with each other, because they fear their action and thus their identities will be marred by the stigma of those who are not-masculine.

"A MAJOR WALL OF NONINVOLVEMENT"

Contemporary Men's Friendships and Cultural Limitations

[Men's friendship] cannot be genuine: it is founded on a misconception and a silent (anti)homosexual complicity (an alienated homosexuality). The liberation of homoeroticism, therefore, is not just the negation of homosexuality as it presently is, it will also overthrow the present forms of friendship between people of the same sex. If homosexuality comes into the open, then a certain type of "friendship" cannot but give way to new erotic relations and open emotions.

— *Mario Mieli,* Homosexuality & Liberation: Elements of a Gay Critique

It is perhaps no coincidence that the name of the first known gay newspaper in America, a 1924 Chicago publication printed by Henry Gerber for the Society for Human Rights, was *Friendship and Freedom.*[1] The concepts of freedom and friendship are intertwined in a variety of personal and social ways. With the diffusion of Freudian ideas on sexuality, the rise of heterosexual masculinity, and a growing exclusion of homosexuality from public spaces,[2] twentieth-century men were not as free as their predecessors had been to develop expressive friendship with other men, especially in the middle-class communities in which concepts about gender and sexuality became more explicitly bounded. While he is not typical of most of the gay men in my study, one respondent, Fred, told me about the lack of emotional expressiveness of one of his friends, who "has a major wall of noninvolvement. He is somewhat aloof emotionally. But perhaps this is why he is such a good friend; he provides the distance and objectivity I sometimes lack."

32   This description of emotional noninvolvement may be more

typical of the kinds of relationships that began to develop between heterosexual men whose transgressions met with official resistance and social marginalization. Romantic and intimate friendship between men slowly disappeared as one model of allowable masculinity in America. That this may have been connected to the increasing recognition of same-sex relationships as an illness is captured concisely by Danish sociologist Henning Bech: "The absence of friendship is thus an indication of the presence of homosexuality."[3]

For an emerging category of men who loved other men, friendship was one source of personal and social freedom. It was a search for other selves, and it led to the creation and social reproduction of community through a type of civic friendship. Freedom forcefully characterizes the concept of friendship in our culture. Friendship is free of the legal, religious, and social ceremonies linked to romantic love. It is typically viewed as something we choose to engage in, and with whom we want to. We are free to decide how to live out our friendships with others without the limitations imposed by custom and formalized rituals; freedom of choice in matters of the heart is a central tenet of American culture. We might conclude that an organizing principle of how we view friendship is that it has no organization or structure, that it is free of constraints, or, as anthropologist Robert Paine describes it, "The reason that we do not institutionalize our friendships is that to do so surely, would smother their ideal aspect—as personal and private relations."[4]

But this stereotype of friendship is not entirely accurate. Friendship is not simply a personal, psychological enterprise of unlimited choices; it is a social process, embedded in a culture of meaning and delimited by a society's gender, sexual, and political scripts. And, as anthropologists have demonstrated, "Friendships are a reaction against the engrossing demands of kinship ties."[5] In other words, the availability of friends is connected to where people are located within the social structure; social and material conditions of individuals' lives shape and constrain interpersonal ties.[6] Friendships in other cultures, men's friendships in American society, and evolving notions of masculinity illustrate this sociological view and go beyond the limiting psychological analysis of how people feel about their friendships.

Cross-Cultural Friendships

Cross-cultural explorations highlight the social dimensions and meanings that can limit and define the nature and structure of friendship.[7] Since it would be impossible to cover all the diverse ways men organize their friendships in various cultures and societies around the globe, my goal here is simply—as a way of highlighting some of the key concepts most relevant to a study of gay men's friendships—to illustrate with a few examples how friendship is conceptualized and organized in several societies. One point that does emerge from a cross-cultural analysis of friendship is that the way men relate to each other (and to women) can vary greatly among cultures with different concepts of masculinity.[8] Yet while it is not unusual to see men walking arm-in-arm around the piazzas of Italy, to pick one frequently mentioned cultural custom, this does not necessarily mean that Italian men's friendships exhibit the intensity, intimacy, and emotional power of women's friendships, or that their friendships are significantly different from men's friendships in countries that do not allow such expressive behaviors among men. Other structural conditions, especially the organization of kinship in a society, may have more impact on friendship than does the amount of physical contact tolerated between men.

Many anthropologists view friendship as a universal phenomenon, depending, that is, on how it is defined and how it is interpreted in a context of other culturally patterned interpersonal relationships, such as kinship.[9] For example, Erik Schwimmer argues that "A universally applicable definition of friendship is difficult to arrive at. . . . But even if the sentiments are universal, it is impossible to designate categories of persons, recognized in all cultures, between whom the sentiments of friendship normally prevail. The term 'friend' is, in many languages, nonexistent or indistinguishable from 'kinsman.'"[10]

Although contemporary American culture has few ceremonies that are linked to friendship, anthropologist Robert Brain believes that "Many societies consider friendship to be as important as marriage and hedge it in with oaths, ceremony, and ritual. Blood brotherhood has been a well-nigh universal means of both formally and magically cementing close friendships and alliances between two or more men."[11] In some cultures the relationship between the men is not a substitute for kinship between two actual brothers. Rather, such relationships are intimate, equal, mutual, and sometimes more intensely emotional than are kinship relationships: "Blood brothers are friends and not kin because their relationship is one of absolute equality; between kinsmen there is always superordination and subordination."[12] In cultures that valorize consanguine kinship, raising the importance of non-kin friendships to a higher status often requires some ritual that uses kinship concepts.

J. H. Driberg reported on the institutionalization of a best-friend relationship among the Didinga in Africa.[13] Around the age of eighteen junior warriors must select a life-long friend from among the twenty-three-year-old senior warriors who become instructors in military conduct. But even in those societies where inequality in status characterizes some friendships—including instrumental ones of patron and client—complementarity becomes essential. The Didinga also must look after each other's interests, warn about dangers, be ready to sacrifice their lives to defend their friend. Any betrayal would result in the friend becoming a social outcast:

> They share all their thoughts, designs and enterprises: there can be nothing kept secret from the best friend. Anything that each has can be demanded by the other and the demand cannot be refused on any pretext, since theoretically, all their possessions are held in common. It is not possible for one to ask for too much from the other, as in actual fact he is only asking for something which is just as much his own. The two may be considered then as a legal, social, economic and military unit, and this type of institutional friendship is the strongest bond there is, far stronger than either kinship by blood (or clan) of the in-law relationship.[14]

Since the friendships link two warrior sets of different ages, the whole social system of the Didinga becomes "closely integrated from top to bottom by the institution of best friend."[15] It is no longer just a psychological process of voluntary selection, but a socially and publicly ratified element integral to the functioning of the society.

Some societies certify close friendship through marriage-like ceremonies. For example, in southern Ghana "Nzema men 'fall in love,' form bond friendships, share their beds, and even marry, but they do not have sex."[16] Exchanges of gifts, payments to the friend's parents, and bed sharing would follow a declaration of attraction between one man and another. Perhaps this is not too far removed from the ceremonies uniting two men of the same sex that John Boswell uncovered.

An example of Aristotle's idea of an "other self" might be found among the Bangwa in Africa. The Bangwa value friendship more than kinship, exchange gifts and ceremonial courtesies, fulfill an "endless" list of obligations and duties, and bond for life.[17] In fact, a friend instead of a relative is called upon when a man is dying. For the Bangwa, these bond friendships are associated with twins in their cosmology. Twins are another self characterized by equality: "The Bangwa call twins 'best friends.' Best friends are known as 'twins' and elevated to the miraculous status of the products of a dual birth."[18] Usually the person born closest in time to someone becomes his best friend—the "friend of the road" as opposed to the more achieved "friend of the heart."

In India, friendships are typically characterized in familial terms; a friend is a brother, an adopted member of the family, not simply "like" a brother: "While such a socialization of friendship gives it considerable stability and social depth, it also subjects it to social jurisdiction and control, including specifying who should be one's friend, within what limits, and what one may expect of him or her."[19] Friends are expected to provide mutual help and loyalty, to care for each other, and to promote each other's well-being; friendships are relationships of the heart, not of the intellect.

S. N. Eisenstadt has observed that "while friendship and

kinship appear to be both symbolically and organizationally distinct—even opposed—many of their characteristics are ideally similar."[20] Until recent times the Maori of New Zealand, had "no friends whom they could not define as kinsmen," although there was a wide range of recognition of kinship, whereas the Telefolmin in New Guinea "do not think in terms of kin and non-kin, but in terms of 'friends' (that is, kin with whom there is a long history of close association) and strangers (who may be known kin)."[21] On the other hand, another New Guinea people, the Orokaiva, have distinctive, institutionalized kin and non-kin categories, while the cooperative, reciprocating, and interdependent types of friendship (some of which are hereditary) that Schwimmer describes correspond to basic categories of kinship.[22]

Although many of these ethnographers, and Eisenstadt in particular, might propose that friendship is a public relationship essential to the survival of a culture and to social control, others have argued that "friendship, no longer institutionalized, provides the individual with a refuge from the glare of public life and its burden of institutional obligation."[23] It is the ultimate personal and private relationship, but always in the context of a society's structure and its relation to the kinship system. Friendship is what Paine calls "a kind of institutionalized non-institution" and one that in our Western middle-class culture "exists in greatest independence of kinship and other institutional arrangements (and takes care of our affective needs tolerably well)."[24]

Contemporary Men's Friendships

Not too long ago an article appeared in *The New Yorker* about the creation of an advertising campaign targeted to get men to buy Dockers-brand slacks. As always, the ad agency needed to create a subtext. The ads that followed focused on what many social scientists already knew: "It's almost as if the Dockers ads weren't primarily concerned with clothes at all—and in fact that's exactly what Levi's intended. What the company had discovered, in its research, was that baby-boomer men felt that the chief thing missing from their lives was male friendship."[25]

This description of the absence of friendship in men's lives is a classic finding in the behavioral sciences literature. Years of research, conducted primarily by psychologists, have demonstrated that men's friendships are "side by side" whereas women's friendships are "face to face."[26] Women are much more likely to spend time with friends, to share feelings, to confide, and to disclose intimate details of their lives, while men look for friends with whom to share activities and interests, such as sports.[27] Many explanations for this difference, including biological ones, have been offered. One example is Lionel Tiger's suggestion that "male-male friendship is of a different order than male-female friendship and that it may be seen as a direct expression or sublimation of male-bonding propensities which are species-specific."[28] Tiger goes on to say that "unless absolutely necessary, male-male relationships are less desirable than heterosexual ones" and that patterns of male friendships reflect species-specific propensities that "with dramatic nonrandomness, exclude females from joining in these patterns."[29] Anthony Giddens reminds us, though, that "There are organisations, like clubs or sports teams, which, because of their all-male character, provide situations in which male fraternity can be developed and consolidated. Yet, fraternity—bonds that come from shared, and exclusive, male experience—is not the same as friendship, considered from the point of view of the characteristics of the pure relationship."[30]

Whether men's friendships are viewed as somehow biological, as social, or as related to cultural concepts of kinship, gender difference remains the most studied—and the most controversial—area in friendship research. Studies offer contradictory conclusions and contest many of the general findings. In order to better understand how gay men's friendships can both reinforce and contest definitions of masculinity, it's important to review some of the key findings about men's friendships that are part of the academic and popular literature.

Decades of research on gender and friendship have uncovered the following differences between men and women and their same-sex friendships:[31]

- men emphasize similar interests and shared experiences; women focus on intimate self-disclosure and mutual help and support

- men rate friendship higher with those who engage in similar activities, women with those who share abstract values

- men's friendships are less intimate, self-disclosing, physically affectionate, other-enhancing than women's

- men tend not to focus on the friendship relationship itself as a topic of conversation; women talk more about the friendship itself

- men talk with male friends about women, the news, music, art, sports, daily activities, and work; women talk about feelings, men, food, family, fashion, relationship problems, personal appearance, and daily activities

- at the beginning of a friendship, men are more concerned than women are about whether or not their friends prefer the same activities as they do

- men use less intimate touch with and sit farther apart from their male friends than do women and their female friends

- men are less willing to talk about intimate or personal topics with other men than are women with other women

- men spend less time with friends, and especially less time talking with them on the telephone, compared with women

- even when they are engaged in an activity (such as shopping) women talk more with friends than men do

- men have fewer affectional supportive relationships and receive less help from supporters when compared with

women; women provide more emotional support compared to men

- young unmarried men's same-sex friendships are rated
the lowest in quality; older women's are rated the highest

- men rate the meaningfulness of and satisfaction with
their same-sex friendships lower than women do

- men view their cross-gender friendships as closer and
more intimate than their same-gender ones; women see
their same-gender ones as closer

- men are less affectionate, close, loving, and nurturing
with their friends than women are

These findings should not be misinterpreted or overgenera-
lized to mean that women engage exclusively in self-disclosure
with same-sex friends and that men do nothing but engage in
activities or talk about such activities with same-sex friends. One
of the problems with research that sets up contrasts between
two groups is that the focus on differences between groups
often masks the differences within a group.[32] Also, similarities
between groups are ignored, since the rules of statistical analysis
privilege findings that reject the null hypothesis of no difference
in average scores; acceptance of no differences is reported
much less often. Hence it is important to remember, for example, that most men and women talk about topical events (movies, work, political events) with their friends, even though men
are more likely to focus on these subjects more often than
women do.[33]

In a review of studies on friendship, psychologist Beverley
Fehr lists several possible explanations for the different degrees
to and ways in which men and women display intimacy: (a) men
are as intimate as women, but only in their closest friendships;
(b) men are as intimate as women, but they just don't like the
word; (c) men appear less intimate only because intimacy is defined in a female way; (d) men simply are less intimate regardless of the definition; (e) men define intimacy in the same way
as women but have different thresholds for intimacy; (f) men

are less intimate, but they like it that way; and (g) men can be as intimate as women but simply choose not to be.[34] However, Fehr says, each of these theories is supported by some studies and contradicted by others. Fehr concludes her review this way:

> [O]verall, the evidence seems to suggest that men's friendships are less intimate than women's. It is not the case that men are reserving intimacy only for their closest friends. It is also not the case that men simply are reluctant to use the word. Nor is it a matter of being evaluated by the wrong (i.e., feminine) metric or having a different threshold. Instead, it appears that men are less intimate than women in their friendships because they choose to be, even though they may not particularly like it.[35]

Clearly, the cultural bias is to value women's styles of friendship and to problematize men's styles and definitions of intimacy, rather than to view both styles as important modes that could be integrated into relationships. Barry Wellman says that the climate today is such that it treats "friendship as a relationship in which women excel."[36] Compare this to the historical accounts of loyalty and bravery that praise heroic men's friendship and its emphasis on shared activities and emotional connections.

What explains gender differences in friendship more accurately is not some innate biological difference, but differences in how masculinity and femininity are constructed and related to social structural arrangements in a particular culture. As philosopher Marilyn Friedman puts it in her feminist analysis of friendship, "patterns of noncommunicativeness in close relationship seem not to be part of the cultural conception or idealization of friendship but to derive instead from other contingently related social conditions, such as the practices of masculinity."[37]

Some studies support the relationship between those who enact androgynous gender roles, and "intimacy, self-disclosure, friendship quality, and various positive attitudes toward friendship, particularly cross-sex friendship."[38] Parallel (but not always consistent) findings occur for feminine gender roles, but the results for masculine gender roles are highly variable. Part of the problem, however, with using gender role explanations (as most of the psychological literature does) is that many times people's observations, interpretations, and expectations of differences are based on already-held cultural assumptions about gender, thereby creating a more static and one-directional model of society imposing its norms without resistance or modification.[39]

Certainly other factors modify a culture's definitions of gender, as Karen Walker's work on friendship has demonstrated.[40] She found that women also engage in many activities together and that men do a lot more talking than other studies may suggest. Social class was closely related to the differences in the ways that men and women approach friendship. Among the people she surveyed, women who did not work outside the home or who gave priority to family over labor-market work were more likely to exhibit traditional forms of intimate friendship with other women. On the other hand, middle-class women who were more occupationally and geographically mobile tended to have friendship that lacked intimacy. Working-class men in dense social networks with limited resources for social activities spent more time talking to their friends about feelings.

Walker warns about overemphasizing intimacy as something to assess when evaluating gender differences in friendship: "The narrowness of the debate has limited our understandings of why men's friendships have been meaningful and important to them. Working class men's reliance on friends for services and material support becomes invisible."[41] When one of my respondents, Ed, told me about how he regularly repaired and did things for one of his friends, he was illustrating how close their relationship is: "Whenever he's expressed a need, I've supplied whatever it takes. . . . I know he's on a fixed budget; little perks go a long way when given freely."

Differences among types of friendships can be explained in part using a more sociological interpretation. Rather than looking at friendship formation as something explainable solely in terms of gender roles or personality theories or some species-specific genetic codes between men and women, consider British sociologist Graham Allan's claims that "the different social positions routinely occupied by the two genders tend to lead to their developing different friendship practices."[42] In other words, a comprehensive analysis of friendship should also include the influences that differences in race/ethnicity, age, social class, location in the occupational and residential spheres, sexual orientation, and so on might have on the relationships. Robert Max Jackson takes this perspective when he writes that friendship is a result of the personalities of those involved and the situations in which people interact, situations that "are themselves the products of the 'formal' structures of society—including the economic, ethnic, and age structures. Consequently, the patterns of personal relations—in a sense, the 'informal' social structures—are shaped by the formal social structures."[43]

Studies consistently report that friends are similar to one another—that they are perhaps an other self, to use the Aristotelian concept. Little evidence suggests complementarity. Even cross-culturally, "Complementarity is foreign, both affectively and organizationally. Thus, friends are friends because they are similar."[44] Our understanding of how people choose among others who are similar to themselves may be enhanced by considering personalities, tastes, values, and other individual attributes, but these social psychological models are not sufficient when it comes to "uncovering the *conditions* under which they are similar, and, most important, the social *processes* that create this pattern."[45] In fact, the characteristics friends share appear to be related to the context of the origins of their friendship, so that friends who meet through work, for example, are more likely to be similar economically, while those who meet through kinship networks are more ethnically alike.[46]

People meet people in specific social contexts: at work, at school, in the neighborhood, and through recreational organizations. Access to these situations is constrained by certain age, education, class, and gender requirements, among others. One is thus limited to some degree to meeting people whose position in the social structure is similar to one's own. Initially these interactions may be primarily instrumental-convenience friendships (short-term, not very intimate, frequent contact in neighborhood or work settings). Some such interactions may eventually become expressive-commitment friendships (more enduring, intimate) that depend less on the initial context and role relationships.[47]

As these friends become part of someone's network—that is, as the exchange value of the interactions remains rewarding—this network in turn becomes a social structure that constrains future interactions and friendships. A description of this "choice-constraint" model is succinctly summarized by Jackson: "Positions in social structures affect what people value in exchanges, their capacities to sustain the costs of maintaining reciprocity in exchanges, and their opportunities to meet and interact with people in different social positions. Existing networks place pressure on friendship selection that reinforces these processes."[48]

Thus, for example, studies of social class show that financial circumstances affect people's interest in and their ability to engage in certain kinds of activities. In addition, the kind of work people do and how it is organized similarly constrain or contribute to friendship formation. Working-class friendships tend to be "bounded by the initial setting of interaction. . . . [W]orkmates are not seen elsewhere unless they also happen to share other activities in common"; they are rarely invited into the home, and neighbors are not usually included in other social activities.[49] Intraclass differences in access to transportation, housing, and employment, and the ways in which these are structured in their lives, also result in friendship variations within class.

Middle-class friendship styles tend to emphasize the relationship over the setting in which it occurs. In such relationships, then, resource reciprocity is less of a worry than it might be among working-class people who need to monitor resources more carefully. Since reciprocity is a key aspect of friendships, class-related resources become salient in the development and maintenance of friendships. As Allan puts it:

> [W]ithin working-class culture there is a greater need to limit the possible claims that might be made on scarce resources. . . . Es-

sentially, where interaction is defined as being as much about the setting in which it occurs as about the relationships it involves, then provided individuals have control over their entrances and exits to those settings they will also have greater control over the call made upon their resources.[50]

Furthermore, resources such as education and income consistently create conditions that can mediate social commitments and constraints: "A lack of resources encourages involvement with kin, neighbors, and, for workers, co-workers, while a wealth of resources leads to secular organization members, just friends, others, and perhaps co-workers too."[51] And related to education and income is the role of the workplace in forging friendships. Consider the unique case of male athletes and how the structure of their work environment affects certain displays of male friendship, some of which directly relate to issues of gay men's friendships.

Michael Messner's research on sports and athletes is a good illustration of how structural conditions and cultural norms shape friendships among men.[52] Among the team members he studied, a love-hate relationship was evident; while they presented themselves as a cooperative "family," the athletes also exhibited a high degree of competitiveness with each other. This often led to descriptions of their friendships as close but not intimate: "Competitive activities such as sport mediate men's relationships with each other in ways that allow them to develop a powerful bond while at the same time preventing the development of intimacy."[53] Yet what emerges is a form of "covert intimacy" characterized by closeness through doing things together. However, Messner argued, it becomes necessary for the athletes to monitor any "feminizing" of their closeness by the reassertion of the larger gender order of heterosexual male power through displays of sexual aggression toward women and through homophobic comments directed toward gay men. Closeness, or intimacy, between heterosexual men is fine, until it crosses the boundaries that demarcate "real" (hegemonic) masculinity as distinct from the gender of those who challenge it, that is, women or gays.

In addition to social class, gender, and occupation, race and ethnicity may contribute to an explanation for differences in how people develop and maintain friendships. Clyde Franklin found that "black men's conceptions of themselves, their identities, and their commitments all were critical variables related to friendship formation."[54] The outcome was closely related to the intersection of race and class; that is, working-class black males had warm, nurturing, holistic, and intimate friendships, whereas upwardly mobile black men, as they adopted the roles of hegemonic masculinity, became less comfortable with close same-sex friendships. The interactions among the men in Chicago's Valois cafeteria that Mitchell Duneier studied similarly illustrate the importance of race in our understanding of friendship formation. Here in the cafeteria, the working-class black regulars gained respectability through their sincerity, honesty, and receptivity with one another, while developing friendships based on surrogate kinships.[55]

Thus, if race and class are salient variables in the organization of men's friendships, and if such other structural considerations as where people meet (at work, at play, through sports, in the neighborhood, etc.) and how people are connected to family and kin make a difference, then sexual orientation should play a significant role in the friendship process. It is reasonable to hypothesize that the ways society evaluates same-sex relationships in its religious, legal, political, economic, and healthcare institutions would make a difference in how people organize their emotional, romantic, and sexual lives. Yet, despite the fact that much work has been done on romantic and sexual relationships among gay men, very little research on their friendship relationships exists.

The remaining chapters begin to address this topic in the context of the ideas discussed above about men and masculinity. For many gay men friendship raises salient questions about gender and sexuality, family and relationships, and value and status similarities and differences. While gay men's friendships reproduce core aspects of hegemonic masculinity, I argue that they also challenge these normative dimensions. Heterosexual images of masculinity intersect with more expressive and intimate modes of relating. Containing as they do elements of passion, sexuality, and eroticism, many gay men's friendships contest the dominant norms that typically maintain barriers between men. At the same time, many gay men continue to act in ways that reinforce their status as men and privilege the more side-by-side ("instrumental") modes of interaction.

Two areas that highlight especially clearly the ways in which gay men's friendships challenge and reproduce heteronormative masculinity revolve around the construction of concepts of family and sexuality. Many writers use the "friends as family" metaphor to talk about gay men's friendship networks. But how unique to gay men is the blurring of the distinction between friends and family, and how is this distinction actually manifested? I turn to this topic first, and to the ways the gay men in my sample talked about friends in kinship terms.

"A CHANCE TO CHOOSE
MY SIBLINGS"

Friendship as Kinship

> He asked me how I could live without a family and I said my family is all
> the guys I was telling him about. Isn't it? But he didn't get that. He said
> no—a family like playing with them and learning from each other and liv-
> ing with them inseparably, and I said that's what we do. And finally he sort
> of got it, that my family is my buddies.
>
> — *Ethan Mordden,* Buddies

People often describe their friends using the language of family.
Although few gay men in my study spontaneously spoke of their
friends using kinship terminology, others did speak about
friends as family when asked about it directly, especially when
talking about gay identity and the support and understanding
expected of, but not received from, the family of origin. One
of my respondents, Bill, stated it most clearly when asked if he
thought of his friends in kinship terms:

> My gay friends are like family. I do think that gay men look to
> friends as surrogates for an understanding family. The closeness,
> the acceptance, the unconditional love that is typical of family is
> often mirrored in gay friendships which last. I would bet that
> there is a difference in attitudes toward this across different gen-
> erations of gay men, although I'm not sure which way it would
> cut. Some families will accept their gay child, etc. and some really
> never do. Perhaps this is a telling clue about the respective posi-
> tions of family and friendships.

Or consider this response from Fred, who at sixty-two has
adult children and young grandchildren: "Having been married

48 ... the most categorical answer is that there is no clear distinc-

tion between family and friends in terms of closeness. Towards
Jay [my closest friend], I feel psychologically and emotionally
closer than towards any current members of my family, though
I love my children and grandson intensely. There are distinct
differences in outlook, part of it related to the gay orientation."
And Greg said that before he reconciled with his family and they
began to accept him, "I truly came to know and understand the
importance and meaning of having my gay brothers and sisters
act as surrogate family members."

To talk about friends in kinship terms, however, is not a
trope unique to gay men. Lillian Rubin said it was the most
common analogy used by her heterosexual interviewees in her
classic study of friendship, *Just Friends,* and Karen Lindsey ti-
tled her research on friendship, *Friends as Family.*[1] But are
these merely metaphorical ways to explain the importance of
friends in people's lives, or does the "family" language in fact
reflect a new form of kinship structure? Some might argue that,
for gay men, "friends as family" is much more than the metaphor it is among heterosexual friends, that it is a reconceptual-
ization of family, that for many gay men rejected by blood kinship, friends are indeed their only family. It is one of the few
ways other gay selves get reproduced culturally and politically.

Gay and lesbian relationships are often described as "families we choose."[2] If this is in fact what they are, then this new
kind of family must have political, social, and psychological implications for individuals as well as for society. Before discussing
these implications, however, it is important to understand exactly what it means to say that friendships are like kin. Kinship
terms among gays and lesbians are used in today's culture. Legal recognition of alternative family structures continues to increase. Many American companies, cities, counties, and states
have institutionalized the concept of "domestic partner" by
providing a variety of benefits to the same-sex relationships of
their employees. In several U.S. court cases lesbian and gay
romantic relationships have been verified as a form of family
with the entitlements that may accrue to such a designation.[3]
Some countries, including the Scandinavian ones, have insti-
tuted legal marriage for same-sex couples.

However, redefining gay *romantic* relationships as being similar to heterosexual married couples or families does not necessarily translate into networks of *friends* being identified, legally or socially, as families. While there may be no official way of determining if two gays or lesbians applying for domestic partner coverage are actually romantically involved or are "just friends," such criteria as the merging of income, the sharing of a mortgage, and cohabitation are often used to assist in the designation of someone as a "domestic partner." Yet none of these criteria in and of itself creates a distinction between a couple of friends and a romantic couple, and none are necessary elements of a romantic couple's relationship.

In practice (if not legally), those considered part of a family are whoever those in the relationship say are members. Anthropologists often refer to such so-called family members, since they are not legally or consanguinely related, as fictive kin. Biogenetics are not required in order for one to be so designated, just as they do not determine relationships created through adoption and marriage.

Family Images in Friendship

In contemporary American society, against a backdrop of numerous religious-based organizations that focus on the family, phrases such as "blood is thicker than water" and "we're just friends" have entered our language. These phrases privilege the ideology of the family over other kinds of relationships. As Mary Hunt puts it in her feminist approach to issues of equality in friendship and family, "Social structures which undergird marriage and family life in a patriarchal, normatively heterosexual culture are constructed to prioritize marriage and to relegate friendship to a noble but lesser plane. . . . [P]utting friendship first—and of course permitting, even encouraging, marriage as well—is fundamentally more suited to the complex needs of our society."[4] But in a climate that privileges family ideologies, to appropriate the language used to describe "family," to apply it to gay friendship networks, and to give "just friends" a more important role in the social system become difficult tasks.

The notion of friends as family can never become more than an analogy or a metaphor when the original meanings of the words "friend" and "family" are so firmly entrenched in the culture. Structurally, statuses in blood families persist regardless of actual contact; they are usually ascribed. One's sister remains so, even if contact has been severed. If this person is the only remaining kin, legal ties also remain binding if they are not severed intentionally. However, one can cut ties with a friend much more easily, often by simply failing to return calls or to make further contact, as I report in chapter 7. The relationship then ceases to exist; since friendships are basically achieved or chosen, they can also be unchosen. You can quickly become an ex-friend, but to become an ex-sibling or ex-son/daughter—as some gays and lesbians do—requires complex legal procedures. Similarly, DNA testing cannot uncover a tie between two members of one's family of friends, as it can between two blood relatives who have never set eyes on each other and have no social relationship whatsoever.

We utter such phrases as "she's been a second mother to me." "He's just like a brother." "You are the daughter I've never had."[5] Our American society offers many opportunities for the creation of surrogate families and for use of the metaphor in several different friendship networks. It may be useful, then, to look at how Lindsey distinguishes among three kinds of nonbiological families in her study: the "honorary relative" family, the workplace family, and the chosen family of friends, and to suggest how these categories may be relevant to gay friendships.

"Honorary Relative" Family

Many consanguine families have included friends of the family in their lives by asking children to call these friends "uncle" or "aunt." Sometimes these are courtesy names that reinforce respect between people of different generations rather than indicating a close attachment. Other times these "aunts" and "uncles" are people who share in the everyday lives of the family and become honorary kin or godparents. Structurally, these extended families of honorary relatives often replicate the age diversity of the biogenetic family, but rarely do the honorary relatives have any legal relationship with other family members.

Lindsey argues that "In cultures of poverty, fictive kin have often played an important part in kinship networks, probably because people need each other more in practical ways, which then translate into emotional ties."[6] William Hawkeswood found that his gay male informants in Harlem regularly referred to friends in kinship terms, and that calling other African Americans "brothers" or "sisters" was also part of black culture, "Thus the metaphor of 'family' is extended beyond the boundaries of the gay community to link the gay population to the larger 'family' network that encompasses the entire black community."[7] Mitchell Duneier's study of working-class African American men who gathered regularly in a cafeteria in Chicago also demonstrates the way they adapted "one of the ghetto's prevalent social forms, the substitute kinship tie, to show, through little acts of caring, an alternative conception of civility and of what it means to be a black man."[8] These studies highlight the structural reasons for the emergence of friends as honorary kin and demonstrate the important social-psychological outcomes of these friendships in terms of identity, social support, and masculinity.

In many gay communities it is not uncommon today nor has it been uncommon historically for people to signal that others in the group are also gay or lesbian by suggesting that they are "a member of the family," and sometimes with more explicit kinship terminology. George Chauncey has described the way that many gay men in the 1920s adopted fictive kinship terminology, calling other gay men of around the same age "sisters" and elderly men "aunties."[9] Note that both of these categories of people remain protected from sexual involvement by "incest" taboos. With the exception of "brother," none of the gay men interviewed in my study used kinship terms to describe their gay male friends, and none invoked a familial incest taboo when talking about sex with friends. (see chapter 4 for a discussion of this topic). However, such terms certainly have their place in the lexicon of gay relationships.

Studies conducted in the late 1950s and early 1960s also make use of family images, even if they don't actually use the word "family." Take for example the work of Evelyn Hooker, who notes that gay men regularly gathered in "cliques, groups, and networks of friends" to celebrate anniversaries, birthdays, and other special occasions, as families of origin typically do.[10] Carol Warren found kinship concepts among the gay men she got to know in "Sun City" from 1968 to 1973: "Several words used to describe community relationships are social kinship words like mother, auntie, and sister. . . . Gay people are bound by bloodlike ties of fate and community as are aunts and nephews or mothers and sisters, and their sociable interaction has the same formal and obligatory character as visits from relatives."[11]

For the most part, kinship terms are one way of differentiating between two people whose friendship doesn't include sex ("just friends"), and those who are "more than friends," in a sexual sense. A definition of "sister" in one gay dictionary illustrates the "incest" taboo associated with this fictive kinship term: "He will share anything but his bed with friends. A sister is sexually neutral with his comrades; he is a chum, not a lover. Sisters are in the same business, but only as competition."[12] Other entries in the book include such terms as "auntie," "sugar daddy," "brother," "mother," "mom," and "daughter," some of which are used by lesbians and others by gay men.

Differentiating lovers from friends who are like family is evident in Mart Crowley's 1968 play, *The Boys in the Band:* "No man's still got a roommate when he's over thirty years old. If they're not lovers, they're sisters."[13] It is not unusual for gay men to separate those who meet their sexual needs from those who meet their social ones.[14] And Kath Weston has observed that "This reservation of kinship terminology for nonsexual relations represents a very different usage from its subsequent deployment to construct gay families that could include both lovers and friends."[15]

Interestingly, in the years after Stonewall, as gay identity became more politicized and as sexuality and friendship began to be more openly discussed, many of these kinship terms became "camp" references to preliberation years or were transformed into political and community terms, for example by the gay ("we are family"), women's ("sisterhood"), and civil rights ("brother to brother") movements. Other transformations in kinship terms also occurred. Unlike "sugar daddy," which refers to "an auntie with money,"[16] the contemporary term "daddy" reflects a physical type with an intergenerational attraction to a "son" or younger man.

Workplace Families

Viewing workplace friends as family is common in many people's lives. It is also a recurring image in popular culture. Look no farther than the successful television sitcoms—not the traditional ones about families at home in the 1950s and 1960s, but those of the last decades, that take place at work.[17] For example, the surrogate family is represented in the characters of the 1970s "The Mary Tyler Moore Show," with its images of the father figure (Lou), the daughter (Mary), the sibling (Murray), and the crazy uncle (Ted), all of whom work at the same office, which is the setting of the show. These roles are replicated in other successful 1970s and 1980s shows, including "MASH," "Cheers," and "Taxi," inter alia, and they continue to be replicated in some of today's comedies (which might, as "Spin City" does, include one gay—and in this case, also black—character in the workplace "family"). In fact, one could speculate that the success of these sitcoms has depended on their presentation for the generation of the 1970s, 1980s, and 1990s of workplace friends as family, perhaps as people's real-life families are breaking apart more often as the result of divorce, geographic mobility, and domestic violence.

Friends in the workplace are also referred to as "associative friends," that is, friends made because of status rather than because of personal qualities.[18] Thrown together to accomplish certain work-related tasks, many may become more personally involved in each other's lives: "Whether the workplace is a big-city publishing office, an army camp, or a suburban home, it can create a family in its midst. When people spend daily time together, sharing a common chore, and when that time expands to many months or even years, bondings can take place that are deep and loving. They can be as nourishing and enriching as any biological bonding—and they can last long after the job itself is finished."[19]

Research studies illustrate the importance of work as a source of friends. Beverley Fehr summarizes several surveys that show that the workplace and the neighborhood are the two most important loci for the development of friendships.[20] For men the workplace provides a pool of people who became friends, while women who are homemakers find more friends in the neighborhood.[21]

Many of the friendships made at work, however, do not carry beyond the workplace. Changes in job status often result in the end of the friendship. Hence they are more fragile structurally, legally, and socially than are biogenetic families or fictive kinships. Furthermore, as Gary Alan Fine argues, "Work, with its centrality of instrumental activity, imposes ecological and normative constraints on friendship."[22] Friends at work develop their own traditions, jokes, jargon, and meanings, in other words, a minisociety of norms, values, and ceremonies.

One tension that exists in the workplace centers on sexual interactions among employees (and the co-related issues of sexual harassment) and the increased potential of such occurrences in this setting. Power inequalities among workers, concerns about mobility and promotion, and competition among employees for resources may all impede the development of intimate friendships, since "it is far easier to develop friendships among those who are status equals."[23] Perhaps employees that function as a family exist only as an image in popular culture or, at best, perhaps the image is a metaphor for the closeness of daily interaction, although without the personal disclosure required to develop and maintain close and best friendships.

For many gays and lesbians a nongay workplace is even less likely to be a source of support than it is for heterosexuals,[24] and indeed, among the respondents in my study, close and best friends were much less likely to come from work than were casual friends (see chapter 5). James Woods' study of gay men in the workplace concludes that "gay professionals find that they miss out on the friendships that often develop in work situations" and that, for many, relationships with coworkers are different from friendships.[25] Certainly, in a society that does not provide the protection of federal nondiscrimination laws, a person's colleagues are not a family of friends when that person feels that to disclose his or her gay or lesbian identity might result in termination. Given the absence of comfort and of mechanisms for identity maintenance that many gay employees find in a predominantly heterosexual workplace, for them, the workplace rarely becomes a source of friends that are more than acquaintances.

Friends as Family

In addition to workplace families and families that form as a result of the bestowal of honorary kinship, there are families of choice. Utopian communes—from the Oneida group to the rural farming collectives of disenchanted young people—have long established extended families of choice and have been written about extensively. Although most of these families have been composed of heterosexuals, one researcher portrays a lesbian residential community in Oregon as "a partial alternative form of family unit . . . a psychological kin group" made up of "sisters," many of whom were lovers and ex-lovers.[26]

Lindsey defines chosen families as people who do not live together (as opposed to members of a commune), are not absorbed into the nuclear family structure (as are honorary uncles and aunts), and are not like the duplicate family members of the workplace who live together all day and are defined primarily by that place.[27] Neighborhoods, voluntary associations, hobby clubs, and other similar arrangements are likely sources of people who can become meaningful members of an extended family of choice.

Continuity, history, accessibility, availability (especially in emergencies), stability, and commitment are some of the attributes that characterize friends as family, according to the interviews Lindsey completed: "Often people don't realize that they have a need to create family until they find themselves alone in a new city or town, far away from the family and friends they have been used to. Alone, without their familiar support networks, they are forced to deal with the need to re-create what they had with their parents or, perhaps less consciously, with their friends."[28] What appears to be a personal, voluntary choice, then, is partly constructed and constrained by a variety of social forces.

Furthermore, Lindsey noticed, "some of the people I talked with who were consciously forming families were lesbians and gay men, who felt that their sexual preference not only precluded their living in a traditional family structure in which they were the spouse/parents, but also weakened, and in some cases severed, their ties with parents and siblings."[29] As one lesbian respondent in her study said, "When I moved into lesbian feminist circles . . . , it was so clear to me that the ties of friendship could be so much stronger, and that in fact there was an expectation that they should be."[30]

Structurally, families of friends are not as age diverse as are biogenetic families; friends tend to be of the same age. Also, in terms of social psychological processes, self-disclosure varies quite a bit. Rubin found that the respondents in her study believed friends were more likely than were family members to accept them for who they were: "How much more easily they can share important parts of themselves with friend than with kin."[31] This was especially truer for her gay and lesbian respondents, and it is something that my respondents often stated, as well. ("My closest friends encourage me to be myself," Aaron said).

However, Rubin goes on to say that her respondents often contradicted themselves when they reported that they avoided conflict more with friends and presented their darker sides more frequently to their relatives. Since most of my respondents claimed not to have had serious conflicts with their friends, I wonder if they too are less likely to display a wider range of emotions with their friends, despite Jim's remarks that "you're more honest and don't have to walk on eggshell with your friends. If friends are too hurt by things you say, they're not a close friend." In general, among Rubin's heterosexual sample, there was typically a stronger sense of permanency and obligation associated with kinship relationships than with friendships. Or to use Rubin's economical phrasings: "Friends *choose* to do what kin are *obliged* to do," and "kinship falls into the realm of the sacred, friendship into the arena of the secular."[32]

The relationship between kinship and friendship structures has been debated by anthropologists and sociologists, as I point out in chapter 2.[33] S. N. Eisenstadt writes that, "while the moral obligation implied in friendship may not be more forceful than that of kinship, it often seems to be more 'pure,' not only because the obligation is voluntarily undertaken but even more because it is seemingly disconnected from collectivities with clear interests, boundaries and power."[34] Cultures with weakened kinship ties typically have stronger friendship ties, although some anthropologists have argued that friendships are more likely to occur when kinship structures in a culture are strong and people need a break from them.[35] Cora Du Bois, however, states it the most succinctly:

> From the viewpoint of friendships, their assimilation to kinship represents an extension of the dominant context within which interpersonal relations have been learned in a society. The more interpersonal relationships are dominated by ascribed kinship ties, the more likely friendships are to be patterned on kin affiliations. Institutional friendships constitute a social recognition of this wider tendency. On the other hand, from the viewpoint of kinship, friendship is a voluntary affiliation that can extend and reinforce the formal kinship structure.[36]

But within a society that values kinship institutions, friendships are more likely to be defined as family-like when individuals feel distant from, alienated from, or lacking in biogenetic family members. After all, not everyone has strong ties to family or a sense of permanence, obligation, and stability. Yet there is an American cultural ideology connected to the family that gives it a more powerful role in our lives than friendship has—and that provides the "friends as family" metaphor with its energy. Even if people do say that particular family members have become friends, families are rarely described generally as being "like a friendship group," although anthropologist Ronald Schwartz, in describing the centrality of friendship in a New-foundland fishing community, says that "it is not that friendship is comparable to 'fictive kinship'. . . but that in some of its aspects, kinship becomes a kind of 'fictive friendship.'"[37]

This brings us back to the original question: are friends for gay men and lesbians more than a metaphorical family? For some of those whose families reject them or who live far from kin, friends do indeed become their substitute family. For others, friends become integrated with families. For still others, there remain two separate domains, one of friends and one of family, and loyalty to family comes before loyalty to friends. But given the intense role that friends play in the lives of gays and lesbians, for most of them friends are like their ideal families and on a daily basis are more likely than is a biological family to provide material and emotional assistance, identity, history, nurturing, loyalty, and support. It is the friendship network in which gay men find their other selves, reproduce cultural identity and history, create political and economic communities, and enact both hegemonic and gay masculinities.

Gay Men's Families of Friends

For some time gay men's friendship have been characterized in terms of families and kinship.[38] In 1983, as the growing AIDS epidemic took its toll, gay writer Larry Kramer called attention to the importance of hospital visitation rights being extended to those other than blood relatives: "Hospitals and health-care facilities should be advised that gay people consider lovers, partners, and friends as members of their primary family."[39] David McWhirter and Andrew Mattison's popular book on gay male couples is dedicated to "our growing family," and one of the index entries under the word "Friends" says, "*See also* Gay families."[40] Many of the white, middle-class couples who took part in that 1983 study talked about spending holidays with members of their "extended family," who were "treated like blood relatives with mutual responsibilities to one another."[41]

Martin Levine's late 1970s research on gay clones describes the saliency of same-sex friendship circles or cliques serving as surrogate families for urban gay men and meeting their basic social, emotional, and material needs.[42] Within the group, people took on family-like roles: there was the "big brother" or "mother," who most likely was the oldest and who mentored the "kid brother," who most likely was the youngest and newest member of the friendship circle. The "best friend" was usually the devoted "brother" or "cousin" who served as someone's constant companion and who acted like a lover but was not involved with him sexually. And the rest were "sisters"—the ones they hung out with, depended on for comfort and material aid, and did not have sex with. These cliques were relatively stable, especially when the members remained single and did not become romantically involved with someone.

In perhaps the sharpest analysis that exists of "families we choose," Weston writes, "What gay kinship ideologies challenge is not the concept of procreation that informs kinship in the United States, but the belief that procreation *alone* constitutes kinship, and that 'nonbiological' ties must be patterned after a biological model (like adoption) or forfeit any claim to kinship status."[43] For her, gay families are not fictive kin but are rather transformations of kinship relations in which biogenetic criteria no longer remain privileged. Kinship includes friendship and not the usual opposition of kin versus friends, or the relabeling of friends in kinship terms.

In response to societal changes that allow for more open disclosure of gay identity, to attempts to build urban gay community, and to a lesbian baby boom, the images and discourse related to families have been transformed—from "lesbians/gays = no family" to "lesbians/gays = chosen families."[44] While some gays and lesbians—particularly those from ethnic, racial, and class backgrounds that emphasize strong concepts of family—continue to apply family terminology only to biological kin, the language of kinship among friends and lovers has developed quite visibly in the past decade. But it's not just language that has changed. Weston's emphasis is on relationships that "consciously incorporated demonstrations of love, shared history, material or emotional support, and other signs of enduring solidarity. Although many gay families included friends, not just any friend would do."[45] So, rather than being an inclusive concept, friends as family became a conscious decision. And social class and the availability of biogenetic family members affect whether or not people redefine their friendships into kinship terms.

Some lesbians and gay men actually do create a family of choice that is not fictive. Conceptualizing their friendships as alternative family forms, and not just as metaphorical sibling relationships, has been a significant part of the "house" subculture of drag balls and vogueing for some time. It is best depicted in the documentary *Paris Is Burning*. The predominantly Latino and African American working-class men organize a kinship structure in which a " 'mother' and 'father' supervise the training and activities of their 'children.' "[46] For many of these men, who have often been alienated by and rejected from their families of origin, these houses are not metaphors or fictive kinship structures, derivative of "real" kinship, but are transformations of kinship relations organized around the principle of choice. The critical role of the friendship network as a family for those who are rejected is similarly uncovered by Annick Prieur in her ethnography of transvestites in Mexico City.[47] There she found that friends provided skills training, self-respect, an authentic and consistent self, food and shelter necessary for survival, and frames of reference to help each other understand their differentness.

The saliency of families of choice has also been recognized in the therapeutic professions and in the national movement in the alcohol- and drug-rehabilitation fields toward family therapy.[48] Many agencies and recovery programs restructured during the late 1970s and early 1980s to incorporate family members of clients in individual and family therapy sessions in the belief that the entire social unit contributed to the problems and that the abusing was not simply an individual pathology.[49]

Many, if not most, of these family programs allowed for a broader definition of family, encouraging friends, lovers, and even housemates to participate in the recovery program.

These programs have become increasingly open to lesbian and gay families as well. Around twenty years ago an article on lesbian families claimed that "As the traditional nuclear family declines as the norm in this country—in numbers if not in influence—members of alternative families are appearing with greater frequency in the agency offices and clinical practices of social workers."[50] And to this day the therapeutic literature continues to make use of family metaphors. A 1997 workbook on growth and intimacy for gay men tells its readers that networks of other gay men "become substitutes for family ties and provide us with the kind of support others may look to their families of origin to provide" and give us support that "may be unlike any kind we have ever felt before."[51]

For Henning Bech, however, friends are distinct from family; he strongly argues that "A network of friends is no 'substitute' for family: it is altogether something quite different from a family. It is not a unity, rather a 'plurality.'"[52] Certainly, for those living in urban areas and separated by distance from blood kin, friends can provide the structures typically found in kinship relationships. But perhaps, as Bech observes, calling friendship networks families is culturally specific to the United States, where appropriating ideologies of the heterosexual family and the associated traditional values of myth and media serve a political purpose.[53] Apart from situations involving parenting, most gay men appear not to create actual families of friends but to make occasional use of the metaphor and image of the family in regard to their friendships, primarily to indicate the importance of friends in their lives.

Friends as family may indeed be a strongly American concept; it became an especially prevalent notion when AIDS emerged as a medical and social issue. Responding to the common 1980s reaction to AIDS as a threat to family values, Larry Kramer wrote: "[Gay people] feel particularly blessed by so many and such strong friendships. We have turned to our friends to take the place of families. 'Your friends are your family' is something often heard in conversations of gay people gathered together."[54]

Yet some gays and lesbians of color, in particular those from Latino and Asian cultures, often remain in close contact with their families, thereby creating some possible tensions around identity and illness.[55] Usually the family is defined as those who are available to offer care, money, and emotional support during the illness, regardless of biology (see chapter 7 for a discussion of social support and friendship). For some, the family of origin is not the major source of assistance, and conflicts can arise over care; if death occurs, "disputes over whether families we choose constitute 'real' or legitimate kin can affect wills, distribution of possessions, . . . listings of survivors in obituaries, and disposi- tions of the body."[56] Hence the rise in importance of domestic partner legislation in the 1980s.

What once was a debate within the gay and lesbian commu- nities over what defines a family soon became larger political, religious, economic, and media issues. Newspapers were chal- lenged to redefine family members and next of kin to include "longtime companions" in obituaries.[57] And courts were asked to rule on whether lesbian and gay couples were families, as the New York State Court of Appeals (in *Braschi v. Stahl Associ- ates*) did in 1989 when it held that unmarried cohabitants con- stituted families under the state's rent-control law.[58]

What has also become evident, however, is that the way families of choice are viewed is changing. Once a larger ex- tended collective, families of choice are now more often taking the form of a more traditional couple, and typically with chil- dren. This shift is illustrated by the legal and social challenges related to the birthing and raising of children, especially among lesbians. Definitions of what constitutes parents and kinship, in the absence of heterosexual intercourse and of both sexes, have been challenged by the "gay-by boom" among lesbians and gay men and by court cases seeking to clarify the legal rights of a same-gender coparent.[59] Legalization of second-parent adop- tions in New York and California, and a New Mexico ruling granting nonbiological parent visitation rights have occurred, leading Elisabeth Nonas to conclude that "lesbians and gay men

with children are one more segment of the population redefining what constitutes a functional family."[60]

Advertisements in gay and lesbian publications also illustrate the shift in kinship terminology toward the reference to
more dyadic relationships. The back cover of the 1993 *Community Yellow Pages* (Los Angeles' lesbian and gay directory) features an ad for a medical group claiming that "Families today
are different. So are their Doctors." The tag line reads "Family
Practice for Today's Families" and it is accompanied by four
photographs, one of a lesbian couple with a cat, one of a man
and a baby, another of two women of very different ages (possibly a mother with a teenage daughter), and one of a gay male
couple with a dog. All imitate traditional heterosexual images
(including gendered stereotypes about pets). None is a photo
of a group of friends.

Soon after the 1992 Republican Convention's attack on the
lack of "traditional family values," more ads in the gay press
began appropriating the concept of family values, but usually
in terms of coupled relationships, rather than in terms of the
collectives that often described the lesbian and gay community
of the 1970s. The October 8, 1992, cover of *Frontiers,* a Los
Angeles gay newsmagazine, for example, is emblazoned with
the word "family" and a framed photo of a black man hugging
a white man and holding their dog. An old family photo of mom,
dad, and baby sits on top of a television set in the background.

Other ads in the magazine include one encouraging people
to vote for Bill Clinton headlined "Defend *Our* Family Values"
and illustrated with a photo of two women and their young boy;
another one for gay and lesbian greeting cards offers "Family
Values to put your stamp on" and shows a card with two men
walking arm in arm accompanied by their two dogs. And several
chapters of the Gay and Lesbian Alliance Against Defamation
put up billboards on which appeared a lesbian couple, one preg-
nant, and the phrase "Another Traditional Family."

Again, what is missing from these photographs and captions
are depictions of gay families made up of friends as well as lovers. The dichotomy of family and friends seems to have been
enhanced rather than broken down by the images in gay and

lesbian (white, middle class, urban) commercialized culture; based on these ads, it is not clear how gay families might be constituted by gays and lesbians of different races, ages, and social classes. Although some claim that "for lesbians and lesbian couples, this network of friends, children, and relatives constitutes a chosen family,"[61] the discussions and images have decidedly been toward portraying gay and lesbian families primarily as couples with child and/or pets and rarely as more collective and inclusive groupings, thereby fulfilling Weston's prediction:

> If gay people begin to pursue marriage, joint adoptions, and custody rights to the exclusion of seeking kinship status for some categories of friendship, it seems likely that gay families will develop in ways largely congruent with socio-economic and power relations in the larger society. . . . The most likely scenario would involve narrowing the definition of gay families to incorporate only couples and parents with children, abandoning attempts to achieve any corresponding recognition for families of friends.[62]

As do all groups, gay men organize their relationships in a variety of ways. Some form units mimetic of those of heterosexual couples, they adopt children, hold wedding-like commitment ceremonies that include registration at the local department store, merge their checking accounts, and buy property. Others form dense networks of a few close friends—some of whom may be involved sexually with each other, provide emotional and tangible support, and celebrate holidays together. Some have a large network of loosely connected friends that include "one to joke with and one to confide problems in; one to live with and one to romance with; one to go to the cinema with and others to dine with,"[63] yet do not consider any part of this diffuse and large set a surrogate family.

What is clear, though, is that images emphasizing friends as family often appear in gay popular culture, including in novels, plays, and biographies, even if they are absent in the heterosexually produced stories of gay people. Writers strain to make the connection with traditional family values. Consider the

"Boys in the Band" genre of theater: a group of gay men gather at a home for some extended weekend or ritual event (holiday, birthday). Invariably there is an older gay man, a youth, other young to middle-aged men, an effeminate or campy man, a straight-appearing and conflicted one, and an assortment of other people with secrets (alcoholism, HIV, self-loathing, cheating on the partner).

How can one *not* see this as a replica of kinship structures? The setting (a home) is one that has been embodied to signify a family; the story revolves around a traditional moment of family ritual (a birthday in Crowley's *Boys in the Band;* Memorial Day, Fourth of July, and Labor Day weekends in Terrence McNally's *Love! Valour! Compassion);* generational and gender roles are portrayed (the campy, domestic "mother" quoting Broadway musicals or opera, the father/son couple); and, like members of any family, the characters possess a long history of dysfunctional behaviors, cultural knowledge, rituals, and emotional support. Friends are almost always family in the popular culture depictions of gay life.

While more of my respondents agreed with the statement that "friends are family" when it was presented to them directly, relatively few actually stated it that way spontaneously. Of the thirty respondents I interviewed (this question was not part of the survey questionnaire), only six explicitly referred to their friends as their family or used a kinship term (usually "brother") without prompting; five of these were people of color. And one man, Will, said that friends were *not* family, when I asked him directly; "I'm close to my extended family," he said, "so my friends are not family. I tend not to combine family with friends, but that's because they don't live nearby." His friends often moved on and did not remain linked to his life, as relatives did. While his response is typical of the way many married heterosexual men might answer the same question, it does also represent the sentiments of a segment of gay men, especially those in partnered romantic relationships.

Ed emphasized his connections to his Asian family of origin, although he did not bluntly state that friends were not family. He told me about the preponderance of family members, in comparison to friends, who were at his fortieth birthday party, and about how "friends don't ask to borrow money; that's reserved for family members." His definition of friendship "can include family members," he said. And Ben said, "Friendship for me, as an only child, has always been a chance to choose my siblings."

Many gay men whose cultural backgrounds stress family traditions and who have positive relationships with family members gave priority to family of origin over friendships. On the other hand, Carl, an Asian/Latino, said he spends holidays with "friends because my friends have tended to become my family." Harry, a Native American, responded that "friendships are quite serious. I view close friends as extended family," and John, an African American, said his "best friend is the brother neither one of us actually had."

Saying that friends are family does not necessarily mean that they replace or take priority over family; rather, friends in almost all the cases extend family. For example, Greg, who survived a nearly fatal accident, listed one friend and several close family members as those who were there for him during his crisis. Although family members outnumbered friends, he saw his best friend as important enough to be included in a list of family members.

I felt that the respondents who mentioned kinship terms without prompting when describing friends and friendship were appropriating the American emphasis on family to indicate the importance of a select few friends in their lives rather than describing a larger, more abstract "brotherhood" of all gay men that fills gaps in their emotional lives. For example, Charles said the friends whom he would include in the "inner sanctum"— the ones who "know everything about me"—"are my family [and are] more than just friends." But he also said that "For me, friends are, outside of family, the people I love as opposed to [the acquaintances] for whom I care." Note that the phrase "outside of family" was not meant to suggest replacement but rather addition. In other words, friends are not substitute family, but they are *like* family, and only very close friends would be included in what Charles termed his "inner sanctum."

Similarly, Aaron said his best friend "is like a brother to me. . . . In a sense, we grew up and came out together." For both Charles and Aaron friends are people they can be honest with and tell everything to, and with whom they share things in common, including age, schooling, hobbies, political views—which suggests that friendship is different from rather than similar to family. Families are made up of people whose ages, genders, degrees of power, and experiences are diverse, while homophily characterizes most close friendships.

Still, the fact that the word "family" or other kinship terminology does not, based on my survey, appear to be widely used among gay men to describe friends should not prevent our looking for other things that might communicate just as clearly that gay men's friendships fit into family ideologies. The gay men who did not talk about their friends in kinship terms also elaborated on the ways the friendship worked for them and used phrases and words similar to those used by the ones who did describe friends explicitly as family. That is, the former group described family-like commitments and processes, as Charles did: "They're the people from whom I seek advice, solace, understanding. . . . They're the people I would call if I were in a crisis, or to share good news. . . . My friends are also people for whom I would drop anything in my world and come to their aid." These are sentiments many would say describe family members, and many of the gay men I talked to used them when discussing their close friendships.

What I conclude from the interviews, then, is that many of the functions, feelings, testimonials, and descriptions of close friendships are similar to those that my respondents attributed to close family members. At the same time, friends are often the people gay men can tell anything, especially things about their gay lives; they talk to friends in ways they wouldn't to family members. Structurally, friendship circles do not look like families; they certainly do not have the legal, ceremonial, or religious attributes that characterize the family institution in American society. To say they are like family may serve, then, as a shorthand form of communication.

But given the negative or mixed feelings of those whose families do not recognize, approve of, or tolerate homosexuality, why would some gay men even want to describe friends as family? Why use what may be a negative term to label a positive experience, unless of course the term is meant to transform and reconstitute the institution that failed them? If this in fact explains some gay men's use of "family" words and concepts to describe their friendships, perhaps it suggests the strength of the ideology of the family in American culture, thereby substantiating Bech's comments quoted above as well as lending support to the theories of those anthropologists who argue that cultures with strong kinship institutions also make use of kinship terms to define friendship, or create friendship structures as "time out" from family.

It is important to remember that because friends provide each other with identity support and with opportunities to be themselves, friendship in practice can be emotionally and structurally different from family. They are not the same thing. Friendship has its own structure and meanings in gay men's lives and does not need the metaphor of kinship to give it substance. Like the heterosexuals in Rubin's book, those gay men in my study who invoked family-like functions of friendship or the "friends as family" trope may have done so to stress the importance of friendship in a culture that upholds family as the ultimate and fundamental institution. It also became evident that people wanted to somehow indicate how important friends are in providing continuity and stability to their lives.

But gay men contrasted their friendships with romantic/sexual relationships almost as much as they compared these friendships to families. Bill said that friendship "is the most fundamental and substantial relationship that somehow is even more meaningful than romance." And Mark commented that friends are important because "lovers come and go." The implication is that friends are "always there for you," just as family is—or is supposed to be. Despite the fact that we live in a culture in which families often break up or stumble along in between bouts of instability, the image of family permanence persists; kinship terminology and comparisons with romantic relationships are used to emphasize the continuity and stability of friendship.

Because the ideology of the family, with its constructs of stability, permanence, power, and continuity, remains a central component of American society, it dominates the discourse of assimilation and cultural tolerance. Family concepts are strongly linked to hegemonic heterosexuality and its images of a gendered order privileging masculinity and patriarchy. In some ironic and contradictory way, gay men's interpersonal relationships with other gay men simultaneously contest the dominance of compulsory heterosexual masculinity and its institutions and also reproduce them and embrace their structures, discourse, and images. While holding each other in an embrace of friendship, gay men subvert the emotional distance required of masculinity; yet in speaking of these friends with the power of kinship concepts (if not in family terms), they reinforce the importance of family ideologies.

Since our language does not have the concepts or words to indicate the saliency of friendship, kinship terminology is used because of its privileged status in our culture, just as writers appropriated family terms to describe the heroic friendships of classical antiquity.[64] That the link between family and friendship appears quite frequently in writings about the abstract, collective gay community, and less often in individual narratives, suggests to me that "friends as family" is a political and social metaphor that gays and lesbians use as a rallying cry for each other. It is a way of presenting a sense of coherence and solidity to the larger society, and perhaps of appropriating the "family values" discourse invoked by those who oppose equal rights for gays and lesbians.

At the same time, using kinship terms also reflects a psychological and behavioral reality; it creates an explicit distinction from family of origin, especially when gay men report that they could only really be themselves (i.e., be gay) in their own recreated family of friends. Friends are not like kin in this situation, however; they are a retreat or "time out" from family. Say-

ing that a friend is "like a brother to me" or that "my friends
are my family" is declaring that "my real brother isn't a brother
to me" or "my family isn't there for me." In comparison to my
family of origin, which doesn't support me for who I am, some
are saying, friends act and feel like my family should. Family
of origin images are displaced and become reduced to images
of friendship, as David Halperin puts it.[65] And when the comparison is with work acquaintances, especially heterosexual
ones, friends might seem even more important in terms of giving one the space to be oneself. So gay men invoke the family
metaphor or concept to distinguish these closest of gay friends
from the people who don't provide the same depth and emotional connections (or sometimes as a way of indicating how
much more meaningful gay friends are to them than friends
supposedly are to heterosexual men).

Except for those gay men who are separated from their family of origin (through death, because they've been thrown out
and disowned, or simply because of geographical distance),
friends for most gay men compose an extension of, not a replacement for, family of origin. This became evident when more
than half of those I interviewed said they spend holidays (such
as Thanksgiving and Christmas) with both friends and family,
sometimes mixed together and sometimes separately, for example getting together with family members for one meal and with
friends for a meal later in the day. As George said, "I am lucky
to be close both emotionally and geographically to my family
of origin and spend most holidays with them. I also spend holidays with close friends (e.g., afternoon Thanksgiving dinner or
Christmas Eve, and then go on to my parents from there)."

The remaining respondents were evenly split between
those who spent time with friends only and with family only.
(Rick stated that he spent holidays with his boyfriend, his boyfriend's family, or his own family, "but most of my friendships
are old and on the wane.") Those who lived far from family or
whose parents were no longer alive opted to spend more time
with friends, but family clearly remained an important part of
the majority of these middle-class gay men's holiday events.

Frank said he socialized with friends "before and after the holidays, but usually not during. Everything's too busy with family" and with his lover.

In an era during which more gay men are open about their sexual orientation and can integrate their friends and family members more easily than was once possible, the opportunities for mixing friends and family have increased, especially for those with family nearby. David for example, reported spending holidays "with my family, my partner's family, friends, or any combination of the three." Most of the respondents who mentioned a lover said they spent the holidays with their lover, and many of the men who were coupled viewed romantic partners not as a friend but as a family member, that is, as a spouse. Although Vince said he spent the holidays "with my lover, who I consider family. No other family," Ed's comments captured another way that some gay men manage both family and friends: "When I did have a relationship, we typically shared time among the two families, but on the actual date (e.g. Christmas), we'd separate for the day and spend it with our respective families."

In short, the use of family terms and concepts to describe friends is best understood as a relational phenomenon. How much it occurs depends on whom the friend is being compared to (blood relatives, workmates, the larger community of gay men, a romantic partner/lover, heterosexual men), whether or not the person doing the comparing has surviving kin, and if he does, whether they live nearby or not. "Friends" and "family" do not exist as exclusive terms on a continuum. There are times when friends are family; there are times when they are not. And those times can vary within a day, or across one's lifetime.

Friends are not family when one is close to relatives, geographically or emotionally; friends become family when parents and siblings have died or when friends provide an escape from the opprobrium of family members. Gay men may compare friends with family to illustrate how important and meaningful friends are in their lives or to indicate their sense of commitment to their closest friends—the permanency associated with such friends. Gay men might also distinguish friends from family when they describe how they can tell their friends (and not their family members) anything and truly be themselves (i.e., gay) with these friends, which is not always possible with family even for those who are open with their families.

There are also occasional moments—while marching together in Washington with strangers or rallying against a local injustice—during which gay men invoke kinship terminology to indicate the brotherhood of all gay people as an important social and political statement. I have heard gay men talk about and have experienced the "family of gay men" when it comes to traveling. I have looked up gay friends of gay friends while visiting other countries and have been welcomed into their circle as if I were a long-lost relative who had just returned. And I personally know several gay men who have opened their homes to other gay men they did not know but who were friends of their friends, and invited them to stay at their house when in town. Or consider the story Ed told me about Art, a friend of his who was HIV positive and who lived in an area of the country with limited health facilities and AIDS expertise. Ed told another close friend about Art, and "when he heard of Art's plight, he immediately offered to take this man he didn't even know into his house, so that he could avail himself of the superior treatment climate in the city."

The fact that some gay men label their friends family in order to emphasize the significance of the friendship, while others do so because friendship is in fact a real alternative to their family of origin, is just one dimension in the understanding of gay men's friendships. Another is uncovering the multiple ways gay men structure their friendships: how they begin, how they are maintained, how they dissolve, what these men do with friends, and what meanings they attach to their friends. I turn to these topics in the next few chapters after first exploring the role of sexuality in friendships and the "incest" implications of viewing friends as family.

4

"And We Never Mentioned It Again. Ever."

Friendship, Sex, and Masculinity

[T]he friendship of one gay man fiercely drawn to another is as tense as any heterosexual passion, whereas a sexless, more disinterested gay friendship is as relaxed, as good-tempered as a friendship, say, between two straight men. Gay men, then, do divide other gays into two camps—those who are potential partners (lovers) and those who are not (friends). But where gay life is more ambiguous than the world at large . . . is that the members of the two camps, lovers and friends, are always switching places or hovering somewhere in the margins between.

— *Edmund White, "Sexual Culture," in* The Burning Library

Jim's response to the question of how sex among gay friends was viewed generated a lot of supportive nods from the other men in the "over-fifty-five" club: "Going to bed together is worth two years of acquaintanceship." The men agreed that many of their friendships started sexually, and that this helped them quickly get beyond a superficial friendship and into something closer. But most felt, as Jim did, that "friendship and lover don't mix; sex ruins friendship." Wayne, an eighty-eight-year-old gay man in the group, said, "My friends are my extended family. I don't fuck friends, they're family."

Even though potential friends are also potential sexual partners for gay men, statements about sex ruining friendships consistently emerged in gay men's responses to questions regarding whether they have sex with their friends. In the popular literature an "incest taboo" is offered as an explanation for why gay men are not more involved sexually with close friends. But only a couple of times did any of my respondents make remarks that would lend credence to such an explanation. Does this perhaps support sociologist John Alan Lee's argument that a breakdown
74

of the incest taboo accompanied the rise of gay liberation and that having sex with a friend became a desirable and legitimate way of getting to know that person?[1] Maybe gay men are having lots more sex with lots more friends today than they used to. Or does their silence on this topic rather indicate that they no longer need to use family metaphors to justify not having sex with friends, especially since we are in the midst of an AIDS era, and gay men are allegedly seeking intimacy more than sex?[2] Without comparable data over time, it is difficult to show whether the incidence of sex between friends has increased, decreased, or stayed the same, let alone whether the change— if in fact there has been one—is related to any kind of incest taboo.

Probably the most common question gay men ask me when I tell them about my research is that of whether I'm going to talk about gay men's friendship and sex. To me this suggests that some powerful connections exist in their minds between gay friendships and gay sexual relationships. When I press them on this issue they typically tell me that many people they know seem to have friends who were once, but are no longer, sexual partners, men with whom they had an affair, or one-night stands. In some ways much like cross-sex friendships among heterosexuals, the same-sex friendships of gay men introduce a sexual component that usually does not characterize the same-sex friendships of heterosexuals or the cross-sex friendships of homosexuals. And embedded in the subject of the relationship between friendship and sexuality are important insights into how gender and sexuality are constructed in contemporary society. Information on the ways gay men handle the attraction, the sexuality, the passion, and the emotional intimacy that can often develop between them and their same-sex friends contributes to a theoretical and empirical understanding of how masculinity gets defined, reproduced, and transformed in American society.

While gay men's friendships typically don't begin sexually, sex is often a starting point for many same-sex friendships. And the signal that a sexual affair is about to end is the often-used expression, "let's just be friends" (or as Michael says in *Boys in the Band*, "just friends, lovers no more").[3] Some ex-lovers really do become "just friends," many gay men have friends who are also sexual partners, and some have sex with men who are neither romantic partners nor intimate friends (fuck buddies). On the other hand, as Jim, one of my respondents, bluntly stated, for some gay men the rule is, "Don't fuck your friends and don't be friends with those you fuck."

Sex-and-friendship is arguably one of the most controversial and emotionally charged issues in friendship research—if the paucity of studies is any reliable indicator. Only 1½ out of about 200 pages in Beverley Fehr's book reviewing studies on friendship are devoted to the topic of sex and friendship, and these pages deal only with cross-sex friendship among heterosexuals.[4] Some of this research focused on the transition from a romantic/sexual dating relationship to a friendship one, or on the problems that are inherent in cross-sex friendships because of sexual tensions. (As Harry said when he met Sally in the eponymous film: "Men and women can't be friends because the sex part always gets in the way.") No research focusing on a sexual relationship begun between people who are already close friends is mentioned.

There is also no mention of sexuality between friends of the same sex—a topic that introduces into our discussion important questions about gender and how it is constructed and enacted in a culture. It's a topic that lends itself to offering salient insights into the multiple ways that "homosexual masculinity simultaneously depends on and disrupts the existing gender order," as R. W. Connell has written.[5] But most of the research on sex and friendship has focused on heterosexual interactions. In general men are more likely than are women to see the sexual dimensions of cross-sex friendships, and cross-sex friendships are often initiated because of a sexual attraction on the part of the man.[6] However, if sexual attraction is the most often-listed impetus for developing cross-sex friendships, it is rarely named as a reason for maintaining the friendship: "Both sexes kept most of their friendships and sexual relationships separate."[7] According to Fehr, women are more likely than men to view sexual behavior and intimacy as troublesome to a friendship, whereas men see sexuality as being more closely linked to friendship.[8]

Of course, culture plays a central role in the organization of cross-sex friendships. In our society, when a man and a woman like each other as friends and are sexually involved, there is social pressure to define the relationship as a romantic one rather than as a friendship.[9] If one is married, this friendship could be relabeled as one that is a threat to the marriage; hence close cross-sex friendships tend to be rare among married people. As Robert Bell has phrased it, "Privacy and exclusiveness are seen by many as important qualities of a love (or sexual) relationship between a woman and man and therefore such a relationship is often assumed to exist in almost all situations involving adults of the opposite sex."[10] Although gay men are subject to similar cultural pressures to couple and to define an ongoing sexual relationship as a romantic one, some gay cultural norms (and highly debated ones at that) allow those in committed relationships flexibility to explore outside sexual relationships (that is, to be nonmonogamous) and to have sexual affairs that remain nonromantic.[11]

In cross-sex friendships involving sexuality, when the sexual relationship ends the friendship often ends, too, especially when the woman initiates the breakup. But if the source of problems in the relationship is sexual tension, sometimes ceasing the sexual behavior helps preserve the friendship.[12] Bell found in his interviews that women were more likely than men (31 percent as compared to 20 percent) to see sexuality as a threat in their cross-sex friendships, even though many women also reported that they wanted (and in a few cases did have) sexual involvement with some of their male friends. Many heterosexuals, however, welcome the underlying sexual tone that cross-sex friendships sometimes bring.[13] Scott Swain said it well when he concluded that "cross-sex friendships are both enriched and plagued by fluctuating and unclear sexual boundaries."[14]

These findings from research on sexuality in cross-sex friendships can contribute to an understanding of same-sex friendships among gay men by focusing our attention on the cultural norms pertaining to sexuality, friendship, and masculinity in gay subcultures, and on the gendered order of the larger American society. In a pre-Stonewall ethnography of interpersonal relationships in a gay male community, David Sonen-schein argues that first-order friendships (those between best friends) and second-order friendships (those between good friends but that are less permanent than are first-order friend-ships) are entirely nonsexual, while extended encounters (for example, "being kept," or perhaps a relationship with a fuck buddy) and brief affairs (one-night stands, tricks) are unstable sexual relationships with those not in one's friendship clique and are without the kinds of emotional support that good or best friends provide.[15] In other words, gay men tend to separate those individuals who serve their social needs (friends) from those who serve their sexual needs; rarely did Sonenschein en-counter gay men having sex with men with whom they were already casual friends. He also wondered whether friends are "really a residual category of individuals who did not work out as sexual partners or whether there are differential expectations through which individuals are initially screened to become ei-ther 'friends' or 'partners.' "[16]

Kath Weston similarly concludes that gay people contrast feelings of erotic and nonerotic love: "A person could then theo-retically sort relationships into two groups: 'just friends' (not sexually involved) and 'more than friends' (lovers)."[17] Thirty years later, data from my study tend to support many of these observations. Typical of the responses to my question about sex and friendship is John's: "I have been involved with a couple of my friends. One friend actually is an ex, the other I've known since high school. The high school friend and I don't fool around any more because it seemed to get in the way of how we felt about each other as friends, and then we both started long-term relationships."

The survey data and interviews, however, suggest that gay men, as a whole, experience more than just two categories of lovers/friends. The diverse range of relationships is evident and includes, for some gay men, relationships in which sex and friendship coexist. This chapter focuses on these issues of at-traction and desire, sexual behavior, and romantic relationships among gay friends, and raises questions about the way gay men simultaneously reproduce and challenge the gendered order of hegemonic masculinity.

Attraction, Sex, Love, and Friendship

George told me the following:

> I have been sexually involved with close friends on several occasions. With some friends who are close but geographically distant, it can be fairly easy to do this comfortably. There is only one very close friend whom I see often with whom I've had sex. We did it for a short while, but he decided it was uncomfortable for him, so we stopped. For myself, I do not actually see any bright line dividing the "friend" category from the "lover" category, and it makes perfect sense to me to have sex with a friend as a recreational activity and as an expression of strong feelings for each other. I find many of my close friends sexually attractive and would be perfectly happy and comfortable having sex with them, but none of them share this view. It saddens me that I cannot share this experience with these friends, but I accept that they have a sense of boundary between friends and lovers which I don't.

This statement encapsulates several key issues and captures the range of emotions relating to sex and friendship. For many gay men attraction is strongly present among friends. For some that attraction is translated into sexual expression once or twice or sometimes on an ongoing basis, but for many others a formidable boundary is created between lover roles and friendship roles, especially for close or best friends. But as will become clear from my findings, there are many different ways in which friendship and sexual relationships—and the way in which the two are connected—can evolve.

To assist in the discussion, I map out the complex variations in a diagram derived from the many combinations of relationships my respondents described. Throughout the next sections I refer back to this figure and to the boxes that best capture the

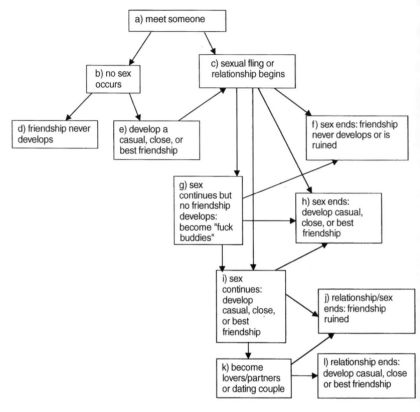

Figure 4.1 The relationship between friendship and sexual activity among gay men: possible scenarios.

shifts the respondents go through as their relationships evolve. I begin by discussing sexual *attraction* between friends (using the categories casual, close, and best friend as defined in the Research Methodology appendix), then talk about sexual *behavior*, and finally discuss *romantic* (lover/partner) relationships and friendship.

It is important to note that the closest or best friend of some gay men is not another gay man. This, of course, does not preclude sexual attraction between the two friends. In fact, Kevin said, "I have had a close sexual involvement with a friend once in my life. This friend was straight, married, and interested in the 'gay lifestyle.'" Paul mentioned that his closest friend was female and that he was "receptive" to having sex with her, but the circumstances were never right. Harry's response is more typical of those who have friends who are not gay: "Most of my closest friends are heterosexual, so I haven't been involved sexually with them."

That Harry's response describes most gay men's attitudes toward their nongay friends is confirmed by the survey data, which indicate that of the 7 men whose *best* friend was a heterosexual male, only 1 had ever been involved sexually with such a friend (0.6 percent of the entire sample of 161 gay men); of the 14 men whose best friend was a heterosexual female, 3 once were involved sexually with their best friend but no longer were (around 2 percent of the entire sample). Only about 10 percent of the entire sample said they had ever had sex with a *close* female friend, and approximately 8 percent had ever done so with a *casual* female friend. Since the overwhelming majority of men in the study reported that their *best* friend was also a gay man,[18] and since almost 90 percent of those surveyed said that the majority of their *close* friends were male, the data presented in this chapter are based on these friendships, unless stated otherwise. (Chapter 5 presents more details about who gay men's friends are.)

Sexual Attraction

In general, the process of forming a close friendship is not unlike that of forming a romantic relationship; that is, an initial attraction (physical, emotional, intellectual) can often serve as the catalyst for continuing a more intense interaction.[19] And for most gay men current friendships start either with minimal sexual attraction on one or both person's part, or with a sexual attraction that is either unfulfilled (box *a* to *b* in figure 4.1) or consummated (box *a* to *c*).

Coming-out narratives often include statements about early attractions to friends.[20] Aaron's is one such story (illustrating a shift from box *b* to *e*): "I think that Ralph, my best friend from college, is attracted to me sexually. He essentially told me so when he came out to me, and a couple of times since. But neither of us has ever acted on it. I think that we believe that it would change our relationship substantially, and would ruin it if we later became sexually involved with someone else." He claimed that he and his friend avoided sexual contact out of a belief they both supposedly held that their friendship might end if one or the other got involved with someone else at some vague future point. Note, by the way, that nowhere did Aaron say that he was actually attracted to his friend. Based on this and several other narratives, it seems to me that many gay men invoke the "sex will ruin the friendship" line when at least one friend is not attracted to the other, thereby saving face and avoiding possible rejection.

Fred told a story similar to Aaron's of initial attraction that did not lead to sex between himself and his closest friend (box *a* to *b*) and that later got redefined into "some attraction or at least curiosity," although "it was not strong on my part." Fred believed that "resentments over unrealized physical disappointments can often be the issues on which imperfect platonic relationships falter and break. More intense and physical relationships may raise us to higher transports, but they also expose us to sharper falls. I am content, even well-pleased with what I have with my closest friend, and I do not believe it would be improved by transmuting it into something else."

Another form of the attraction story—but a much less common one (box *a* to *b* to *e* to *c* to *h*)—was told by Ben, who mentioned long-standing feelings of unfulfilled attraction toward a friend he knew for three years that finally led to a sexual fling when they shared a bed: "I was always attracted to him, but I don't think he was attracted to me. . . . We did have sex once. . . . It was great and we never mentioned it again. Ever." Although the sex did not lead to the much-feared loss of friendship, note how the two friends played out stereotypical masculinity roles by avoiding intimate and emotional conversation about what had happened between them.

Some gay men are not attracted to their friends. (Steve said, "Never have been. Not sexually attracted to them.") But for many others attraction has been and remains a component of their friendships. Respondents to the survey indicated the degree of their sexual attraction, if any, to their *best* friend in the

past and currently. Almost 80 percent of the respondents reported that they had experienced some sexual attraction to their
best gay male friend in the past; about half said they were currently sexually attracted to that same person. Of those who were
attracted, 58 percent had been "very or extremely" attracted in
the past, but only 38 percent were currently "very or extremely"
attracted to their best gay male friend.[21] (Of the twenty-one gay
men with heterosexual male or female best friends, only three
said they were currently sexually attracted to their best friend,
and seven said they had been so in the past.)

The survey data also confirm a physical expression of closeness and possible attraction among male friends. Almost 78
percent of the respondents said they "frequently or usually" expressed affection by touching their best male friend. Seventy-
five percent did so with close male friends and 44 percent with
a casual male friend. Despite cultural norms about masculinity
that discourage men's touching, these numbers were much
higher than were corresponding numbers (51 percent and 33
percent, respectively) related to affectionate touching between
close or casual female friends, and about the same as were the
corresponding numbers for those few gay men in the survey
who had a best female friend (75 percent).

Louis responded, "All my best friends titillate me. There is
an attraction, a passion, even without sex." Attraction has long
been associated with friendship. Many psychological studies
have demonstrated that physical attraction plays an important
role in the development and number of friends adults and children have.[22] But here I want to focus less on what attracts people to one another in terms of shared values, hobbies, or physical attributes, and more on the idea of passion or *eros*. As
Charles said about his attraction to his close friend with whom
he has not had sex (box *a* to *b* to *e*): "The moment passed
[shortly after we met] and we've not gone back. . . . There's a
tension existing between us. I'm curious about his body, . . .
but perhaps my curiosity is in the appeal he has to other men.
He seems to have this quality, sexual energy, which defies my
analysis."

But sexual passion may be one of the driving forces behind

the formation of close friendships for many gay men, even if it is not constitutive of the friendship itself. The concluding lines of Plato's *Phaedrus* declare that "friends should have all things in common," and when this common end is *eros* directed at the Good (that is, the desire for truth and beauty), true friendship emerges: "The passion, the *eros*, the sublimated sexuality is a condition not of the friendship, but of the common desire for the rational ideals which the friendship augments and sustains. . . . The *philia* which binds friends doesn't really bind them at all; it is the means whereby the *eros* driving each separately toward the Good is augmented and sustained."[23]

Yet *eros* is not the same as *philia;* passion is not friendship, certainly not something shared in a political friendship. Gilbert Meilaender argues that "unlike friendship, *eros* is a love that is jealous and cannot be shared."[24] And *philia*, especially to Aristotle, is a bond that joins people in a civic friendship. But surely *eros* and *philia* are not limited to gay men.[25]

Although attraction—physical, erotic, passionate—between heterosexual men was historically more culturally acceptable than it is today, by the mid-twentieth century for a heterosexual man to acknowledge any form of such erotic or physical attraction had become taboo. Allan Bérubé discusses the way in which psychiatrists during World War II recognized the erotic undertones and sublimated homosexuality of the "buddy relationships" that typically formed in military situations between men who openly expressed sentimental bonds but were prevented from engaging in overt sexuality.[26] As Anne Seiden and Pauline Bart write, "There is probably an erotic component in most close friendships, . . . but this appears to be disturbing to many people and is denied or repressed."[27]

It is possible, then, that attraction continues to play an important role in men's friendships but that it must remain, especially among most heterosexual men, an attraction that dares not speak its name. Or as Connell phrases it, "Heterosexual men must deny desire except for the gendered Other, while making a hated Other of the men who desire them (or desire the embodied-masculinity they share)."[28] Gay men are freer to express erotic attraction with same-sex gay friends (and to fulfill the attraction sexually), thereby subverting culturally held definitions of masculinity while simultaneously reproducing the gendered sexual energy (instrumental, hierarchical) constitutive of hegemonic masculinity.

Harry, for example, had no problem talking about his attraction in a way that at the same time made him sound very much like a "stereotypical" male who focuses on sex: "I do have one close friend who is gay, and I have hopes that our relationship will become sexual eventually, as I'm highly attracted to him." This doesn't seem likely, given the direction most gay friendships usually go. Attraction does not always lead to sexual behavior, and it typically fails to do so frequently among those who have already established a friendship. However, there are many exceptions, as I now discuss.

Sexual Behavior

Gay men's erotic attraction to their gay male friends appears to be a component in the earlier stages of friendship formation, yet in most cases it does not seem to be sustained or transformed into sexual behavior as friendships develop. Some gay friends never pursue the possibility of engaging in sexual activity with one another because at least one of them is not attracted to the other or because they fear it will ruin the developing friendship. Sometimes the failure to consummate sexual desire for a friend comes about because one of the friends already is involved in or is starting a romantic relationship, as David explained, "I wouldn't even consider having a sexual relationship with a friend. If I wasn't partnered, I probably still wouldn't. Sexual relationships can complicate and roughen up a friendship—too many issues of jealousy and fidelity crop up." Or sometimes it's because both are in a relationship and lack any attraction; Charles said he has not had sex with one of his closest friends because the friend "is involved in a long-term relationship and truly not my type."

As I discuss in the previous section of this chapter, some gay men claim to have felt no initial attraction or interest in having sexual relationships with their friends. Again, these are among the people who later become close or best friends (box *a* to *b* to *e*). It's very possible that for another set of people a lack of physical, emotional, or personality attraction prevents any kind of friendship from forming at all (box *a* to *b* to *d*). (See chapter 6 for discussions of how friendships start.) Information is rarely collected in friendship studies about those people who do not become friends (as opposed to information about friends who cease being friends).

Most gay men, though, report attraction *and* sexual contact with some of the people who later became casual, close, or best friends (box *a* to *c* to *h*). Indeed, for many men, short-term encounters are a common way of discovering a life of gay sexuality and identity.[29] Not as many (less than a third of those interviewed), though, continue having sex with another person once the two become friends (box *a* to *c* to *i*) or even begin a sexual relationship *after* they become close friends (box *e* to *c*). And almost no one told of a friendship or relationship having been ruined because of a sexual relationship (box *f* or *j*). But consider this story told by Mark, who clearly was attracted to one of his established friends and waited for the right time to follow his feelings:

> In an odd moment, last Friday I slept with the most unlikely person in my group of friends—someone I've known for several years. Some background: a few months ago, my friend Drew suddenly dumped Jon—much to everyone's surprise since they were for over three and a half years so coupled they were regularly referred to as Drew-and-Jon. So, Drew kicked Jon out of their apartment. Drew, meanwhile, has taken a new boyfriend and has alienated many in our little group because of this. Now, I had always found Jon attractive (do you see where this is going?), but never thought of him in that special way 'cause he was taken, and I am not one to break up couples. Anyway, I went to Jon's party last Friday and had a wonderful time hanging out with him. We went to the local disco, and before you know it, we're making out at the bar. Then all of a sudden, the rest of our friends entered the bar and found us hot and heavy all over each other. Needless to say, everyone was shocked, stunned, petrified, horrified, etc.

by the turn of events. So we quickly made our escape, and somehow ended up at a beach where we continued where we left off (picture a gay version of "From Here to Eternity"). After deciding that I was not such a cheap fuck that I would actually have raunchy sex in public, I recommended we go back to my place, where much indoor pleasuring was had. And had and had. We were both surprised by the intensity and compatibility we shared. While I am not really looking for a relationship, I do think that Jon and I will be exploring all things sexual in the coming weeks, months.

Only time, of course, would be able to tell whether this sexual relationship would translate into a dating romance or whether Jon and Mark would become a committed couple (box *e* to *c* to *i* to *k*), whether their friendship would become nonsexual, as it once was (box *e* to *c* to *h*), whether sex would cause a rift never to be healed, as many gay men believe happens when sexuality enters into a friendship (box *e* to *c* to *f*), or whether the relationship would continue as some form of a nonexclusive sexual relationship with a good friend (box *e* to *c* to *i*). In this case, time actually did tell us something about what happened, even if it has yet to provide us with the conclusion of Mark's saga. During a follow-up interview that took place several months after the first one, Mark said:

> I have dismal-love news about myself to report. I mentioned before to you I had started dating a friend of mine, and we had been dating for several months until last week when he said he couldn't handle seeing me as both a friend and lover. He wants to go back to where things were; I want to take this someplace much more. Sigh. So we had words; I said some uncharacteristically nasty things, and now he won't answer my calls or E-mails. I'm heartbroken and feel I have lost both a good friend and a potential husband as well. Never again will I date a friend.

But getting involved sexually with men who later become casual, close, or best friends when the sex ends (box *a* to *c* to *h*)—the "let's just be friends" scenario—is much more common, according to the results of my survey, than is starting or continuing a sexual relationship once people become friends (box *e* to *c* or box *a* to *c* to *i*). Almost three times as many of the gay men surveyed (60 percent) reported that they had been involved sexually in the past with their *best* gay male friend, compared to those who reported that they were involved sexually with their best gay male friend today (20 percent). Furthermore, 75.8 percent of the gay men said that they had engaged in sex with some of their *close* male friends (only around 9 percent said with "many or most") at some point, and 62.5 percent said that they had done so with at least some of their *casual* male friends (only 7 percent said that they had done so with "many or most").[30] Of course, some of the sexual relationships with best and close friends were in the context of a romantic coupled relationship, as I discuss in the next chapter. A comparison of gay men's past and current sexual relationships with casual and close friends is not available, but given the very small percentage of respondents who said that they had engaged in sexual activity with "many or most," of their friends, the point remains that very few currently have sex with their established friends. Although men under thirty were slightly less likely to have had sex with friends compared with men over fifty-five, and although urban men were slightly more likely to have had sex with friends than were rural men, these differences were not statistically significant. There were also no significant differences among men of different income and educational categories (social class).[31]

For most gay men who become friends with one another, then, it seems that an initial attraction and sexual fling is as far as it goes before the relationship gets redefined into a casual, close, or best friendship (box *a* to *c* to *h*). Very few continue to have sex after they become best friends, and very few gay men have sex even once with many or most of their casual and close friends. In percentage terms, it makes sense that so few casual and close friends have been sexual partners: network size increases as gay men get to know more and more friends of the people with whom they may have had an initial sexual contact, but not all new members of a clique have sex with each other. Martin Levine found in his study of gay clones in New York that "The men became friendly with each other after an initial sexual relationship, and gradually introduced one another to mutual friends and acquaintances over the course of their friendship. Those men who were compatible coalesced into a clique."[32]

Sex may gain someone entry into a particular circle of people who then become that person's casual and close friends, thereby decreasing the percentage of friends he has had sex with. Having sex with friends of friends can get very complicated, as Andy realized when his friend Ken learned that Andy had a crush on their mutual friend Howard and that Andy and Howard had actually "trysted" (to use Andy's word). Andy said, "I had absolutely no intention of acting on that crush. I had a crush on Howard from the first time I saw him at the gay students meeting. I thought I had an obligation to ignore/hide how I felt about him because he was Ken's friend." But Andy's friendship with Ken was changing, and Andy thought it would be okay to get involved with Howard. It made things awkward between Ken and Andy, but they were able to talk about it and begin working it out, as the discussion in chapter 7 about friends dealing with conflicts shows.

For others, though, sexuality and friendship can lead elsewhere. If romance becomes part of an ongoing series of sexual encounters, the relationship is then redefined as a lover/romantic one (box k)—one between more than just friends. Perhaps Sonenschein's statement quoted above is accurate today as well; friends may be the residual category for many of those who did not work out as sexual partners. But this simple dichotomy seems to assume that all friendships begin sexually and then end when the friendship develops, or at least that they begin with the desire for a sexual relationship that goes unfulfilled. This overstates the erotic component in gay friendship formation and understates the numerous other reasons for why certain people become close or best friends (as I discuss in chapter 6).

Still, the ruination of a good friendship appears to be one of the most consistently echoed cultural beliefs about the consequences of sex with friends (box f or j), despite the fact that I heard few stories indicating that this sequence of events actually occurs. It is part of the mythology and moral storytelling about friendships in American society and in gay subcultures. It also reflects the strong emphasis on equality and reciprocity that characterizes friendship in our society—an equality and reciprocity that can become unbalanced in sexual relationships.

Over and over again, gay men of various ages, races, and regions of residence reported that they wouldn't have sex with friends because, as Bill put it, "Once you get into that status it's difficult to retain friendship as it used to be. It's more of an act that potentially jeopardizes rather than enhances your friendship." Tim also concluded that "sexual involvement will damage or harm the friendship." Notice how the answers focus on sexuality once the friendship has been formed; continuing sex with a close friend (box i) or starting sex with a close friend (shifting from box e to c) are not common behaviors among gay men. As soon as the people involved define themselves as friends, then the possible harm sex can cause is discussed.

Yet with the exception of Mark's story about dating a friend, which may or may not result in the friendship being ruined in the end, not one other person interviewed offered an actual story about a friendship that went wrong because of a sexual relationship or because of sexual tensions.[33] Of course some self-selection occurs; it's possible that in those sexual relationships that ended badly friendship did not develop at all (box f); in such a case no respondent could rightly claim then that the sex caused a friendship to end, when they had never even become friends. Since sexual problems may prevent some friendships from even beginning, these experiences may explain why people feel that sex could hurt an already established friendship. Despite the firmly held belief that close friendships are based on honesty and trust and can withstand crises, the implied message is that the friendship might not really be strong enough to survive the emotional intensity of sexual relations.

It appears that, for most respondents, sex doesn't ruin a friendship, probably because people become "just friends" as soon as the sexual relationship turns problematic and ends (box h). Or the relationship starts off as a nonsexual friendship (box e) when at least one of the people does not allow the new friendship to become sexual. It may be at this point in the friendship that phrases about the potential of sex to ruin friendship are invoked to explain and justify the absence of or the end of sex in the relationship. What sex or its absence probably ruins, though, is the potential for a romantic relationship (moving to box k), not the friendship. If there is a sexual relationship, friendship might develop along with it (box i) and may possibly become redefined as a romance or as a committed partner relationship (box k).

Some of this discussion may be one of semantics—by definition a friend is someone you are not involved with sexually or romantically, so sex can't be part of the friend role. This may explain why some respondents seemed confused when they were asked if sex with friends were possible. If there is a sexual relationship, in their minds, then the person with whom you are having sex is either a lover, someone you are dating, or a nonfriend sexual partner (box g)—anything, that is, but a friend. Switching to the "just friends" label ends the sexual aspect of your relationship and publicly announces that you and your friend are not involved sexually or romantically. A friendship is usually a nonsexual relationship, even though gay people once commonly used the word "friend" to designate a romantic lover or conceal a same-sex lover, and some communities, and other languages and cultures, may still employ it in this way. For example, John noted that "in the African American gay community, 'friend' and 'lover' are often synonymous. People often refer to their partners as 'my friend.'"

But not everyone separates sex and friendship. Remember that almost 20 percent of the gay men surveyed reported that they were currently involved in a sexual relationship with their *best* gay male friend, and around a third of those interviewed mentioned having had at least one sexual experience with an already established friend. While our language does not allow the concept of friendship to include a sexual component in its definition (what are people in box i called if they are not dating or coupled?), there is a label for people involved in nonfriend—possibly casual friend—sexual relationships (box g); they're called fuck buddies. Ben talked about this: "I have and do still have fuck buddies, but they don't qualify as 'friendships' of the caliber and quality that I felt you were studying. These relationships will by necessity be on the perimeter of my relationships. These relationships are narrowly defined and single purpose and that is the antithesis of close friendships, which run the full range of life experiences."

According to Levine, fuck buddies "related sexually not romantically. They repeatedly rendezvoused for erotic contact. A fuck buddy was a long-standing trick, and this relationship therefore involved neither commitment nor emotional attachment."[34] It's the availability of sex without the emotional demands that makes this particular type of friendship possible in gay communities, but that at the same time represents one stereotypical characteristic of heterosexual men, namely the ability to have instrumental and hierarchical interactions rather than expressive and solidary sexual interactions.[35] Love and sex can be separated more successfully in hegemonic masculinity, thereby illustrating the contradiction of gay men enacting such gendered scripts while simultaneously subverting the very definition of heterosexuality, i.e., by being intimate with someone of the same sex.

There are also some men who manage a sexual relationship with people who are already part of their friendship network. These are the friendships we don't have a word for (box i). Vince is a good example of someone who maintained a sexual friendship with a man who began as a trick (illustrating the shift from box a to c to g to i): "We started out as fuck buddies, and the relationship evolved into friendship, although we still occasionally have sex." Notice, also, how his use of the qualifying "although" implies a cultural norm about friendship not being sexual.

Several others interviewed in my survey also appeared to balance friendship with sex (box i); their doing so illustrates the complexity of reproducing hegemonic masculinity (e.g., sex without commitment) while also challenging it by invoking stereotypically nonmasculine emotions of comfort, sharing, and friendliness—or perhaps by mixing hypermasculine roles with elements of trust and danger, as one of my respondents who is into wearing leather clothing and engaging in S&M told me he does. Ben went on to say that "sex with friends can be very comfortable and satisfying. It's not the scary, my heart-is-on-the-line risky business." The lack of commitment that occurs in romantic/love relationships is what attracts Rick to sex with friends, as well: "I've worked on being able to share sexuality with my friends instead of all the 'tall, dark strangers.' It's friendly and superficial sex." And Nick, who is bisexual, said that he has been involved sexually with his closest friends because "they are the closest friends I have. I am comfortable with them. It feels right." None of these men reported any loss of a friendship due to sexual interest and involvement.

For these gay men who managed to combine sexual behavior and friendship (box *i*), their relationship might continue as it was or might develop into a committed romantic relationship (more on box *k* in the next section). If sexual attraction and activity should begin to diminish, though, the relationship could end, and one of the friends might never hear from the other again (the feared ruination, brought on by sex, of the friendship [box *j*]). Or the relationship could become a casual friendship, with occasional nods of recognition being exchanged when the two ran into each other in public situations. Alternatively, it could change into a close or best nonsexual friendship filled with the characteristics of mutuality, intimacy, and sharing that characterize committed friendships (box *h*). As Ed succinctly phrased it: "It may be a cliché that having sex with a friend can negatively alter the friendship, but it doesn't apply to everyone. With some friends, it's been a single instance and the friendship endures and continues to grow [box *h*]. . . . I don't view sex as taboo, but instead see it as an expression of friendship on a physical level. If the other person is of the same mind, we can have great encounters, however infrequent they might be [box *i*]."

Thus, in light of all these possible combinations, it becomes very difficult to make generalizations. We can say, however, that while the traditionally expressed *fear* of sex and friendship not mixing may characterize what most gay men feel, there are enough cases in which sex is combined with friendship to call into question the universality of the cultural dichotomy of sex *or* friendship. This statement made by Leo, one of the working-class men I interviewed, best captures the range of possible sex-and-friendship relationships I've been discussing:

> I have been sexually involved with people who were close friends at the time who have since become distant over time [box *i* to *j*] and with people who are still close friends [box *i*]. It is the way I met some of them. There are other close friends with whom discussions of possible sexual activity have taken place, or the sexual tension has been talked about, but the decision was made that the friendship was more important and we would not pursue any sexual activity for fear of it destroying the friendship [box *a* to *b* to *e*].

Lovers, Ex-Lovers, and Friends

For some gay men erotic attraction, sexual behavior, and a developing friendship give rise to romantic feelings that result in a partner/lover or dating couple relationship (from box *i* to *k*). Not only can this shift the nature of the friendship, but it might also seriously impact other friendships. Many friendships change and some end when one of the friends becomes romantically involved, as I describe in chapter 7. One of my respondents, John, said he had sex with someone he has known since high school, "but we don't fool around anymore because it seemed to get in the way of how we felt about each other as friends, and then we both started long-term relationships." And Fred told me how one of his close friendships ended when that person "developed an intense personal and sexual relationship that preempted our already somewhat fragile and conditional friendship." He admitted to feelings of jealousy and of being left out and "extraneous." Key characteristics of friendship—reciprocity, trust—were shaken (or perhaps had never fully matured) as a result of Fred's friend's getting involved with someone else.

Romantic relationships are often on a different order of intensity than friendships, and negotiating current and ex-lovers in one's friendship networks can become an emotionally charged task, the outcome of which varies depending on how solid the friends have become. Around 19 percent of the gay men surveyed said that their *best* friend was an ex-lover (median of eighteen months together, mean of thirty-eight).[36] The percentage of close or casual friends who were ex-lovers (as opposed to sexual partners) was not measured. John stated that, "one friend actually is an ex. It does seem like friend equals ex-lover to a lot of gay men." Although a higher percentage of gay men aged fifty-five and older and of those with more education and a higher income said that their best friend was an ex-lover as compared to those under thirty and to those with less education and a lower income, the differences were not statistically significant.[37] Obviously, older men—the ones who are more likely to have accumulated more income and years of schooling, as well—have had more time to cultivate romantic relationships and thus are more likely to have friends who are ex-lovers.

About 37 percent of the gay men interviewed and 47 percent of the gay men surveyed were currently coupled.[38] Of the coupled men in the survey, 71 percent considered their partners to be their best friends. There were no significant differences based on age, income, or education in the percentage of coupled men who said their partner was their best friend.[39] Studies confirm that when people get coupled they have less time to develop and maintain friendships, especially more casual ones with single people.[40] This held true to some degree in the survey. Coupled gay men were significantly less likely to have as many casual friends as single gay men did (58.5 percent of the single men reported twenty or more casual friends, in comparison to 43 percent of the coupled gay men who reported the same thing), and the coupled men were also significantly less likely to have had sex with their casual friends (47 percent of coupled men said they never had sex with any casual friends, compared to 27 percent of single men).[41] Age, income, and education were not statistically significant in predicting differences between single and coupled men in terms of whether or not they had sex with casual friends and in terms of the number of their casual friends.[42]

For those gay men who were coupled, asking about friendship raised questions about their relationship and about what made it different from and the same as a friendship. Ask people what the difference is between a lover and a best friend, and the immediate response is "sex" or "sexual attraction." But then they think it out and sometimes question what the distinction actually is and whether one exists at all. For many in companionate romantic relationships there is little difference. Yet Mike said, "I think that a friend differs from a lover in that there is more sexual attraction with a lover but, more importantly, the amount I am willing to reveal to a lover is greater. I'm willing to risk more with a lover and show more emotion. It was tough to even think of someone who was my best friend because my lover kept coming to mind."

Sex, Equality, and Masculinity

From the data, some conclusions about the relationship between friendship and sex emerge. First, among gay men, there is a persistent fear of sex ruining friendship (Harve said, "sexual relationships make friendship more tenuous and/or difficult to maintain"). Second, most gay men who have had sex with friends did so in the earliest stages of friendship formation (Frank: "My best friend and I made love when we first met and then one other time, but that was it. The others, no"). And finally, some gay men continue to enjoy sexual relationships with fuck buddies or with people who are already friends (Ben: "Sex can be great with friends, and I think that it is an extension of intimacy"). To understand the role of sex in gay men's friendships it's important to grapple with a set of contradictions about how gay men view sex with friends that, in turn, introduces yet another set of contradictions about the way masculinity is both contested and reproduced in American society.

Of course, one explanation for the range of sexual behaviors with friends is that different folks make use of different strokes—generalizing about *all* gay men is a dangerous and misguided enterprise. Having sex with friends works for some gay men; for many it works only at the start of the new acquaintanceship, and then the "let's just be friends" mantra is invoked. For others it is possible to have sex with some friends, but not with other friends—that is, it works for those between whom there is some mutual attraction and whose fear that sex will ruin the friendship is minimal. But what is it about sexuality and friendship that creates such passionate and polarizing beliefs?

As I explore in the next chapters, friendship in our culture depends on, and is defined by, inter alia, trust, reciprocity, authenticity, similarity, and loyalty.[43] Although sexual relationships can enhance these attributes, they also have the potential to distort them and to uncover their opposites, especially if one of the people involved feels more passionate and demands more exclusiveness than the other does. Allan Bloom argues that friendship, unlike love, is reciprocal by definition: "You can love without being loved in return, but you cannot be the friend of one who is not your friend."[44] Fehr concludes in her review of research on friendship that "romantic relationships are more likely than friendships to involve exclusivity and passion,"[45] very possibly the attributes that could lead to an imbalance in a friendship.

If a person were suddenly to reveal a sexual interest to a friend after the relationship had already been established, it might be interpreted as a sign that he has not been entirely honest and disclosing in the friendship. It could raise issues of trust—have you really been interested in me as a friend, or were you just befriending me to get me in bed? And when the possibility of having sex has been brought into the open, and the other does not feel the same way about it, reciprocity and equity are threatened. On the other hand, sex can be the very thing that could bring greater intimacy, trust, and reciprocity to a friendship, as those who successfully manage an intermingling of sexuality and friendship attest.

But this is a gamble it seems few are willing to take, given the number of people who repeat the belief that sex ruins friendship. Where does this belief come from? Part of it may be definitional; friendship is defined in American culture as a nonsexual relationship. One might come away from this discussion arguing that, rather than being a word the meaning of

which is vague, it is one whose meaning is very clearly defined—
a friend is someone you don't have sex with but might feel attracted to, perhaps passionate about, and certainly loyal to. But
as soon as the friendship becomes sexual, the person is redefined as either a fuck buddy, someone you are dating (a boyfriend, as opposed to a boy friend), or an exclusive romantic
partner (a lover). By definition, he is not a friend; he is *more
than* a friend, indicating some hierarchical order. If two friends
are really passionate, attractive to one another, trusting, and
loyal, why would they not become a couple? If one or more of
these is missing, well—let's just be friends. And then let's save
face and rationalize our lack of passion for and attraction to each
other by invoking the refrain that sex potentially ruins friendship, and avoid all those awkward and honest discussions about
how we really feel, which might throw the equality and reciprocity of our friendship further out of balance.

Another reason for why this belief about "sex ruining friendships" persists can be located in the self-selection process of
friendship formation and in the methodological problems that
ensue. People respond to surveys about friendship, including
this one, keeping in mind the individuals who are their friends
now, that is, those who made it through the stages of friendship
formation without becoming alienated or ruining the interaction along the way. Those between whom problems and tensions did arise are not friends now, so it is possible for people
to honestly say that sexual issues have not created any problems
for their current friendships. The friends they have now are
the ones who, by definition, most likely made it through the
friendship process without problems and ultimately became
their friends.

Another part of the explanation for the contradictions in
the way gay men view friendship and sex is that many may be
reflecting on affairs that went wrong and in which issues of sexuality were at the center of the breakup. Friendship did not
result in these cases; sex is used to explain why the interaction
did not develop into a friendship. People then generalize this
experience to their current friendships, which so far have survived without sexual problems. In other words, people may be

articulating their fear that sex will ruin a friendship simply be-cause they are afraid it will ruin a *potential* friendship, even if they have never experienced sex ruining an already established friendship. If sex can ruin those relationships that never be-came friendships, they may reason, then it can also ruin existing friendships.

In addition, people may be generalizing about what hap-pens (emotionally and physically) in the actual sexual situation itself and transferring that to what might happen in their estab-lished friendships. Sex is about pleasure with elements of trust, reciprocity, intimacy, and caring. So is friendship. What more could one want in a good friendship? What better way to en-hance a close friendship and reinforce the pleasure, intimacy, trust, and loyalty that go along with it?

Well, on paper that sounds terrific, but in reality many sex-ual encounters, even if they occur between people whose over-all relationship is positive, raise concerns about equity, reciproc-ity, and trust over time. Michel Foucault said that "Friendship is reciprocal, and sexual relations are not reciprocal. . . . [I]f you have friendship, it is difficult to have sexual relations."[46] In the process of rationalizing, negotiating, and discussing sexual rela-tionships, imbalances can emerge. Issues of power and control, as well as "disruptions of orderly gender relations,"[47] begin to show up with repeated sexual encounters with the same person. Connell says, "In short-term encounters, in which giving and receiving pleasure is the only agenda, there is an approximate equality of position."[48] The risk of exacerbating power and con-trol differences with someone who already is a close friend might not be worth the possible pleasure that adding a sexual element to the friendship could bring. Is putting to this kind of a test a friendship just beginning with someone you like, but don't like enough to be involved with in a romantic relationship, any way to nurture the friendship? Again, if the passion, equity, reciprocity, trust, attraction, and sexual intimacy are all present, it would not be "just a friendship"; it would be a dating or lover relationship.

Of course, as the data show, many gay men have had sex with their friends, especially in the early stages of the friendship, so the possibility of reestablishing a sexual relationship is of little or no interest. Levels of physical attraction decline, and seeing the person on a routine basis reduces the excitement level of a sexual adventure. Indeed, any attempt to have a sexual fling might jeopardize the relationship or minimally reawaken the tensions that may have caused the sexual relationship to end all those years ago. Furthermore, if the person has developed into a close friend, an other self in Aristotelian terms, perhaps the "incest taboo" of no sex with friends (who are "like family") actually refers to no sex with someone who has become too much like another self.[49] Exploring another man's body is not unlike exploring one's own—a "mirroring of lover and beloved";[50] it is even more so if the other has become a close friend.

A more daring explanation for why people fear that sex will end a friendship—despite the fact that this rarely happens—is that many have just not tried sex with their established friends. Perhaps they would cease to use "sex will ruin the friendship" as an excuse if they knew how wonderful it could be to have sex with these friends. So say those who have managed to balance sexuality with friendship. Sex will be enhanced by the intimacy, trust, reciprocity, and balance of the already existing friendship, they say; and the intimacy and trust (the friendship) will be enhanced by the sex. This is a radical proposition in a society that strongly influences men to treat lovers and friends as distinctive categories. It is radical because sex with friends can lead to a renegotiation of gender in relationships. Sex with friends can lead to a unique combination of the culture's stereotypical characteristics of masculinity and femininity, the emotional with the physical, the sexual with the intimate. In this process hegemonic masculinity is contested.

But in resisting this radical transformation of the gender order—in avoiding sexuality with those to whom one is intimately and emotionally connected—in some contradictory way gay men continue to reproduce the very characteristics of the masculinity they sometimes challenge. Adolescent boys, for example, who learn the norms of heterosexual masculinity are more likely to believe that sex will lead to intimacy, while adolescent girls who learn the norms of heterosexual femininity wait for intimacy to be present before sexual relations occur.[51] If gay men get to know their potential friends from the starting point of sex and then refrain from sex when they get to know a person too intimately as a friend (as an other self), they end up reproducing compulsory masculinity. Issues of sex and friendship, therefore, reveal the intensity of gender in American society and perhaps give meaning to Connell's thesis that "Gay men are not free to invent new objects of desire any more than heterosexual men are—their choice of object is structured by the existing gender order."[52]

A study of gay men's friendship and sexuality can uncover the contradictions in the ways that various masculinities get constructed, reproduced, and resisted in American society. In terms of the number of sexual contacts with potential friends, fuck buddies, and nonfriends, gay men often reproduce hegemonic masculinity (e.g., sex without intimacy or love), while at the same time subverting the very notion of compulsory masculinity just by having sex with other men and by seeking passion, emotional intimacy, nurturing, reciprocity, and equality in the relationships.[53] They want it, as Rick said above, both "friendly and superficial."

Attraction, sex, and romance, though, are only part of the story of gay men's friendship. While they are important sites for understanding how masculinity is played out among gay men, there are other dimensions to friendship that also simultaneously contest and reproduce cultural constructions of masculinity. The next two chapters explore these other aspects of friendship. They include profiles of gay men's friends, and they discuss how the friendships begin, grow, are maintained, and sometimes end.

5

"THE MAGIC OF SYMPATHY AND IDENTIFICATION"

Profiles of Gay Men's Friends

"[P]eer relationships [in the gay community are] marked by a higher level of reciprocity than that characterizing heterosexual relations. Reciprocity is emphasized as an ideal and is to a large extent practiced. The conditions for reciprocity include similar ages of partners, shared class position, and shared position in the overall structure of gender."

— *R. W. Connell,* Masculinities

With friends we test out boundaries, discover who we are, and blend our souls in the development of a self—creating a "synergy between people," as my respondent Paul put it. Most research confirms that people's friends are like themselves; that is, to use the ironically appropriate jargon, friends exhibit homophily.[1] Fred spoke eloquently about the shared connections and power of friendship. For him, friendship is

> the human capacity to see oneself in the other. . . . [There is] a certain homology of experience and response to the world and to other people. . . . A deep friendship is an unspoken pact to be involved in and to participate in another's unfolding life through the magic of sympathy and identification. . . . It enables us to ratify and affirm the value and importance of another, while receiving reassurance about the value and importance of our selves. It is a miniature society in which we can test our ideas and emotional responses about life in general, refine and correct them in a context of candor and support.

Ben said, "Friends are people that I share my life—experiences, as well as space—with and who share theirs with me. I think it's accurate to say that we share a similar world view, and our values are similar, although our styles might be very different. . . . Friendships have been a tremendously important part of my life and will only continue to be so. It's a vital part of loving and living for me." And Ed said something that was explicitly echoed by half of those interviewed (when they were asked to define a friend), "[A friend] is someone who shares some of my values and perspectives."

No word came up as frequently in the interviews with the gay men as did "sharing." And through the use of words or phrases like "bond," "common interests and values," "similar," and "mutual," virtually everyone I talked to sought to emphasize some strong connection and similarity with their friends. But to reduce the complex process of friendship formation to a simple "birds of a feather flock together" maxim overstates a psychological choice in which people purposively select those who reinforce their own image and sense of self, and misses the dynamics of social structure and social interaction—the "miniature society" Fred talked about. Since most of us live in segregated neighborhoods, attend functions and select activities based on social class, and espouse certain values depending on our location within the social system, the fact that we meet potential friends who resemble us in many ways should not come as much of a surprise. Studies of friendship offer little empirical support for the "opposites attract" maxim.[2]

As Ed told me, "Since birds of a feather flock together, there is a natural selection and filtering process where we tend to be of like minds in many senses. At some point, the characteristics and personalities eventually diverge outside of my preferred comfort zone, but that either contributes to personal growth through diversity, or I rein in the 'circle' by dissociation, ignoring, or excluding." In general, there is stronger evidence for status homophily; friends are often of the same gender, ethnicity/race, religion, age, and class: "Friends tend to be relatively similar to one another along whatever dimension is measured. . . . There is little evidence that friends have complementary attributes; *similarity* pervades friendship selection."[3] Charles, an African American respondent, for example, spoke about the first time he met his close gay male friend: "I recognized someone who, like me, didn't fit in with the rest of the black students on campus. My instincts weren't wrong, and we became fast friends."

Paul Lazarsfeld and Robert Merton demonstrated almost forty-five years ago that a "process of mutual or unilateral accommodation of originally conflicting values" often occurs with friends; there is "a motivated tendency toward the formation of common values" resulting in a "prevailing pattern of value-homophily among current relationships, because the opposition of deeply held values tends to disrupt the friendship."[4] The degree to which friends are similar in status and in values depends on different social conditions, so that friendships developed through neighborhood contacts tend to be more ethnically diverse than those developed through kinship; work-related friends are more similar to one another economically and more diverse in terms of age and ethnicity.[5] This makes sense, since reciprocity and balance of exchange in friendships demand some overall equality: "It is much easier to treat as equal those who in fact are equal: who have the same economic resources, the same sorts of domestic commitment, the same status in the wider society, and so on."[6] Given the economic and social stratification of contemporary American society, the opportunities for people to meet others who are different in these respects are limited.

Yet variations, as always, persist. College students often find themselves in situations more conducive to cross-sex friendships, middle-aged people are more likely than are younger or older people to have a more age-diverse and race-diverse set of friends, and lower-status people have more heterogeneous networks than do higher-status people.[7] Furthermore, according to Letty Cottin Pogrebin, some people reported on how similar another person may be to themselves even when he or she is different in status terms. This is either because they perceive the person to be similar and report it that way or because they are speaking about a much deeper congruence of value similarity.[8] And it is at the intersection of shared values that the friendship is maintained, not just because friends are similar in terms of age, race, gender, and other status characteristics.

Maybe it is in this arena, in which shared values prevail, that gay men's friendships fall; many gay men report that they feel closer to other gay men, sometimes regardless of their other status characteristics, because of a shared identity and set of values developed in a culture that has routinely marginalized and oppressed them. The expressions of camaraderie and brotherhood expressed by many African American men who have experienced an outsider status come closest to illustrating the kinds of bonds that can emerge among gay men.[9] However, this is not to suggest that those who also share additional experiences of oppression related to race/ethnicity, social class, and religion feel akin to all gay men. For many of these people, identification with those who are typically represented in the dominant images of gay culture may not come easily, even though they share a sexual orientation.[10]

Interestingly, several of my respondents of color were the ones who highlighted the importance of being oneself with friends. John, an African American, said, "a friend is someone I can be myself around, cruise guys with without feeling just a touch of insecurity about it, to share my thoughts and dreams with." And Harry, a Native American, also emphasized the fact that friends are those who "take the time for getting to know me . . . and accept me for being gay." What many of the gay men appeared to be saying is that there are values and behaviors—resulting in part from the experience of being a gay man in a society that is institutionally and culturally structured around heterosexual masculinity—that can create the potential for a bond to develop at a level of intensity not typically present between most heterosexual male friends. In practice, these values and behaviors are rarely the same across categories of gay men, since they get mediated by other characteristics that mask sexual orientation and since they privilege some men, such as those who are white, middle class, and more "masculine."

Because gay men have historically congregated in a limited number of public spaces and institutions, like bars, baths, parks, and, increasingly, social and political organizations, they are more likely than others are to meet people of diverse backgrounds and thereby to develop a more heterogeneous network of friends. However, this may have been more the case in the years before the contemporary gay movement, when there were fewer places in which gay men could meet others, although even then various types of bars attracted different subcultures, especially in large cities.[11] Now many more gay organizations, clubs, political groups, and bars exist, resulting in status differentiation and greater specialization. Today it may be more likely than it once was for gay men of various educational and income levels, races, and ages to join different organizations, go to separate bars and baths catering to various styles and tastes, and participate in political movements at different levels, thus resulting in a self-selection into subgroups of gay men who tend to resemble each other.

R. W. Connell points out that, unlike in earlier eras, in contemporary society "men can adopt, negotiate, or reject a gay identity, a gay commercial scene, and gay sexual and social networks."[12] Despite all the diversity and heterogeneity in gay communities, when gay men choose which networks and spaces they want or don't want they often end up with other people who look more like themselves in terms of values, tastes, behaviors, and statuses. They may encounter (but do not always pursue) people outside their usual circles. This is not simply a personal choice but is often one constrained and shaped by a social system. For example, meeting friends through other friends—one of the most common way of making friends[13]—would typically result in a perpetuation of homophily rather than in diversity. When people are already connected by class, education, income, race, and styles of masculinity to specific institutions and value systems, their choices are not as voluntary and free as they are believed to be. This becomes evident in this chapter as I describe who gay men's friends are and where gay men meet these friends.

Gay Men's Friends: Who They Are

It should come as no surprise that gay men's close and best friends are other gay men who tend to be like themselves. Of

Table 5.1   Profile of Sexual Orientation of Survey Respondents'
Best Friends

Identity of Best Friend	Percentage of Respondents
Gay male	79.3
Heterosexual female	9.7
Heterosexual male	4.8
Lesbian	2.8
Bisexual male	2.1
Bisexual female	1.4

the 30 men interviewed 65 percent said their *best* friend was a
gay man, and of the 161 men who completed the questionnaire
almost 80 percent reported that their *best* friend was a gay man,
as Table 5.1 shows: [14]

The survey data on *best* friends also confirm a high degree
of homophily, even when one includes those 20 percent of best
friends who are not gay men. Best friends look like each other
(see Table 5.2).

Homophily is also supported by the interview sample on
age and race. The mean age of the thirty participants was 40,
and 73 percent were white. The mean age of their best friends
was 38.6, and 78.5 percent of the friends were white. Other
characteristics were not assessed.

Table 5.2   Profiles of Survey Respondents' Best Friends and Best Gay
Male Friends

	Respondent	Best Friend	Best Gay Male Friend
Age (mean)	40	37	38
Education (percent college graduate or more)	72.5	66.9	68.1
Income (percent under $34,000)°	44.4	43.6	41.6
Income (percent over $54,000)°	25.6	23.6	26.5
Living with a lover/partner (percent)	34.2	36.7	37.0
Ever legally married (percent)	26.1	27.6	23.0
Live in rural area (percent)	7.5	6.2	5.1

° Income is yearly before taxes, adjusted for 1997 dollars.

Table 5.3 presents information from the survey about close and casual friends. In response to questions about *close* friends, 22 percent of the questionnaire respondents mentioned more than twelve close friends, and 10 percent listed fewer than three, with a median of around six close friends. Studies of men's friendships (which are presumably based on mostly heterosexual samples) indicate that men have on average around three to five close friends and that about 10 percent do not have any close friends.[15] About 60 percent of the gay men in my study had two or fewer close friends who were women; around 3 percent said that the majority of their friends were women.

When it came to *casual* friends, approximately 51 percent of my survey respondents reported twenty or more casual friends, 10 percent said they had fewer than five, and the median stood at around twenty casual friends. About 21 percent of the gay men who responded said that two or fewer of their casual friends were women; around 2 percent said that the majority were women. In short, most gay men's casual, close, and best friends are men.[16] Women are more likely to be part of the larger network of acquaintances and casual friends.

Most of the men I surveyed, except those who had fewer than five casual friends and three close friends, said they were satisfied with the number of casual and close friends they had. And those with the fewest casual and close friends were also the least satisfied with the quality of their relationships. Overall there was a significant relationship between the number of casual and close friends and feeling satisfied with the quantity and quality of them; it seems that the more friends you have, the more satisfied you are with your friendship network.[17] And the

Table 5.3   Profile of Survey Respondents' Close and Casual Friends

	Close Friends	Casual Friends
Median number	6	20
Percent with very few	10.0	10.0
Percent with very many	21.9	51.3
Percent for whom majority are female	3.1	1.9
Percent for whom two or fewer are female	60.9	21.3

satisfaction with the quality of the friend significantly varied by type; as expected, respondents were the most satisfied with best friends, compared to close friends and casual friends.[18]

These findings about the similarity of friends replicate those of studies completed before the development of modern gay communities; they are not just a function of the emergence of gay organizations and neighborhoods in contemporary urban centers. In their study of gay men in San Francisco almost thirty years ago, Alan Bell and Martin Weinberg provided one of the first surveys with questions on gay men's friendships. Most gay men responded that the majority of their friends were male and homosexual and that they had five or more good, close friends (defined as "people you can talk to or go to for help about relatively intimate matters"). Differences were not significant between the white gay men sample and the black gay men sample, but gay men overall had significantly more friends than did the heterosexual men in the study (most of whom stated that they had three or fewer friends).[19]

Other studies completed in the same era also found that gay men have more close friends than do heterosexual men and that the majority of gay men's friends are other gay men.[20] In the late 1960s and early 1970s, when most of these studies were completed, gay men often found it difficult to express their sexual orientation in public heterosexual settings and typically sought out networks of other gay men for socializing, sexual contacts, and recreation.[21] This was still true in the late 1970s, when a study of gay male couples also found that gay men's best friends were other gay men or gay male couples, and about two-thirds of the participants reported that they spent almost all their time with other gay men.[22] Around 12 percent had nongay friends and couples as their closest friends. Those couples who were together over eleven years had "the most friends identified as 'ours' rather than as 'his' or 'mine,' including a higher percentage of heterosexual couples."[23]

But not all gay men have many friends. During our interview, Will forthrightly stated his opinion that "gay men don't make good friends because of competitiveness, insecurity, and envy." He had lost many friends in his life, and always around issues of jealousy or failing to reciprocate socially. Others just don't have an easy time making friends. Rick said, "I may be at one end of the scales. I often wished I was more sociable but it just never seems to engage me. . . . I'm actually more of a loner than anything else. I adapted to isolation as a child and unfortunately the habits have stuck." And Nick, a bisexual married to a woman, identified his wife as his best friend and reported that he didn't have "any 'real' close friends." This is similar to what most research has found to be typical about heterosexual married men.[24]

Among the gay men surveyed, those who said they had no best friend were more likely to be single (88 percent were single compared with the overall sample of 52.5 percent), older (mean age of forty-six compared to overall sample mean age of forty), and more lived in rural areas (11 percent compared to 7.5 percent of the total sample). Those with fewer than three close friends were also older (mean of forty-five). Gay men with the fewest casual friends (five or less) tended to be single (67 percent) and fewer were college graduates or higher (50 percent, compared to 72.5 percent of the total sample).[25] Since most people in coupled relationships view their partner as their best friend, it makes sense that most of those without a best friend are single; similarly, those in couples are more likely to know other couples, increasing the potential number of casual friends, as well. College is also a source of friends, and those without college degrees had fewer casual friends. Younger gay men were more likely to list college as a place they met their friends; this may account for why older men have fewer close friends (younger men are more recently graduated than older men, so more are likely to still be in touch with college friends).

Where They Met

Who becomes friends with whom is partly related to where they meet, and where they meet is usually related to their location in the social structure. Take social class as an example: studies show that the friendships between men of higher social classes generally are initiated from more diverse sources, although higher-status men have fewer friends who are kin and neighbors compared to lower-status men. In general, most people meet their friends through work and in the neighborhood, and many retain them from childhood and adolescence.[26] Friendships developed in childhood and through kinship are of the longest duration and are the most intimate ("friendships of commitment"), while work and neighborhood friendships are the least intimate and are of shorter duration, despite more frequent interaction ("friendships of convenience"). A study of networks by Claude Fischer also found that full-time working respondents met most of their nonkin friends at work, through friends, and in the neighborhood (in that order).[27]

This is mostly true for Ed, who works full-time: "I met most of my closest friends either at work or through the gay book club I belong to." His closest friends he met through the club, but "there's also a slight, expanding circle of acquaintances through my few friends from work." Ben, who grew up in the South, knows most of his closest friends from college, graduate school, and even the seventh grade: "He was the new boy, so shy and a Yankee. So I welcomed him to our little town like a proper Southern gentleman should. We became instantly inseparable and we later both turned out to be gay. He's family."

Harry met one of his closest friends in a "tearoom" (a public bathroom known for being the site of sexual encounters) while he was in graduate school: "He slipped me a piece of paper underneath the stall that said 'suck my dick,' and I wrote coyly 'I don't think I know you well enough for that yet'—bluffing is important, you know. So I wrote 'tell me about yourself' and he said 'I'm a first-year business student,' and I said 'so am I. Which major?' I invited him back to my apartment and we talked for hours—no sex. Can you believe it?" And Charles talked about meeting his closest friend fifteen years ago in college on a bus when he went up to Aaron and introduced himself: "I had seen him on campus but had never spoken to him." Charles felt Aaron was also someone who didn't quite fit in with the other black students. He was right, and they became "fast friends."

According to the survey data presented in Table 5.4, most

Table 5.4 Survey Respondents' Main Sources of Friends (Percent, with Rank Order in Parentheses)

	Best Friend°	Close Friends	Casual Friends
Other friends	32.3 (1)	69.4 (1)	68.1 (3)
Clubs/organizations†	30.7 (2)	63.1 (2)	71.3 (2)
Work	19.7 (3)	53.1 (3)	81.3 (1)
Parties/dinners	15.0 (4)	35.6 (4)	41.3 (5)
Bars	12.6 (5)	29.4 (5)	29.4 (7)
College	11.8 (6)	29.4 (5)	25.0 (8)
Church/synagogue	10.2 (7)	27.5 (7)	31.3 (6)
Adolescence/high school	10.2 (7)	17.5 (9)	8.8 (12)
Graduate school	6.3 (9)	16.3 (10)	13.8 (11)
Sports/gym	3.9 (10)	10.0 (13)	18.8 (9)
Neighbors	3.1 (11)	18.1 (8)	45.0 (4)
Childhood	3.1 (11)	13.1 (11)	6.9 (13)
Friends of family	3.1 (11)	12.5 (12)	14.4 (10)

° Percentages are much smaller for best friend, since respondents were asked to select one or two best friends (who were not their lover/partner) to answer this question, and to indicate where they met most of the people who were currently their close or casual friends.

† Percentages for clubs/organizations are very likely much higher than corresponding figures might be in other surveys, since the sample was selected mostly from organizations and clubs (although this does not necessarily mean that they would be a source of best and close friendships).

gay men met the majority of their best, close, and casual friends through friends of friends, clubs and organizations, work, and dinners or parties.[28] Neighborhood and the workplace were sources of friends, especially of casual friends, while other friends were the largest source of close friends and best friends. Educational settings, including high school, college, and graduate school, were a better source of close friends, and sometimes the neighborhood was a good place to meet close friends. Bars, once one of the most likely places in which gay men could get involved with a social circle, continued to be a venue in which to meet friends, especially close and casual friends, but were not nearly as important for this mostly middle-class sample as were personal networks of other friends, dinners, parties, clubs, or work. In general, for gay men, other friends are the main source of close and best friendships, work is the main source of close and casual friends, and the neighborhood is where they find most of their casual friends, although the neighborhood appears to be a less likely source of friends for gay men than it is for heterosexuals.

While for nearly every category of gay men, friends' introductions were a source of casual, close, and best friends, there were some differences in the ordering based on education/income (social class) and age. Compared with the overall sample, gay men over fifty-five were more likely to have met friends through clubs and organizations, less likely to have done so at work (many are retired) or at college, and more likely to have close friends from the neighborhood. Younger men (under thirty) were much more likely to list college and less likely to list clubs and neighborhood as meeting places for various kinds of friends. Younger men were also more likely to say they had met some of their close and casual friends during childhood and adolescence. These data are consistent with studies showing that over time and distance people lose touch; younger men are closer, in terms of time, to their college days and to their childhood and adolescent experiences.

Those with less education (a few years of college or less) and lower incomes (under $34,000 annually, 1997 adjusted) were slightly more likely to list bars as a place to meet close friends, and they had more friends from adolescence, compared with the overall sample. Gay men of a higher social class were slightly more likely to list parties/dinners as a source of close and best friends. But clubs, work, and the introductions of other friends continued to be the primary avenues by which gay men met most of their casual, close, and best friends.

So far I have focused primarily on the male, mostly gay, friends of the gay men in the study. But what about the heterosexual male and female friends of gay men? One of the few studies about gay-straight friendship is discussed in Letty Cottin Pogrebin's popular book *Among Friends*. Almost a third of the respondents to an early 1980s *Psychology Today* volunteer survey said that they had a gay or lesbian friend. Close friendships between gay and straight people appeared roughly in the following order: straight women–gay men; straight women–lesbians; straight men–gay men; and lesbians–straight men. Friendship between lesbians and gay men was just slightly more common than was that between lesbians and straight men.[29] Using data from my study and from other research, I now discuss the friendships of gay men with straight women, straight men, and lesbians, even if such friendships are not typical of the urban middle-class gay men in my study.

The Friendship of Straight Women and Gay Men

There is perhaps no more persistent stereotype about gay men's friendships than the notion that gay men and straight women make good friends. When I discussed my research with heterosexual women, one woman after another told me about how many straight women she knew (including sometimes the woman herself) who had gay male friends. And straight men also said they thought that friendships between straight women and gay men were particularly common but rarely mentioned any friendships between heterosexual men and gay men. Edmund White writes that the friendship between straight women and gay men is "straightforward, amiable, and totally disinterested. In such a friendship neither person stands to gain anything except companionship, support and simple fun."[30] Could Oscar Wilde have been so inattentive when he wrote in *Lady Windermere's Fan* that "Between men and women there is no friendship possible. There is passion, enmity, worship, love, but no friendship"? Maybe this is so in the case of stereotypically heterosexual men, as the research on cross-sex friendship suggests, but it seems that gay men may be the exception to this profile.

Not all gay men's friends are other gay men. In fact, more and more, gay men are integrating their friendship networks and including lesbians and heterosexual men and women among their close and casual friends. Some have argued that this has been one of the outcomes of the AIDS epidemic, since it brought together lesbians, straight men and women in health care institutions, gay organizations, AIDS agencies, and political alliances.[31] It also reflects perhaps a "queering of friendship," by virtue of which today's postmodern younger generation increasingly blurs the boundaries between male and female and among bisexual, gay, lesbian, and transgender categories.

However, only 10 percent of the gay men in my study (remember, the mean age is forty) said that their best friend was a heterosexual woman, and a very small percentage responded that women composed the majority of their casual or close friendships. How different are these findings from a survey completed almost thirty years ago in which more than 90 percent of the gay men surveyed said that *most* of their friends were male? In addition, 71 percent of the white gay male sample and 76 percent of the black gay male sample in that study reported having at least *some* female friends. (A higher percentage of heterosexual men than homosexual men had women friends, suggesting the inaccuracy of Wilde's statement.)[32]

Who They Are and Where They Met

The fourteen gay men in my survey (and the one from my interview sample) who said that their best friend was a heterosexual woman were much younger than the rest of the sample (their mean age was 30.4), and their female best friend was similarly young (with a mean age of 31.3). They were also matched on educational level, current living arrangements with a spouse or partner, and living in rural areas, as Table 5.5 indicates. A smaller percentage of the women had higher income levels, compared with their gay male friends, although more of the men earned at the lower-income levels. The women were more likely than the gay men to have been married at some point in their lives.

In comparison to the entire sample, gay men with "many or almost all" close female friends tended to be younger, were less likely to have a college degree or higher, earned less money (were of a lower social class), were more likely to be living with a partner, and were more likely to live in a rural area (see Table 5.6). Those with "many or almost all" casual female friends were less likely than the sample as a whole to have ever been married and were slightly more likely to live in a rural area.

Table 5.5 Profile of Gay Survey Respondents Whose Best Friend Is a Female Heterosexual ($N = 14$)

	Respondent	Best Female Heterosexual Friend
Age (mean)	30.4	31.3
Education (percent college graduate or more)	78.6	71.4
Income (percent under $34,000)°	64.3	50.0
Income (percent over $54,000)°	21.4	14.3
Living with a lover/partner (percent)	28.6	28.6
Ever legally married (percent)	21.4	50.0
Live in rural area (percent)	7.1	7.1

° Income is yearly before taxes, adjusted for 1997 dollars.

Other friends and college, as well as the workplace, were the primary sources of these heterosexual female friends (see Table 5.7). For those with "many or almost all" female close friends, other friends, work, and clubs were the best sources of most of their close friends; work, clubs, and other friends were the primary sources of casual friends.[33] In general, other than the facts that college is a better source of gay men's best female

Table 5.6 Profile of Gay Survey Respondents Reporting That "Many or Almost All" of Their Close and Casual Friends Were Female

	Respondents with Close Female Friends ($N = 20$)	Respondents with Casual Female Friends ($N = 42$)
Age (mean)	35.5	38.1
Education (percent college graduate or more)	40.0	73.8
Income (percent under $34,000)°	65.0	50.0
Income (percent over $54,000)°	15.0	30.9
Living with a lover/ partner (percent)	50.0	28.6
Ever legally married (percent)	20.0	17.1
Live in rural area (percent)	30.0	11.9

° Income is yearly before taxes, adjusted for 1997 dollars.

friends than it is of their gay male friends, and that bars are less important sources, the way gay men meet their female friends is not unlike the way they meet their gay male friends—through other friends, work, and clubs and organizations.

In general, if any overall pattern can be gleaned from these data taken from very small subsamples, it is that younger gay men and those living in more rural areas have more female friends. Structurally this makes sense, as previous research has demonstrated. Those living in urban areas have more opportunities to become involved in communities and subcultures that are more specialized, and that attract people who are similar to themselves. Gay men are more likely to circulate with other gay men in urban areas and with groups composed of both genders in rural areas. Also, younger men are more likely to have female friends because they were more recently or are currently in col-

Table 5.7   Main Sources of Survey Respondents' Female Friends (Percent, with Rank Order in Parentheses)

	Best Female Friend° (N = 14)	Close Female Friends (N = 20)	Casual Female Friends (N = 42)
Other friends	28.6 (1)	85.0 (1)	57.1 (3)
College	28.6 (1)	40.0 (5)	31.0 (7)
Work	21.4 (3)	65.0 (2)	85.7 (1)
Parties/dinners	14.3 (4)	45.0 (4)	38.1 (4)
Church/synagogue	14.3 (5)	20.0 (9)	33.3 (5)
Adolescence/high school	14.3 (5)	25.0 (6)	14.3 (11)
Clubs/organizations†	7.1 (7)	65.0 (2)	76.2 (2)
Graduate school	7.1 (7)	25.0 (6)	19.0 (9)
Sports/gym	7.1 (7)	15.0 (11)	16.7 (10)
Bars	0.0 (10)	20.0 (9)	21.4 (8)
Neighbors	0.0 (10)	25.0 (6)	33.3 (5)
Childhood	0.0 (10)	10.0 (12)	9.5 (13)
Friends of family	0.0 (10)	10.0 (12)	14.3 (11)

° Percentages are much smaller for best friend, since respondents were asked to select one or two best friends (who were not their lover/partner) to answer this question, and to indicate where they met most of the people who were currently their close or casual friends.

† Percentages for clubs/organizations are very likely much higher than corresponding figures might be in other surveys, since the sample was selected mostly from organizations and clubs (although this does not necessarily mean that they would be a source of best and close friendships).

lege, where cross-sex friendships occur more frequently. In addition, there is possibly an emerging "queer" culture, in which categories and boundaries get erased and in which an increasingly large number of men and women (gay, lesbian, bisexual, transgendered, and heterosexual) interact more and share more social spaces. And in the process society's gender order is questioned; men and women do become friends, something not experienced as often in strictly heterosexual social worlds.

The Role of Fag Hags

Before leaving the topic of the friendships between gay men and straight women, I want to consider one particular form of this relationship. Within many gay communities a designated role exists for some straight women who have gay men as friends. Over the years these women have been variously called "fag hag," "fruit fly," or "faggotina."[34] But while the words might be commonly used, how they are defined is not as clear-cut. One gay dictionary defines a "fag hag" as a heterosexual woman who likes to be in the company of gay men and who can be a somewhat plain woman who befriends gay men, *or* someone interested in sex with them, *or* someone in love with gay men.[35] The term has been interpreted as insulting—"[a label] of disdain for a woman who doesn't choose to upgrade herself with a 'real man'"[36]—but is not necessarily meant to be so when it is used by gay men, who define a "fag hag" as "a straight woman who spends a lot of time with gay men, usu. not considered to be a derisive term except by fag hags themselves."[37] In his 1968 book, *The Gay World,* Martin Hoffman defines "fruit flies" as "women who like to associate with male homosexuals. . . . [T]hey are the beneficiaries of a great deal of sociability without being objects of seduction."[38]

Curiously, no equivalent phrase exists for friendship between straight men and lesbians, straight men and gay men, or lesbians and gay men, perhaps indicating that the straight female–gay male friendship is a more common, or at least a more visible, relationship after all. Possibly it requires a special label because it calls into question all sorts of unique gender and sexual identity issues, forcing us to examine the gendered order of American society and how hegemonic masculinity is maintained. Such is the argument in one of the few published academic studies on this topic.

Dawne Moon states that "The term *fag hag* resides at the boundary between who belongs in gay space and who does not, highlighting the tensions within a discourse of gay identity, tensions related to people's experiences of community, gender, and sexuality."[39] The meanings gay men Moon surveyed assigned to the role of fag hag varied depending on the era in which they came out; older, pre-Stonewall gay men used the term to refer to lonely women unable to get dates with straight men and who liked to hang out with gay men for the company, while younger men saw fag hags as women who wanted to date gay men and get sexually involved with them. Both young and old, though, used the term to refer to "unattractive" and "fat" women who don't perpetuate the heteronormative sexist ideal of a woman. They are "women who, like gay men, have been rejected from or have rejected the heterosexual mainstream."[40]

Moon argues that fag hags who express a sexual and/or romantic interest in gay men represent a threat to some gay men's identity and, by extension, to the building of gay community, which requires the unambiguous rejection of heterosexuality and the reification of binary categories (while paradoxically calling for a liberation of sexuality from its narrowly defined categories). Hence, "for a gay man to reject women's presence in gay space may be an attempt to challenge heterosexism."[41] Others see gay men who hang out with fag hags as younger, newly out men who have not yet learned the details of gay men's culture and still need to cling to the heterosexual images of the society.

Sometimes, "where the woman does not challenge her companions' gay identity, and where she is not perceived as a threat to the politically charged reproduction of a community of gay men, she may be accepted as a member of that community," and gay men would use the term fag hag symbolically or ironically, and not derisively, to include the woman in the group.[42] In other cases women friends were not labeled fag hags when their gender or sexuality was not a threat to the cohesiveness of the group, its identity, or individuals' identities. The way in which women who hang out with gay men view the situation is not assessed in Moon's study.

Thus a term that many might say represents a clearly defined role in gay communities in fact has multiple meanings, which vary depending on the age of the respondent and the cohesiveness of the group that includes a woman. Whether it is used humorously or pejoratively, the term raises salient questions about who is or isn't part of a gay-identity community. It also calls attention to the complex and often contradictory dimensions of gay masculinities; gay men enact traditional gendered styles of heterosexual masculinity by appearing with certain kinds of straight women while simultaneously distancing themselves from any misperception that these are women they might be sexually attracted to or involved with.

But before we start overinterpreting the use of this term, I want to point out that no one in my interview sample mentioned fag hags until I directly asked about the label. Harve defined fag hag as "an unflattering, negative term for a straight woman who likes to associate with a gay man. I would never describe any woman in that manner." Greg said, "The onerous vernacular fag hag refers to a woman who is attracted to gay men. The rationale for her attraction varies as much as there are stars in the sky. I have had many fag hags in my life and love them all dearly." On the other hand, Fred did not limit the term to a straight woman, as most do, but described a lesbian fag hag he personally knew who is a regular at one of the gay/lesbian organizations he attends: "She seems to be trying to be more gay than the men. She's into S&M, and promiscuity, and into bringing a 'fiancé' and then fondling another guy while she was sitting between him and her 'intended.'"

All the over-forty-five-year-old men in my sample understood the term as a negative one describing a woman who likes being around gay men for any number of reasons. But Fred's remarks point out the gender issues involved. Not only did he associate S&M and promiscuity with being "gayer than gay"—more masculine perhaps than most gay men, he was saying—but he also called attention to the "fondling" that takes place between a man and a woman, which would in heterosexual contexts be a gender-appropriate even if not a decorous thing to do in public.

Here, at this gay/lesbian public meeting, for a woman to be gayer than the gay men means being more instrumentally masculine in sexual terms (multiple partners, rougher sex play) while her being a lesbian means she should not touch men (and by extension, the gay men should not be touched by a woman). It's not clear whether Fred was reacting more against the stereotype of a "butch" lesbian (one who is more masculine than a woman should be) or against the blurring of gender lines for both the men and the woman. After all, this woman's behavior calls into question the gay men's masculinity, which, like the masculinity of heterosexual men, must set up boundaries in order to preserve its power and meanings. Once again, gay men enact the duality of hegemonic masculinity while subverting its very constitutive elements. While breaking down some of the gender borders they reconstruct the traditional ones at the same time.

The Friendship of Gay Men and Straight Men

If friendship with straight women raises these kinds of issues, imagine what friendship with heterosexual men can do. Gay men's friendship with straight women may challenge the construction of gender and sexual orientation by calling into question what it means to be gay and male when one is emotionally or sometimes sexually involved with a woman. Friendship with straight men is even more so a relationship that contests the very meanings of gender, hegemonic masculinity, and gay masculinity for both the straight and the gay men involved. Listen to the complexities of emotions, the comparisons with women and wife, the homosocial settings of military and fraternities, and the sexual attractions—all of which hover at the intersection of hegemonic masculinity and gay masculinity—underlying Eugene's story about his best friend, whom he met during his freshman year of college in the deep South ten years ago:

I was in a fraternity and he was a candidate being rushed to join. He joined and he and I became fast friends. I was deep in the closet at the time. He had several girlfriends, and we shared sexual experiences with a few of them—although it didn't seem as if he and I were having sex together, if that makes sense. I enlisted after college in the military and was home on leave when I told him I was gay. We were both around twenty-four then. He seemed a bit surprised, but said he thought I was just intolerant of women (laugh). He has been *very* understanding, and our friendship has grown. He has since married, and we are all three very close. Though he is very handsome and I have always been aware of his attractive looks, I have only once or twice thought of him in a sexual way. It just doesn't seem appropriate to think of him that way. He is my best friend because we share an emotional intimacy that surpasses the level of emotional intimacy I have with the other friends in my life. He has most assuredly reached that same intimacy with his wife; I'm not sure though, and I'm not going to ask him that question. I hope they share that though, but I can tell him secrets, thoughts, feelings, questions that I can tell no other person, and he can do the same to me. We both know each other well enough to understand how we both react to things.

Although Eugene claimed that he and his friend shared all sorts of feelings and secrets with one another—after all, they once shared girlfriends in the fraternity—they remained silent about how emotionally intimate his friend was with his wife. Perhaps there is some unspoken emotional and intimate relationship that might be contested if comparisons were to be made. But Eugene's description of his friendship also illustrates the reproduction of some stereotypical masculine limitations between close male friends—that is, the reluctance to talk about really personal feelings—while it was simultaneously being framed in terms of emotions, same-sex sexual attractions, and intimacy, all of which are less typical of heterosexual masculine roles in American society. Gender is as much at work here as is sexual orientation. Even if friendship with a heterosexual male is not typical for most gay men, any gay-straight male friendships could provoke questions about our gendered gay and straight cultures.

Few studies, however, exist about these relationships. And unlike the term fag hag, there is no institutional role or label in gay cultures for heterosexual male friends in gay men's lives. I found one book of letters between a straight man and a gay man that describes the unfolding and multidimensional character of their friendship.[43] The gay man, Chris, reported that he wrote more than his straight friend, Tom, about his personal emotional and sexual development, reinforcing the findings from my study that gay men are more likely to talk about their feelings and to disclose personal stories. But the two did make the case that their "exceptional venture: brothers growing closer in affection and unity" was contributing to building Walt Whitman's invincible city of friends.[44]

In his doctoral research on straight men who have gay friends, Dwight Fee uses the term "coming over" to describe the trip heterosexual men have to make to become friends with gay men. Just as the fag hag role can call into question meanings about homosexuality, gay-straight male friendships disrupt "the process whereby heterosexuality fends off gay-identifications."[45] Focusing on the straight men's perspective, Fee says, "One of the features of straight men who, through the context of friendship, enter gay worlds is that they do not follow the script or norm for heterosexual male behavior. . . . They risk undermining homosociality by pulling the framework out from under men's collective fellowship, thereby abdicating their favored status with the large majority of other straight men."[46]

The men in his study, in general, were not homophobic. They were tolerant and congenial toward others, and they were uncomfortable with trying to be a "regular guy" in traditional male terms. The straight men found their friendship with gay men to be less instrumental, less rigid, more intimate, and more open than their friendships with other heterosexual men: "straight-gay attachments, and a gay-identified masculinity specifically, can undermine men's mundane collusions that maintain hetero-dominated or normative structures."[47] These are transformative and transgressive relationships challenging and deconstructing the culture's concepts about masculinity and sexuality.

But what about the gay men in these relationships? The straight men in Fee's study were interested in the sexual differences between themselves and the gay men, while the gay men were focused on the gendered similarities with the straight men, lending support to Connell's argument that most gay men continue to use hegemonic masculinity as a reference point in their personal and social lives.[48] Because most of the gay men had mostly gay male friends, they recognized that the friendships with the straight men were often not as intimate and affectionate as were their friendships with other gay men. In fact, many "knew they posed a threat to many straight men and knew they could never be sure of their reactions. Initiating friendships with straight men was therefore a precarious and sometimes exhausting enterprise."[49] But some of the gay men welcomed this less intimate friendship with another man, which gave them "time out" from the type of male intimacy expected of them among their gay friends: "Contexts of straight friendship can thus be a place to withdraw from gay loci of experience, but it is not recanting one's gay identification, politics, or anything else."[50] Still others liked having straight male friends in order to keep a diverse range of experiences in their lives; many of them had close, affectionate friendships with the straight men.

Pogrebin's friendship research focuses some attention on straight-gay male friendships. Straight men's responses were not reported, but of the three gay men whose comments are printed in the book, one had straight male friends because he came out at forty-nine and did not identify with gay culture, another grew close to his straight college roommate, and the other found straight friends too trying because their dislike of gays prevented him from being himself.[51]

In my study, less than 5 percent (seven men) of the survey respondents and only three of the men interviewed reported having a heterosexual male as a best friend. Bill and his best (straight male) friend were fellow college students: "He's the best a friend can be. He'll be there for me without any questions asked. His willingness to help is second to none. He's the type of friend you always want to keep and always want to do things for." But the small sample size makes it very difficult to describe any patterns, other than to say that younger men (under thirty) are more likely to have a straight male best friend whose age is around the same as their own and whom they are likely to have met in college. Data on the sexual orientation of casual and close friends were not collected.

The Friendship of Gay Men and Lesbians

And what happens when gay men and lesbians are friends, in either a sexual or an emotional sense? Again, no term exists for gay men who are friends with lesbians (or vice versa), and very little research has been done on the topic. Only seven gay men in my study reported having a lesbian best friend, so it is difficult to offer any patterns other than to say that the gay men who have a lesbian best friend are younger or around the same age as their friend, and that these friends meet through their friends and organizations, suggesting perhaps the changing nature of gay/lesbian clubs. Mike said, "My best friend is a lesbian who I met in a gay/lesbian professional organization. She is the person who comes to mind (after my partner) when I need to talk through problems. She and her partner have been very supportive during tough times, and they are a lot of fun to spend time with. We are all close in age."

Pogrebin argues that lesbians are more likely to have gay men as friends than gay men are to have lesbians as friends, because lesbians "need the political support of the relatively stronger male wing of the gay rights movement," whereas gay men get "supplementary affirmation of their attractiveness" more from straight women than from lesbians, the latter of whom also may turn gay men off with their "personal style and 'stridency.' "[52] Other than a quote or two to illustrate these awkward explanations, no quantitative data are offered to support any of these stereotypes.

In contrast, and to get a glimpse of the greater range of emotional and sometimes sexual attractions that exist between gay men and lesbians, consider the personal stories of friendship that appear in two anthologies. Joan Nestle and John Preston collected stories about the friendship between some gay men and lesbians. As Preston puts it, an erotic response by a gay man to a lesbian "destroyed that illusion of containment" that keeps gay people from expressing attraction toward someone of the other sex. A relationship between a gay man and a heterosexual woman (fag hag) can have the same effect.[53] A collection of writings edited by Sara Miles and Eric Rofes also focuses on the sexual realities that can and do exist between lesbians and gay men and on how these relationships contribute to identities, communities, and culture.[54]

Many lesbians and gay men have come together to form coalitions in the fight against AIDS. Nancy Stoller notes that when the AIDS epidemic began in the early 1980s "most lesbians and gay men were living essentially parallel lives, organized primarily around the separate themes of female values and feminism for the women and masculinity and justice for the men."[55] But some "coalition lesbians" argued for an active involvement with gay men not only to fight the injustices of the health-care system but also to improve the role of lesbians and gay men in other institutions of society. And many did and continue to work with gay men in staffing gay and lesbian organizations, serving as executive directors of major national lesbian and gay groups, and developing working and personal friendships with each other.

Homophily and Gay Friendship

Most previous research on friendship indicates that a high degree of homophily exists among friends. Anthropologist Robert Paine goes so far as to say that a "friend is someone who understands you, who can explain you to yourself; alternatively, a person is able to see himself in his friend."[56] The data presented here from my study and from others' research show that the same pattern applies to gay men who depend on finding similar others to share their sense of self, their sexual orientation, and other identities. The data also indicate the range of friends gay men have and suggest how friendships with heterosexual men and women, in particular, raise provocative questions about the complex ways gender and sexuality are constructed in our society. Through the formation and development of gay men's friendships with straight women, straight men, and lesbians, masculinity is maintained yet transformed, gay identity is defined yet expanded, and sexuality is reinforced yet fluid. The ways gay men rationalize, debate, reproduce, negotiate, and transgress gender and sexual boundary markers are highlighted when one studies their friendships with nongays.

Yet important social, psychological, and political dimensions are uncovered when individuals seek compatible friends whose values, status, and especially sexual orientation, are similar to their own. Reciprocity, equality, and trust are more likely to develop where homophily dominates. Gay men's friendships with other gay men, thus, become important sites for the development and maintenance of identity and community, as I discuss in chapters 7 and 8. Since the focus of my research is on gay men's friendships with other gay men, I want to turn now to how these friendships are initiated, developed, and maintained.

6

"ALL THE GOLD AND GEMS OF THE WORLD"

The Meaning and Maintenance of Friendships

[T]hose in a network of friends are not pre-positioned. . . . They have been chosen; further you are with those you feel like being with and when you feel like it; . . . or else you are with them because you feel bound to them. Or out of boredom and for want of better. . . . And finally, you live both inside and outside the network of friends. You are constantly leaving it again, not only in a physical sense but also in a more fundamental one; for, once out of it, it ceases to exist for you: it will probably still be there tomorrow, but there is no telling. Perhaps they will have made other friends, better friends, no longer feel bound. Its existence needs continual reestablishment; it is not simply there.

— *Henning Bech,* When Men Meet: Homosexuality and Modernity

Friendship supposedly knows no boundaries. It is not like the family, where legal, religious, and social customs more or less dictate who is a member, how members should interact, and which ceremonies should be enacted to verify membership. Friendship does not have such legal, religious, and social structures in American society. It must be created and reproduced by those who participate in it, without the benefit of any formalized guidelines. That is both the simplicity and the complexity of friendship.

Yet, the boundary-free images of friendship are not entirely accurate, as Harry, one of my respondents, illustrated when he stated that he could not be friends with people who couldn't "accept me for being gay." Upon closer inspection boundaries and rules do emerge, and often at the intersection of gender and sexual orientation. Patterns persist in the ways people talk about friendship, how they define it, what processes are at work to facilitate the initiation and development of a friendship, and what they do and what they discuss with their friends. In the pursuit of friendships many people follow implicit norms and scripts constructed by the culture and by subcultures.

Differences based on race, social class, religion, neighborhood, and age also provide variable opportunities for and constraints on the way friendship is carried out. As Graham Allan concludes:

> Rather than being freely chosen, the patterns of friendship, in a generic sense, which individuals sustain, are shaped by the whole interactive complex of material and social constraints that impinge on them. . . . The overall constellation of these structural factors affects not just the opportunities that individuals have for meeting other people sociably and forming friendships, but also the "content" of the relationships in which they are involved—the sort of activities engaged in, the frequency of interaction, and in some instances the emotional depth of the relationship.[1]

But how friendships are defined, formed, and maintained differently or similarly by gay men has not been systematically studied. Anecdotes, personal experiences, and very limited empirical data have defined what we know and believe about friendship among gay men, as I discuss in previous chapters.

Friendship, then, is not as simple as a voluntary choice without boundaries. People are networked to other people based in part on shared social characteristics; these persons in turn influence who else one can potentially get to know: "Relationships are as much a function of person-to-network interdependencies as they are person-to-person interdependencies."[2] How these factors play out among gay men in the development of friendships is the focus of this chapter. I discuss what friendship means to them, how they develop their friendships, what kinds of things they do and talk about with their friends, and how they maintain friendships.

The Meaning of Friendship

Loyalty, intimacy, reciprocity, trust, authenticity, similarity, sharing, acceptance, support. Not as passionate, sexual, expressive emotionally, affectionate, and exclusive as romantic relationships. These are the words and phrases people used over and over again when they were asked, as part of a wide range of academic studies on the topic of friendship among mostly heterosexual samples, to define friendship and to compare it with other relationships.[3] And these are many of the same descriptors the gay men in my study used to define their friendships. Sharing, trust, honesty, intimacy, mutuality, love, respect, similarity, and caring were the most commonly spoken words. As chapter 4 illustrates, though, many of the gay men made distinctions between friendships and sexual and romantic relationships, but they also mentioned passion, attraction, affection, and sometimes sex quite often in response to questions about what friendship means to them.

According to the constraints of hegemonic masculinity, men are not expected nor are they likely to talk about their friendships in ways that disclose their personal thoughts. They supposedly cannot share feelings, reveal emotions and vulnerabilities, or disclose personal information to other men. And they spend time evaluating their friendships in terms of activities, shared interests, and other task-oriented accomplishments. They just will not talk about the meaning of friendship in their lives. Or so the story goes.

But not all men conform to the generalizations about masculinity and play their designated cultural roles. Among these are the gay men in my study, who presented a much wider range of responses than those alluded to above when asked to define what friendship means in their lives. Like many of those interviewed, Fred made important distinctions between very close friends and acquaintances, and in so doing highlighted some of the key characteristics of friendship, especially ones that have to do with sharing and exclusivity:

> [Friendship is] a close personal bond that gives pleasure, enlarges the heart and mind through shared experience and reflection, hu-

manizes and educates us in the Platonic sense—that is, draws out of us what is innate but unrealized and unrecognized. For me, perhaps because of the degree of intensity involved, close friendships have been few in number. They require an investment of time, concentration, and energy, responsiveness and receptivity that by its nature implies a degree of exclusivity. I cannot be that intensively involved with a multitude. I am here, of course, speaking about close friendships—the other, more partial, special-purpose kind exist, but their limits seem to me to be mutually understood and accepted. They are in part defined by the degrees and ways in which they fall short of the core concept; they are defined, limited versions of what is essentially an undefined, open-ended, unlimited ideal.

Leo said that a friend is someone he is "able to talk and share things with in confidence, someone who will listen and reflect with care, someone who I can enjoy being around, share moments—everything from a great quote on the Internet to traveling in Europe with—as well as respecting differences." And Kevin said friendship is "a relationship formed with another in which one shares similar interests, trust, concern for one another. It is the ability to share experiences and thoughts and conversations on a daily basis, our hopes and desires and what we want out of life." Many of these characteristics of friendship—talking and sharing, especially about emotions, hopes, and feelings—have not been associated in recent times with culturally defined masculinity. But other dimensions of friendship have been.

According to more stereotypical masculine definitions of friendship (see the discussion in chapter 2), friends are people who share interests, do things for you in exchange for your doing things for them, and work together on tasks. Gay men similarly speak about friendships in terms of these more "doing" (side-by-side) dimensions, but often along with the less typically masculine (face-to-face) aspects of disclosing and talking. David continued, "Friends share hobbies and interests such as gardening or theater. They are people with very similar interests and similar—but by no means identical—views of life. It's a relationship that has both social and support dimen-

sions." Frank stated his definition very clearly in more hegemonic masculine terms of reciprocated interests and goals, but
also issued a caveat when he realized how his words might
sound:

> A friend is someone with the same interests as I, someone that
> I can count on to do things for me, someone that will allow me
> to do things for them, someone I can hang out with and do stupid
> things if I want and not care about what other people think, some-
> one who is—and this may sound shallow, but what the heck—
> comparable in ambitions, goals, salary, intelligence. They don't
> have to be the same as mine, but they should at least have high
> ones.

Overall, gay men defined friendship as a relationship with
someone they both talked to and did things with; with whom
they shared activities and emotions; who returned favors, and
with whom they disclosed hopes. This all took place in the context of having companionship with those who could accept them
for who they were, or as Greg phrased it, "Friendship is loving
another person and having them love you—without condition."
While reproducing hegemonic masculinity, these men were also
contesting it in their definitions of what friendship meant in
their lives. They were able to articulate a definition of friendship
that appears to capture what has been described in the psychological literature as the features of both men's and women's
friendships.[4] Carl captured this range of definitions and meanings in the following statement:

> Friendship means people that are close and can interact with each
> other to do various things. It also means people who are capable
> and willing to do something for you and you for them. It means
> someone to confide in, talk to, share stuff with and generally expe-
> rience various aspects of life and enjoy yourself. Close friends are
> intimate on other levels than mere acquaintance friends. No, it
> doesn't necessarily mean they engage in sex; it means they are
> more open, more available, more willing to do and share things.
> They are more dependable, more honest, more caring, more
> trustworthy, more appreciating. They are the types that go far and

beyond—they are there through thick and thin. . . . They are special treasures that give life added depth, dimension, and value. Friendships are a great way to offer, share, and express love on various levels. Truly good and awe-inspiring ones are more worthwhile than all the gold and gems of the world.

Forming Friendships

People define friendships based on an assessment of their current friends and on ideal images formulated in particular cultures. Not everyone becomes this kind of perfect friend, though. There are acquaintances or casual friends, and there are close and best friends. Becoming a friend and remaining a close one is a result of ongoing encounters that have to begin somewhere and somehow.

Longitudinal research on the development and maintenance of friendships, however, is virtually nonexistent. In fact, most research on friendship has focused either on the structure of the friendship (quantity, types, outcomes) or on its initiation (how people meet, the early stages of friendship formation) at one point in time; very few studies have assessed the maintenance of friendship over time and space, and, concomitantly, how it becomes closer or more distant.[5] Friendship is not a static event that is captured fully by cross-sectional surveys.

Social psychologists have mapped out some of the processes involved in the formation of friendship. Beverley Fehr summarizes four general sets of factors that affect its development; these factors are environmental, individual, situational, and dyadic. *Environmental* ones revolve around the fundamental concept of propinquity—"people who inhabit the same physical environment are more likely to become friends than those who do not."[6] Hence people's workplaces, neighborhoods, urban environments, other friends, and relatives are the major sources of friendship formation.[7] For gay men, as chapter 5 illustrates, other friends, work, and various gay organizations found in urban environments are also important sources of friends.

Of course, not everyone in these environments becomes

friends with each other. *Individual* factors serve as filters, eliminating those who are not likely candidates for friendship—usually those who are disliked or disregarded because of dissimilarity in values, demographic characteristics, or behaviors.[8] After eliminating some, an individual evaluates the remaining people according to physical attractiveness, social skills, responsiveness, shyness, and similarity. More attractive people, those with good styles of initiating contact and of responsiveness, outgoing people, and those who share similar demographic characteristics and attitudes are most likely to emerge as potential friends.[9] Fred told me about the first time he met his close friend seventeen years ago at a gay organization meeting: "I remember being strongly attracted to him intellectually and emotionally. . . . We seemed to have the closest intellectual and emotional ties, in terms of similarity and congruence of response to art, literature, science, of any others at the event."

Situational factors must also be present for friendship to develop: "Factors such as how often we are likely to see the person and whether we are dependent on the person for something we want are important. Another consideration is whether we are able to accommodate another relationship, given our other commitments."[10] Respondents to my survey were asked if they were unable to spend as much time with their best friend as they would have liked and, if so, what was responsible for this. Around 74 percent replied that they were unable; of those who reported this 67 percent said work and career commitments competed for their time, 39 percent cited voluntary organizations and community commitments, and 30 percent selected daily errands and chores (see Table 6.1). Vince summed it up: "I wish I could have more friends, but I don't have the time. I love my friends." Like most men, gay men accommodate friendship into their schedules around career obligations, but unlike most heterosexual men's, gay men's family responsibilities may not take up as much time and do not involve as many commitments.

For some, distance, and not time, is the problem; about 57 percent of my respondents reported that their best friend did not live nearby. This creates an added problem of keeping in

Table 6.1   Survey Respondents' Reasons for Not Spending More Time with Best Friend

Reason	Percent Who Cited
Work or career	67.0
Live too far apart	56.7
Voluntary organizations/community activities	39.2
Errands and chores	29.9
Obligations to partner (lover)	26.8
Obligations to other friends	24.7
Work-related socializing	20.6
Time with family and relatives	14.4
Hobbies/sports	12.4
Expenses/travel costs	12.4

touch and of finding time to do so. The more frequently we interact with or even just see someone, the more likely is the attraction between us to increase, especially if that person has the power to provide or withhold rewards and sanctions. But we also have to be available for the friendship, and the number of other friends we have, our work commitments, and our romantic relationships all affect the amount of time and space there is to accommodate new friends, as some of the stories in chapter 4, which describe what happens when gay men or their friends get involved in other relationships, demonstrate. Beth Hess frames it in terms of the number of roles a person enacts and in terms of the structural constraints imposed by those roles,[11] and Allan describes the limitations in friendship formation by invoking the concept of "personal space," which is "an image of a bounded area of relative freedom within people's lives. Patterning the boundaries of this space are the demands and restrictions placed on the individual by his or her position within the social structure and the roles and relationships this entails. The space that remains within the boundaries represents the opportunities he or she has to develop aspects of personal life in ways he or she chooses."[12]

Finally, *dyadic* elements become salient as people get to know each other. Breadth and depth of disclosures increase as we perceive that the other person likes us. Reciprocal expressions of liking and sharing develop trust, intimacy, closeness, and ultimately friendship.[13] It is at this point that, depending on the amount and depth of these dyadic elements, the newly met persons evolve into casual, close, or best friends. Ben illustrated this when he said he "hit it off" with his close friends when they first met: "They were interesting to me and I felt a comfortableness which propelled the friendship forward. We laughed and slowly opened up to each other and then our lives became entwined through common situations, such as school or being gay or shared sorrows and hard times."

As can be seen, friendship is a behavioral and emotional *process;* it requires reciprocity, self-disclosure, and intimacy. It is a cognitive process that needs regular interactions, social support, and assessments on the parts of the people involved about how it is developing. The cognitive, affective, and behavioral dimensions of friendship formation are not just psychological categories; they are also "influenced by social structure and the historical context, . . . the structural features of the dyads and networks in which [people] participate, . . . their previous experiences in close relationships, their developmental maturity, and their personality characteristics."[14] Indeed, people already embedded in dense interdependent clusters of friends (that is, where members of a person's network also know and interact with each other) are much less likely to develop new friendships compared with those who are part of a less dense and more loosely knit network of friends.[15] Other friends control access to the clique or group and monitor who can enter it and who cannot. That so many gay men report that their friends were made through other friends and that their friends tend to look like each other suggests that this process is at work here as well.

Reciprocity

An exchange model has been used to describe the development of friendships in which people with roughly equivalent resources interact in mutually rewarding ways, each receiving something in return in an amount commensurate with what they put into the interaction. In addition to descriptions of sharing, trusting, and bonding, reciprocity is regularly invoked as an element of friendship formation. Take for example Tim's definition of a friend: "They're there when I need them, and I am here for them, too," or in Steve's: "being willing to help each other in a selfless manner," or in Vince's: "I help them and hope that they will help me when I need help. They are people who seem to care about and like me and who I care about and like." David succinctly captured the exchange and the need for trust in these reciprocal interactions: "Friendships are based on shared experiences, common interests, and trust. If someone is my friend, I feel that the individual can be trusted to be honest with me, help me when I have a problem, and share life's experiences, good and bad. And in exchange, they get the same from me."

For a large majority of the gay men who answered the survey questionnaire, doing favors for one another and assisting each other in a task or project characterized their interactions with best, close, and casual friends during the two months just prior to their taking the survey, as Table 6.2 indicates. Helping friends professionally and loaning or borrowing money—especially to or from best friends—also describes what many gay men do with their friends. Depending on already existing networks of friends and other contextual factors, these series of exchanges might result in a friendship growing: "Positions in social structures affect what people value in exchanges, their capacities to sustain the costs of maintaining reciprocity in exchanges, and their opportunities to meet and interact with people in different social positions. Existing networks place pressure on friendship selection that reinforces these processes."[16]

But the simple exchange of equivalent resources is not enough. Often the interaction needs to go beyond a balance in benefits to a more communal interaction in which the potential friend takes the other's needs into account and provides benefits he feels the other would find most useful, and which are not necessarily of equal value to those he receives from his friend.[17] When this occurs, the friendship begins to become a closer one. Ed talked about how reciprocity with friends does not mean a one-to-one value exchange:

> My friends are not mercenary, insofar as not expecting every favor to be repaid, and my friends respect my heritage and cultural

Table 6.2   Survey Respondents Who Engaged in Various Activities
Together in the Past Two Months (Percent, Ranked in Order of Results
for Best Friend)

	Best Friend	Close Friends	Casual Friends
Talking activities (face-to-face):			
Had a meal together	95.4	98.7	88.2
Called just to chat	94.7	94.3	61.5
Got together just to talk	87.0	92.4	72.7
Had coffee or a drink	78.6	88.0	70.2
Doing activities (side-by-side):			
Went to a movie, concert, cultural event	79.4	84.8	47.8
Went to a party, bar, social event	71.0	81.6	53.4
Went shopping	67.2	70.9	33.5
Attended a class, meeting, organization	55.0	70.3	65.8
Pursued hobbies or leisure interest	45.8	48.7	19.9
Went away for a holiday, weekend, vacation	38.9	41.8	9.9
Participated in sports or went to gym	20.6	23.4	22.4
Watched sports	7.6	8.9	3.7
Assistance activities:			
Did a favor or errand for each other	73.3	79.7	61.5
Assisted each other with a task or project	60.3	62.0	52.8
Loaned or borrowed money	42.7	36.7	17.4
Helped each other professionally	32.1	41.8	48.4

NOTE: Percentages for best friend are often lower since respondents were asked to
indicate activities they engaged in with one or two best friends, while the "close
friend" and "casual friend" categories can accommodate larger numbers. Also, nearly
57 percent of the respondents said their best friend did not live nearby.

eccentricities. I realize that in the occidental world, wealth is measured by what one owns, but where I come from, wealth is also
measured by what one is owed. In other words, you try to keep
the scales tipped in your favor as far as doing things for other
people. As long as I don't sweat the small stuff, this works well
for me. I don't mind occasionally picking up the tab for a meal,
or repairing things or doing work around their house, as long as
the other person doesn't feel the compulsive need to keep an even
accounting. Conversely, although my friends know they can ask
for the periodic favor, they also know that there is a limit to this
largesse because I don't abide "moochers." . . . To put it another
way, friends—my friends—aren't users.

Ed's words also show that people are aware of the cultural scripts and unspoken rules—in his case, of not exploiting a friend—that govern close relationships. Individuals tend to learn about such rules very quickly and often use them within the first hour of meeting someone, when they make decisions about whether to pursue the friendship in a particular direction.[18] Often, people inquire about others' availability, romantic relationships, and work commitments before pursuing further interactions. Also, asking people to disclose personal information upon first meeting them is typically governed by culturally approved norms of propriety. They decide very early, then, which type of relationship (acquaintance or closer friendship) they want and identify the script that needs to be followed: "One must choose to follow the rules for a close relationship early in order to communicate one's desire for such a relationship to the other, and, consequently, to give it a chance to develop further."[19] Dan said that when he first met his close friend "I was quickly impressed with his trustworthiness and caring for others. We have known each other now for more than fifteen years." People often monitor the other's availability, responsiveness, similarities, and adherence to communal norms and values—trustworthiness, in Dan's case—and decide to communicate a desire to become close friends by following culturally shaped rules of exchange and disclosure in the encounter.

Decisions about the relationship are made along a variety of social and personal attributes that emerge in an interaction. First of all, many people decide to become friends with others because they already have mutual friends in common; they are part of the same interdependent network. Second, what goes on in the interaction when people become acquainted has some impact on the direction of the relationship. According to William Chambliss, people prefer to continue interacting in validating, successful, and effective encounters, that is, in situations where there is a correspondence between the actors' self-images and the impressions of others (validation), where the others' responses are favorable (successful), and where there is a correspondence between the self the actors intended to project and the impression of others (effective).[20] In short, people and their relationships "are embedded within a social system, a system that profoundly influences people, their availability to one another, the choices they make with regard to one another, and the character of their relationships."[21] How the friendship does or does not develop is not just left up to one individual; it is an interaction that incorporates many of the rules and structures of management impression and the dynamics of the social setting.[22]

Disclosure

It is important that the norm dictating that friends must share information be followed during interactions if a close friendship is desired. Information is gleaned either directly between two people or indirectly through other mutual friends. The latter method comes into play especially in denser, more interdependent networks where "Much of what we know about our friends is not necessarily the result of direct communication (self-disclosure) but results from what others tell us about our friends."[23] Indeed, a majority of gay men in the survey reported that they heard about their best friend and close friends several times a month or more from other friends (see Table 6.4).

While many interactions between people meeting for the first time are spontaneous and unplanned, at different points in a relationship's development individuals must make decisions about intensifying or limiting the amount of information disclosed.[24] For the gay men interviewed, and for a very large majority of the gay men surveyed, sharing thoughts, feelings, and experiences are central components of their friendship definitions and interactions. Harve reported that he talked with his closest friends about "serious and trivial topics, but it usually involves revealing personal feelings." And over 90 percent of those surveyed confirmed that, in the past two months, they had phoned a best or close friend just to chat or had eaten a meal with them, and almost as many said they had gotten together just to talk (see Table 6.2). These figures are much higher than are corresponding ones for most heterosexual men according to other studies; heterosexual men tend not to call each other just to talk.[25]

People are agentic and strategic. They know about social rules and use them when they are needed to develop friendships. When unexpected information or behavior that doesn't fit the existing picture of the other person in the developing friendship emerges, or at crucial points of change, people more strategically monitor and plan, depending on their goals for the relationship.[26] This is more likely to occur in the beginning of relationships and less likely to do so in long-standing ones in which a wider range of shared knowledge already exists, and in which, therefore, unplanned interactions occur more frequently than do strategically planned ones. In short, "In a new relationship that might grow, any information might be relevant, any point might be a change point, and, thus, the relative proportion of effort invested will be higher than in an established relationship."[27]

And that's what characterized the early stages of Ed's getting to know Les, who eventually became one of his closest friends: "I don't remember at what point Les became a friend, but I remember him slowly befriending me. I then introduced him to my lesbian niece, and he promptly invited her, her lover, her lover's older brother, and myself to a dinner at his home. When Wayne, my lover, left me, Les took me under his nurturing umbrella and helped me get through a very tough year." And Dan told me how he met Jerry, his close friend, at a gay organization meeting, corresponded with him, and invited him to visit him on the West Coast, but not with any intentions of a sexual relationship: "I courted his friendship." When people met those they were interested in, attracted to, or curious about, they pursued the friendship and constructed opportunities to interact with the potential friend and to develop the new friendship.

Maintaining Friendship

Making new friends is one thing; keeping them and developing them is another. There is work involved; friendships don't always just happen without some effort and adjustments, especially if friends move away, find themselves in other circles, get involved in romantic relationships outside the friendship, and otherwise go through life's transitions, mature, and change. We all have a "we'll always stay in touch" story; we pledge undying commitment to friends during our senior year in high school or college or when leaving a workplace and then later lose track of most if not all of them as newer friends, who more and more closely match our newer interests, more mature personalities, and changes in economic and social circumstances, enter our world. Friends have to remain similar (or to perceive that they are similar) in many ways and to communicate this; changes in values and in romantic-relationship status and shifts in economic and occupational status can alter the closeness and continuation of a friendship. As chapter 5 shows, younger gay men are more likely to have friends from college compared to older gay men, even though older gay men in my sample were somewhat more likely to have graduated from college and graduate school. It takes perseverance to maintain old school ties.

In their review of adult friendship research, Rosemary Blieszner and Rebecca Adams write, "The ways people sustain friendship usually revolve around continued similarity, rewarding communication and interaction patterns, and positive feelings."[28] At the heart of friendship maintenance is communication, that is, managing the range of reciprocal interactions and choices that incorporate sets of dialectical principles.[29] These choices include contextual dialectics—the private and public aspects, the ideal and the real images of friendship—and interactional dialectics—freedom to be independent and dependent in the relationship, balancing affection and instrumentality, negotiating judgment and acceptance, and demonstrating expressiveness and protectiveness. According to William Rawlins, effectively communicating in friendship entails viewing individuals as "conscious, active selectors of possible choices from a field that is partially conceived by them, partially negotiated with others, and partially determined by social and natural factors outside of their purview."[30]

Contextually, friendship has a public marginality in the social role hierarchy, Rawlins argues, yet public roles and societal institutions constrain private decisions about how to act toward friends. Furthermore, the realities of social situations and a culture's value system exert a strong influence on normative expectations that the ideal friendship should be voluntary, personal, equal, mutual, and affective: "Friends may attempt to communicate in ways that conform with the ideals of their era, but in doing so, they create and encounter real constraints and contradictions."[31] A culturally patterned set of images about friendship is produced and reproduced through the dialectics of the ideal and real conceptions, and in the public and private realms.

The reproduction of meanings and behaviors associated with friendship occurs through a set of interactional dialectics: "Communicating within friendship involves a constant interaction between interpretive and behavioral practices to maintain a mutual definition of the relationship as friendship."[32] Talking about the friendship relationship thus becomes an important enterprise in itself, and one that has traditionally varied by gender. One dynamic is the negotiation and enactment of the freedom to be independent and the freedom to be dependent, traits that also have been gendered in our society. Friendship maintenance requires a composite balance of these two freedoms, along with a balance between instrumental and affective behaviors. And unlike much research that supports traditional gender-linked differences in the imbalance between the instrumental and the expressive, between independence and dependence, the data in my study of gay men, as I now report, illustrate the fact that many men are capable of integrating and balancing these interactional dialectics in their friendships.

Doing and Talking Friendship

In order for friendships to continue, people must do things together and talk about their lives. There are obligations—social norms, if you will—to be there for a friend in need, to listen to his or her problems and successes, to provide companionship centered around activities, and to share personal experiences and hopes. Without reciprocity, disclosure, common interests, and nonjudgmental attitudes, the friendship cannot develop into a close or best one; it remains an acquaintanceship or a casual friendship, if it lasts at all. Despite inaccurate descriptions of friendship as entailing only affective components and a minimum of instrumental ones, most friendships include obligations and reciprocity, not simply generosity and spontaneity.[33]

Much of the survey data shows that gay men get together with friends to help out, just to talk, to share activities, and to discuss personal and intimate topics. As Table 6.2 illustrates, when presented with a list of items that included both affective and instrumental behaviors, more gay men surveyed selected typically "face-to-face" activities over typically "side-by-side" ones; that is, while a large majority reported that in the past two months they had been to a movie, attended a social event or party, done a favor, helped out on a project, and gone shopping with their best friend, some close friends, and some casual friends, even more of the men surveyed said that they had called or gotten together with a friend just to talk, and had met for a meal or a drink.

As chapter 2 reports, according to the common stereotype, men are better at doing things together and at talking primarily about work, sports, and shared activities, whereas women are better at talking about personal matters and relationships (including the friendship itself), even when they are engaged in doing tasks together. The gay men in this study illustrate the contradictions of gender in American society in their frequent reports of their both doing things and sharing activities with friends *and* of talking with them about personal events and emotions (and about being gay). Calling someone just to chat on the phone or to have dinner together, disclosing personal information and slowly opening up to each other, as Ben phrased it in the example given above, rarely characterize heterosexual men's patterns of doing friendship, whereas attending a movie, engaging in activities, and pursuing hobbies together typically do.

And, as Table 6.3 suggests, what gay men talk about is a unique combination of normative "male" topics, such as work and politics, and normative "female" topics, such as personal relationships, their friendship with each other and their friendships with others, personal sexual behavior, health concerns,

Table 6.3 Survey Respondents Who Discussed Some or All the
Important Details Pertaining to Various Topics in the Past Two Months
with Different Categories of Friends (Percent, Ranked in Order of
Results for Best Friend)

	Best Friend	Close Friends	Casual Friends
General topics:			
Work problems	73.4	67.8	45.6
Work successes	72.1	66.5	41.3
Politics/ideas/culture	54.7	55.7	29.4
Personal financial success	45.0	31.9	7.7
Personal financial problems	44.2	27.0	8.8
Hobbies/sports/leisure interests	39.1	37.3	22.6
Personal topics:			
Intimate relationship satisfactions	73.0	54.1	19.1
Intimate relationship problems	71.4	54.1	17.7
Personal sexual behavior	71.2	53.4	17.8
Friendships with other	70.7	53.8	19.4
Personal health concerns	65.7	50.6	18.8
Hopes about the future	64.4	61.7	24.5
Friendship with each other	63.2	50.0	13.2
Family (parents, etc.)	60.7	49.7	16.5
Doubts about the future	56.2	49.4	18.2
Personal strengths	51.9	40.8	10.0
Personal weaknesses	48.5	43.2	10.7
Personal body image dislikes	37.6	28.3	10.7
Personal body image likes	35.6	21.9	7.6

NOTE: Respondents were asked to indicate the extent to which they discussed each
of nineteen topics in the past two months using a five-point scale where four equals
"I have discussed this topic in some detail" and five equals "I have discussed all the
important details on this topic."

and thoughts about the future. They engage in discussions
about these more intimate topics with a best friend and to some
degree with close friends; gay men's casual friendships are characterized mostly by talk about work, hobbies, and politics, probably because, as chapter 5 shows, most gay men meet their casual friends through work.

Again, it is evident that gay men reproduce culturally approved norms of hegemonic masculinity while contesting some
of the core dimensions that constitute it and differentiate it
from homosexuality. For example, note the very low percentage
(virtually the lowest figures in Tables 6.2 and 6.3) of gay men
who participated in sports, watched sports, or talked about

sports with their friends. Yet, in keeping with normative images of masculinity, disclosing personal information about vulnerabilities and anxieties for the most part did not occur between many gay men and their friends in the survey. Some of the other least-selected topics were those of body image, personal finances, personal weaknesses, and doubts about the future. This may partially reflect larger American cultural norms that dissuade people from sharing information about personal finances and encourage bragging about personal strengths or body images, especially with casual acquaintances. However, discussing intimate relationship problems, particularly with a best friend or some close friends, was very high on the list. This after all is a core topic of gay identity in a society that doesn't offer many opportunities to talk about such things. Gay men need gay friends with whom they can discuss this subject and who can provide information, advice, and understanding without judgment.

Charles said, "Over the years my best friend and I have done everything but attend sporting events. We talk about everything. We tell each other things we don't tell our partners. In some ways, I'm the stable point in his life. It's a role which has brought me lots of insight into his life, and by reflection my own." Ben stated that he and his closest friends talk about "everything, our lives, the funny stuff, the tough stuff, our sex lives. There is nothing off limits." Will, on the other hand, said that he "is resistant to talk about relationship problems with friends. They may amplify the problem rather than help out." For Will, friends can be envious and jealous, can take sides, and can compete in a way that makes disclosing too much personal information uncomfortable for him, although he acknowledged that "gay culture has an intimacy of friends revealing themselves, especially in the coming-out process."

Will was the only person who felt this way, and Leo was the only other person interviewed who did not explicitly state that he shared personal information and emotional feelings with friends. His response came closest to the way many heterosexual men talk about friends, according to the research on gender differences. He said that he talked with his closest friends about "politics, church activities, incidents at work, movies, music, things we've read, disgust with technology." He went on to say that his closest friends were "people I have met and gotten to know better while working on a project or task—political, religious, social—and in the sharing of working on something together found we had other things in common, or appreciated each other's attitude, outlook, or perspective." John, on the other hand, captured what most gay men say they talk about with friends: "Ideas, dreams, dates, relationship joys and problems, trouble at work, family—everything."

And when it comes to doing things with close friends, most responses focused on entertainment, such as movies, dinners, parties, "anything that's nonsexual" as Frank said, or "lunch and/ or sex" as Nick put it. Fred, though, provided the best summary of and some important insights into doing things with friends, and, in the process, demonstrated how—even when talking about doing things together—many gay men are self-reflective and intimate in the way they interpret the sharing of activities:

> It sometimes seems that the deeper and richer the friendship, the more mundane the things we can find pleasure in doing together. Eating, walking, talking, sharing commonplace experiences, and, less frequently, planning and enjoying certain peak experiences together. More concretely, I think of attending movies, plays, concerts, sharing books, exchanging letters about both ordinary and extraordinary events. . . . It seems to me that a friend is one with whom one can play, interact in a way that gives a sense of "flow" to experience. So it seems to me that it is less the specific things friends do together than the presence of this sense of flow—unconstrained attentiveness—that gives heightened meaning and structure to shared experience.

Besides sharing experiences and feelings, friends are supposed to accept one another for who they are but also are allowed to judge and evaluate: "People value a friend's acceptance, especially when they know the other takes their ideas, thoughts, and actions seriously. They also appreciate judgment and criticism from a person who primarily accepts and cares about them."[34] Revelations about personal feelings often make people vulnerable and sensitive, thus introducing issues about the establishment and preservation of trust in the relationship. For gay men, establishing trust is one of the most important methods of developing and maintaining friendship, since it is with friends that they need to "tell anything and not worry about what they think," as Frank said. Ed captured the various kinds of interactions people have with a range of friends, and who gets to hear what, depending on how trust and closeness have developed:

> With friends that I'm in frequent contact with, we usually don't start with small talk, but jump immediately to the reason for the call. For those of less frequent telephone contact, we have the typical small talk, the conversational "dance" where these conversational gears slowly mesh and synchronize before any comfort is apparent. And there are lulls and pregnant pauses, but with my friends, these lulls are not uncomfortable. It's as if we were enjoying each other's company face-to-face, where every moment would *not* be occupied by a spoken word. For acquaintances, these pauses are awkward, but that's why they're acquaintances. . . . Even among my friends, weeded and culled from hundreds of acquaintances, there is a stratum where my deepest, darkest secrets and fears are not known to all. These concerns only percolate down to a select couple of friends, like Scott. I can relate family, work or financial troubles to these few, without fear of condemnation, reprisal or ridicule. My primary expectation is that they be there for me, be able to hear my side of a story, and not be "too" judgmental.

In Ed's narrative we can see some of the interactional and contextual dialectics (ideal and real, affectional and instrumental, public and private, independence and dependence, judgment and acceptance) involved in the maintenance of friendships. These are usually configured and interwoven differently for various kinds of friendship, at different stages of life, during different phases of the friendship's development, and depending on the individuals' personalities, their social roles, and the cultural norms of their society, to paraphrase Rawlins.[35] The dialectics of the interactions also depend on how connected someone already is to a dense, interdependent network of friends, as is illustrated by the fact that most gay men meet their friends through other friends. Fred related a story about a falling out he had with his friend Elliott's closest friend, Daryl, and how it got patched after he "was reproved by Elliott for wounding Daryl." Relationships in such networks tend to be more enduring and stable and to be monitored by the other members; in short, "structure influences stability."[36]

Keeping in Touch

Similarity, reciprocity, developing trust, and blending the affectional and instrumental are still not sufficient to keep a friendship going. Maintenance of these dimensions, of course, also requires repeated interactions: phoning, visiting, writing cards or letters, engaging in activities, and just plain talking (regardless of the topic that is discussed) contribute to the friendship's endurance and verify the friendship's existence. And in today's technological era, E-mail has jumped to the top of the list as perhaps the primary way of maintaining contact with people not nearby, especially among those who can afford a computer or have access to one at work or school. Nearly everyone whom I directly asked about the methods they used to keep in touch with friends said they did so by E-mail, and the phone was a close second.[37] Virtually no one wrote letters or saw their closest friends on a daily basis. Aaron's best friends were from college and graduate school but were now scattered around the country: "I do not see my three or four closest friends in a typical month. When we are in the same city, we spend time enjoying each other's company. With my closest friend, we talk about once a month and we E-mail at least twice a week. E-mail is the main way I keep in touch with friends. I don't call or write my friends on a weekly basis."

Dan reported that he might see close friends who live nearby about three times a month, talk to them anywhere from once a day to twice a week, and E-mail them weekly, sometimes daily. Fred said "E-mail, a new discovery for me, has been a godsend. Formerly, I was largely dependent on the telephone which is expensive, or correspondence which is a dying—nearly dead—art. For friends who are close at hand, occasional phone conversations and dinner." And Ed, who traveled a lot for work, kept in contact with his closest friends with "many, many telephone calls—judging by my monthly tribute to Ma Bell, way too many—but it's one of the vices I have. . . . I also go through letter-writing cycles where I'll send postcards because of the interminable amount of time spent waiting in airports. . . . E-mails sent to friends are kept to a minimum because there are chances that they can be monitored at work." But Frank put his finger on something else when he said that "it's important that even though my best friend and I don't necessarily communicate daily, weekly, or even monthly, we each know the one is available for the other at any time. There's that comfortable feeling, that knowing feeling—it's hard to explain." Or does this just demonstrate that, for some gay men, traditional male ways of doing friendship persist when the structural demands of work, distance, and time take effect?

Survey respondents were asked how they kept in touch with friends (in terms of telephoning and writing cards), about the amount of time they spent with friends in a typical week, and about how many of their close and casual friends they saw in a typical week. As Table 6.4 shows, on a weekly basis most of the men surveyed spent fewer than nine hours a week with friends, and they spent them with only a few friends. Based on the percentages, I would infer that the gay men get together with several casual friends at a time and get more selective with close and best friends. Since 57 percent of the respondents said that their best friend lived far away, they obviously called him or her more often than they did close or casual friends, but I imagine—based on the interviews—that they did so more frequently with nearby best friends as well. Letter or card writing is indeed a dying form of communication, given that the percentages probably reflect mostly birthday or holiday cards.[38]

In general, physical proximity is more important than is interaction and expressed affection for maintaining casual friend-

Table 6.4   How Survey Respondents Keep in Touch with Friends

	Best Friend	Close Friends	Casual Friends
Time spent socially in typical week (percent saying nine or fewer hours)	70.5	62.8	77.0
Number of friends seen in typical week (percent saying fewer than three close or five casual)	n/a	51.0	34.8
Talk on the phone (percent saying several times a week or more)	64.7	39.6	10.7
Write cards or letters (percent saying once a year or less)	32.8	28.8	57.0
Hearing about friend from other friends (percent saying several times a month or more)	58.4	62.3	42.7

ships, but close and best friends require more interaction and expressed affection, even if they are not physically proximate.[39] Over and over again, as the next chapter describes, people's friendships fade away if contact is not kept up. What the E-mail revolution will do for friendship maintenance has yet to be assessed, but it seems that its potential for helping friends keep in touch and for renewing old friendships is quite high. Several people reported—and my personal experiences confirm this as well—receiving E-mail messages from long-lost friends from college and even high school. Although E-mailing may restart communication between friends, unless more intense interactions including personal disclosures, shared activities, verification of value similarities, and face-to-face (or at least voice-to-voice) contacts occur, my hunch is that the friendship will not develop beyond that of acquaintances and that the friend will remain a cyber version of a pen-pal.

Keeping up contact with people over time and space requires some effort. Consider Aaron's story and how he has been able to form a best friendship with another African American gay man he met in college, and to maintain it despite many changes. I quote it at length, since it is a good way of summarizing the issues I have just discussed:

> Our friendship has endured almost fifteen years of moving here and there, as well as relatively long stretches of silence due to

nothing in particular other than that we were busy. Maurice and I met when we were still young and closeted. In a sense, we grew up and came out together during our college years. We did most everything that typical college buddies do together, including going to the movies, shopping, eating, and just hanging out. Note, however, that we never dated each other or slept together. After college, we lived in different states for about four years. During that period, we mostly wrote letters to each other and phoned from time to time. We visited each other twice during that period—once when he stayed overnight in the city where I lived while he was on a business trip, and a second time, when Tom, my boyfriend at the time, and I were on vacation in the city where Maurice lived, just after I finished graduate school. Later, I transferred from the main office of the company where I worked to its office in Boston. Coincidentally, Maurice had also taken a job in the city. When I moved to the area, I moved into an apartment building that was just a five-minute drive from his apartment building. This added a new dimension to our friendship. In some ways, it reminded me of when we were in college. We talked on the phone almost every day. We saw each other at least a couple of times each week. When my boyfriend came to visit, the three of us would do things like go out to dinner or go to a dance performance. From time to time, he accompanied me to where my boyfriend lived—for example, on weekend trips at Thanksgiving or Christmas. Later, after I moved from Boston to live with Tom in Connecticut, Maurice would visit us—again, on holiday weekends—sometimes bringing a guest such as his beau of the moment. . . . Today we live hundreds of miles apart, but we're still close. Last summer, we spent a week together in Provincetown. . . . We communicate by E-mail frequently. We talk on the phone less frequently.

In general, then, studies confirm that maintenance of friendship depends on a combination of factors that include proximity, interaction, and communication (face-to-face or through E-mail and phone calls), similarity on a variety of characteristics, self-disclosure and openness, assurances that the friendship is important, social support, communal rewards (each friend is concerned about the other's well-being and makes the interactions pleasant), allowing friends to be themselves, following social conventions and rules about friendship maintenance (such as respecting privacy, avoiding jealousies, keeping confidences and trust), receiving rewards and benefits (including reciprocity), engaging in constructive discussions about disagreements, making the effort to keep in touch, and finding time to interact.[40]

And all this occurs in a cultural context that does not provide ceremonies, organizational structures, or formalized norms or laws for the maintenance of friendship. None of the respondents offered any examples of a ritual or a way they certified and celebrated their friendships, other than birthdays and holidays. What keeps friendships together and working, then, are likely the direct and indirect mechanisms of social and psychological support that result from ongoing, positive, and identity-strengthening interactions that take place in structurally sound networks and social contexts. But when support mechanisms and identity begin to get challenged or ignored in the interactions, and when alterations occur in the social structures and institutions that incorporate the relationships, friendships begin to change and fade. There are no couple-counseling programs to help out when such things begin to go wrong in a friendship. "The societal structures that are in place to hold marital and familial relationships together," Fehr notes, "are curiously absent when it comes to friendship."[41] As Will insightfully pointed out, drawing on personal experience: "We need self-help books and therapy sessions on how to deal with the loss of a friendship. There's a lot of heart-on-the-line stuff with gay men's friendships, and I can be an emotional wreck when a friendship is not working out." I turn in the next chapter to these issues of social support and what happens when friendships and support mechanisms begin to unravel.

"WHERE I GO TO KNOW
I'M NOT CRAZY"

*Developing Social Support, Achieving
Identity, and Confronting Conflicts*

> Most friends fade,
> Or they don't make the grade.
> New ones are quickly made
> And in a pinch, sure, they'll do.
> But us, old friend,
> What's to discuss old friend?
> Here's to us—who's like us? Damn few.
>
> — *Stephen Sondheim, from the song "Old
> Friends," in* Merrily We Roll Along *(1981)*

Aaron, an African American teacher, told me what makes his
closest friends his friends:

> My closest friends stick with me through good times and bad,
> tend to tell me what they really think rather than only what they
> think I want to hear, and forgive me for transgressions that I make
> from time to time. For example, my closest friends don't just dis-
> appear when I am depressed. And they cheer me on when I'm
> succeeding at something. In general, my closest friends are people
> who make an effort to encourage me to be myself and to excel
> at whatever I attempt to do.

Support when one is emotionally down; support for being truly
oneself; support by being open, honest, tolerant, and loyal; support to go beyond the limits of what one can do; support to
maintain and strengthen identity—these are some of the ineffable components that many struggle to articulate when describing what friendship is and how it works in their lives.

Friendships are usually a reliable source of social and psychological support and identity development in people's often fragmented and dispersed lives. But sometimes they're not; the very essence of friendship can be put to the test, contested, and modified. This chapter explores how friendships provide social and psychological support, what kinds of support are available, how these may reflect a society's gendered order, how friends contribute specifically to supporting gay identity formation and maintenance, what happens when support begins to change, how conflicts are confronted, and why friendships fade away or end.

Social and Psychological Support

Study after study confirms the importance of friendship for mental and physical well-being.[1] A 1997 report in the *Journal of the American Medical Association* even goes so far as to say that people who participate in more diverse social network relationships (regardless of the actual number of people in the network) are less susceptible than others to upper-respiratory illness.[2] In general, different friends offer different benefits: "We may benefit directly through instrumental aid provided by friends or supporters. Others may serve as a reference against which we may validate our opinions and beliefs. Also, others may be influential in maintaining our self-esteem or providing emotional support in times of need or distress."[3] Ben agreed: "Who I call first on a certain subject will vary. Joe is so cool and levelheaded that I might talk with him about long-term things, while I talk to Kelly a lot about my family 'cause he knows them too. It depends." And as the research reported in chapter 2 shows, often these sources of support are gendered; men have fewer supportive relationships, receive less help from supporters, and perceive less emotional support than women do.[4] Hegemonic masculinity discourages men from seeking all kinds of assistance and support, since to do so might signal vulnerability, weakness, and powerlessness and might blur the cultural boundaries between stereotypes associated with heterosexuality and homosexuality.

In Claude Fischer's important research on personal networks in urban and nonurban areas, he assessed three types of social support—counseling (advising about personal matters), companionship (visiting, doing things together, talking), and practical (material assistance)—and found that married men and women had weaker *counseling* support, but that married men especially had few people to turn to for counseling besides their spouse.[5] As I discuss below, gay men, even those who are coupled, appear to have strong networks of counseling support provided by their closest friends. John said, "I'd truly be lost without my friends to hold me up and strengthen me during difficult times." Others that the Fischer study identified as having minimal support were older people, women with children at home, and women of color; social class differences were not as relevant. Overall, younger single people and those without children were more likely to have networks of counseling support outside the immediate household.[6]

Similar demographics, along with higher education and income, also characterized those in Fischer's study who had adequate *companionship* support and who engaged in more social activities. And younger people, whites, those who worked, and those who joined organizations or associations had adequate *practical* support. Affluent people had fewer helpers, and urban residents (who tend to be younger, single, childless, and educated) were less likely to have practical support, such as someone to pick up mail or water plants when they were away and to help around the house—practical support that is more likely to be available from kin and neighbors in less urban areas. In general, the number of people in the network was not as important as was just having at least one person outside the household who could provide support. Furthermore, there was little empirical evidence showing that urban residents lacked social support, despite common stereotypes about the absence of community in modern city life.

Most respondents in Fischer's study tended to name others of the same gender as offering most kinds of support, but social support was relatively specialized: "companionship from friends, practical help from relatives or neighbors, and counseling from immediate relatives and friends."[7] Overall, those at risk of having marginal or inadequate support were "older respondents, especially older men lacking counselors; parents—that is, respondents with children at home—mothers and low-income parents most notably; non-Anglos, particularly black women; and respondents with less education and income, especially in companionship (but not counseling)."[8] What may be most relevant for a study of urban gay men is Fischer's finding that kin are less important to higher-income adult men living in cities who do not live near their families of origin. The saliency of friends for gay men in the development of a subcultural identity and for social support thus becomes more understandable.

It could be said that friendship for heterosexual men is an option—that their heterosexual male identity depends more on developing and maintaining romantic/family relationships in the context of a network of blood relatives. Key elements constitutive of hegemonic male heterosexuality in American society include marriage, children, and family responsibilities and commitments. And when it comes to seeking expressive and emotional support, heterosexual men usually turn to their wives or other female kin more than to male friends, who typically serve more instrumental support needs. But for gay men friendships with other gay men are a necessity, especially for those who do not live in urban areas, where numerous options and subcultures thrive, but who live rather, for example, in suburban environments that heavily emphasize schools, family, and children and that have few alternatives to the bar scene.[9]

Many social psychological studies conceptualize social support in terms of emotional support (someone to turn to for comfort when one is troubled), tangible support (physical assistance, including financial aid, problem solving), and informational support (comparing opinions, rumors, communications network).[10] In their work, Sheldon Cohen and T. A. Wills define social support as tangible, self-esteem, appraisal/emotional, and belonging support.[11] They found that stress is buffered by combinations of these different kinds of support, depending on the needs of the individual and the specific situation creating the stress. Tangible support is characterized by such things as helping others with a task or when they are sick, belonging support is providing companionship, appraisal support includes sharing feelings and talking about problems, and self-esteem support focuses on having views, beliefs, and interests similar to those of another. It should be clear from chapters 5 and 6 that gay men consistently define friendship and talk about their actual friends in terms of self-esteem and similar beliefs, appraisal through sharing feelings and emotions, belonging by being a part of a larger community of gay men and having people to do things with, and tangible aid in terms of doing favors and providing assistance.

Survey data also confirm the relative importance of best friends, in comparison with close friends and certainly with casual friends, in providing these kinds of social support. Table 7.1 demonstrates that gay men expect a best friend, especially,

Table 7.1 Social Support: Survey Respondents' Expectations of Friends (Percent Responding "Very" or "Extremely Important," Ranked in Order of Results for Best Friend)

	Best Friend	Close Friends	Casual Friends
Appraisal/emotional support:			
Talking about personal problems/relationships	90.3	80.1	10.6
Sharing feelings and emotions	89.5	83.2	21.2
Talking about sexual issues or concerns	76.1	56.0	18.6
Talking about politics, culture, sports, events	48.5	43.2	21.7
Belonging support:			
Providing companionship	74.3	71.9	28.9
Going places together	63.9	51.5	18.6
Having lunch or dinner together	62.4	53.5	20.7
Doing things together	55.3	49.7	14.3
Tangible support:			
Helping each other when sick	66.1	57.8	18.7
Helping each other with a task or project	59.4	50.0	21.7
Doing favors or errands for each other	58.7	42.9	10.1
Helping each other professionally	36.4	35.7	26.1
Lending money or other resources	31.0	20.5	3.1
Self-esteem support:			
Talking about jobs or careers	63.6	47.8	22.5
Having similar views and beliefs about life	62.7	50.3	24.2
Having similar hobbies or leisure interests	48.8	31.2	19.3
Competing at sports or play	10.9	8.3	6.2

(and close friends also, but to a lesser degree) to be available foremost for appraisal support and, in particular, to talk about personal problems, relationships, feelings, and emotions. In addition, there are expectations for best and close friends to provide companionship and other belonging support; offer tangible opportunities to help each other; and be someone to talk with about careers and with whom to share similar views and beliefs. Casual friends are not expected to provide nearly as much of these kinds of social support. Gay men in the survey appeared to expect casual friends to be more available for talking about jobs, politics, and feelings; for providing professional support, for providing companionship, and for helping each other on projects.[12]

Studies focusing particularly on men and their friendship networks have revealed specific kinds of social support: emotional aid, small services, large services, companionship, financial aid, and job/housing information.[13] Friends were most likely to provide companionship and small services (performing minor repairs, lending items), while kin and neighbors were more available for large services such as health-care assistance, and performing major repairs. Male friends also provided emotional support, but female kin were more involved in major emotional support issues (e.g., marital problems).

But for the gay men in my study other patterns emerged. In general, as I show in chapter 6, they defined friendship in terms of personal feelings; the gay men interviewed rarely talked about their friends in terms of material support, and, when they did, they almost always began with descriptions of emotional support, or using Cohen and Wills' categories of appraisal and belonging. Ed said, "I regard as friends people who add value (not in the financial sense) to my life; people who contribute energy, good vibes, well-being. Conversely, people who draw energy from me (when not welcomed) or who otherwise drain or sap me are not friends." It was only after he spoke these words that he talked about more tangible benefits and material support:" It's nice to be needed by friends every now and again, especially when I can use some of my skills to help them. . . . I really enjoy home improvement projects, although

I'd rather it be someone else's. . . . [There's] the great satisfaction of seeing a project come to completion, as well as knowing that someone else is benefiting."

Some men spoke in very rational ("masculine") terms of the kinds of support they get when they're feeling down. Charles, who "rarely tend[s] to process down times outwardly," called on his best friend and "sought advice from him on lots of issues. I value his insights, the rigor of his analysis, the quality of his thinking." Fred spoke of the support he gets from his close friendship this way:

> What I get from Barry I can less readily find a substitution for. Perhaps I am more emotionally needy, more isolated in my specifically gay needs and sensibilities. I think that he—because of his multifarious, multitudinous interests and connections—has amassed a larger store of good will, which he can draw on without even asking. . . . He provides the emotional distance and objectivity I sometimes lack and helps me to deal with sometimes overwhelming emotion.

Sometimes the description of a friend's social support combines the rational with the emotional, illustrating once again the blend of hegemonic and gay masculinities. Ed talked about one of this closest friends this way:

> There have been many times he's been there for me, especially when I was down, disappointed, or needed some wise counsel. What impresses me about Ron is his ability to commiserate with someone, as far as being the shoulder to cry on or having the ear to bend. Although he listens, and offers advice only when asked, he is able to remain detached from the situation and not get consumed in it. . . . I call on him not only when I'm down, but also when I need advice or counsel.

But a few were not always so open with their friends in terms of providing or seeking social support. Will, for example, was less sanguine about his friends: "I need to negotiate distance. How do you tell a friend not now, not today, that he's not getting the message?" He was not willing to be there all the time for his friends, for he felt that they had not always been there for him, or that they hadn't been the most helpful when he had a problem. Insecurity, envy, and competitiveness characterized many of his friendships with other men. Sometimes a friend is not a good source of support because he himself is having problems, as Paul reported, "I am often hesitant to talk with Doug when I am down because his situation often strikes me as a precarious and depressing one. I sometimes feel like I'm whining when I talk with him about things that aren't going the way that I would like."

Attempts to explain such varying differences in social support within gender—let alone between men and women—using biological or psychological essentialism minimize the way a society constructs, reproduces, and legitimizes a gendered order and creates conditions that generate different ways of doing and organizing friendship and support. Graham Allan, for example, argues from a more structural position when he states that, "it is not that friends fail to meet their obligations to one another at times of trouble, but more that the organisation of social life makes it difficult for friends to provide support when the circumstances of their lives differ markedly."[14] Hence, how much material and emotional support friends are able to provide without concern for self-interest is dependent on the rules established by the culture between friends about privacy, about what and how much to disclose, and about the contextual boundaries of the friendship. Also, since friendships are typically seen as secondary relationships with limited claim over people's resources, "most people put their family's interests before those of friends, and indeed feel that occupational demands take precedence over those of friendship."[15] Chapter 6, however, demonstrates that for the gay men in my study, career obligations were much more likely to limit time spent with friends than were family and romantic relationship commitments.

In other words, people do not expect friends to provide the kind of support that would threaten their friends' other primary relationships (such as that with their spouse, romantic partner, parents, or siblings). In fact, they may even be uncomfortable receiving or asking for such support—"I don't want to burden my friends with my problems" is a common statement—since the norms of friendship dictate that there should be reciprocity. They, in turn, would be obligated at a later date to provide similar kinds of support—the kinds that might infringe on their own responsibilities and time spent on more primary relationships and on work obligations. The limits of this exchange is evident in Eugene's statement, in which he said that his closest friends are his friends "because they are giving when they are able to be, yet able to receive my input, words, deeds when they need these things without necessarily feeling as if they are imposing on me. Friends know the meaning of appropriate give-and-take and can apply the appropriate thoughts and actions in the spirit of appropriate give-and-take."

Equality and reciprocity in friendships are taxed particularly dearly if there are requests for more long-term and time-consuming support, as Allan stated: "Managing friendship often becomes more problematic as the provision of regular, non-reciprocated support by one side may threaten the basis of equality implicit in the relationship. . . . Despite the commitment that friends have towards one another's welfare, in practice the basis of solidarity within the tie does not generally facilitate high levels of long-term unilateral support."[16] Studies of the chronically ill confirm that in only the rarest cases are friends providing practical support for and care of a friend: "Care for those who are ill remains very much a family matter. . . . Friends, then, are quite likely to be used as a resource for coping with the care situation, without actually being involved in acts of nursing."[17] Showing concern for the welfare of a friend is different from actual practical care, which, if done on a long-term basis, throws the relationship into imbalance by making one person more dependent on the other and threatens such core components of friendship as equality and reciprocity.

But many gay men may be different in this regard. Greg said, "Recently I nearly died. After I came out of my five-week coma, figured out what the fuck happened to me, the people who I always knew were my friends were there at my bedside, my family and my best friend." When white middle-class gay men in couples were asked by researchers to designate the people who provided social support, the couples as well as the individuals separately listed gay male friends the most; couples listed gay couples the second most; and the individual respondents listed a heterosexual female friend second most.[18] However, when asked to evaluate who had the most influence on the quality of their relationships, the couples listed family members first, but only slightly ahead of "friends" (as a category, not in terms of specific types of friends, such as gay male friend, heterosexual female friend, and so forth). Although other gay men were listed first in terms of support when types of friendships were analyzed separately, and heterosexual males were listed last, the support of any friends appeared to be essential for the gay couples, independent of whether the friend was gay or straight, or male or female.

Research on caretakers of patients with AIDS also contributes some important information about friendship and long-term social support. One study found that 42 percent of the 478 caregivers of patients with AIDS (PWAs) in central cities (using probability sampling) were heterosexual women, 26 percent were heterosexual men, 25 percent were gay men, and 7 percent were lesbians. Since many of the people being cared for were heterosexuals, the researchers estimated that "roughly one-third to one-half of the gay men with AIDS are cared for by gay peers. It is possible that many of the remaining caregivers are family members."[19] Because only 17 percent of the caregivers were over the age of fifty, most did not appear to be parents and were probably younger heterosexual friends or siblings. Many of the gay peers caring for a gay male PWA were likely to be lovers or partners; the percentage that were "just" friends was not assessed.

But data from the UCSF/UCLA AIDS Caregiver Study can clarify the relatively large role friends play in the lives of gay men dealing with AIDS. Around 37 percent of the 642 caregivers of PWAs (about 85 percent of the PWAs were gay men) who responded to the survey in Los Angeles and San Francisco were the gay lovers or partners of the PWA; another 37 percent were friends or acquaintances; 17 percent were siblings, parents, or other relatives; and 9 percent were legal spouses.[20]

Looking just at the 543 gay male PWAs, the data also suggest that most were informally cared for by people who have traditionally not been viewed as "family." Approximately 42 percent of the gay men in their sample were cared for by gay lovers and around 41 percent by friends (22 percent of the friends were female). Less than a fifth were being cared for by either legal or blood relatives.[21] Despite some limitations associated with a convenience sample, the data clearly support the general patterns of AIDS caregiving uncovered in research that has attempted to draw conclusions regarding the prevalence of AIDS caregiving in the general population using probability samples.[22]

In short, the majority of people caring for gay men with AIDS are likely to be their romantic partners/lovers (for those in relationships), followed by friends (other gay men and younger heterosexual men and women) and family members (typically sisters and mothers). In other words, friends are less likely than are same-sex lovers to be involved in long-term and time-demanding care of the ill. Comparatively, however, nonkin, nonpartner friends make up a larger proportion of those providing support for gay men than do family of origin members: "People are more likely to seek help from and give help to individuals with similar characteristics as themselves. . . . Although certainly many parents do care for their gay sons, a history of conflicting values and attitudes concerning lifestyle and sexual orientation may create barriers that make them less likely to serve as caregivers."[23]

Several of the gay men I interviewed spoke about AIDS and how they were able to be there for their friends, talk to them about their HIV status, and help them out when needed. Ed told me about how he "was seeing a friend through a difficult time with AIDS. I visited him as often as I could during frequent business trips." Sometimes, just having friends is sufficient for psychological well-being, even if they do not necessarily provide actual tangible assistance, since friends help relieve stress and enhance physical and mental well-being, as Table 7.2 shows. Almost all the gay men in the questionnaire study responded that having a best and close friends was very or extremely important, and that a best friend was especially impor-

Table 7.2   Importance to Survey Respondents of Friends for
Psychological Support (Percent Responding "Very" or "Extremely")

	Best Friend	Close Friends	Casual Friends
How important is it to have . . . ?	94.7	86.4	55.3
To what extent do you feel you are open, trusting, and "truly yourself" when with . . . ?	93.3	83.3	29.8
In times of stress, how helpful are . . . in helping you relieve the stress?	83.4	67.7	14.3
Do you believe your physical and/or mental well-being is enhanced by your relationship with your . . . ?	88.0	80.8	38.8

tant in terms of relieving stress and enhancing physical and mental well-being. It is important to have casual friends, as well, but they are not perceived as being as vital a source of psychological support.

Friends are important for helping out and for being there to talk to, especially in difficult times, or as Steve phrased it—in a way that went beyond specific health problems and touched on a larger political idea of unity—"Friendship is one of the things that differentiates man from beast. That is why mankind has overcome the great odds against its survival. Friends working together to overcome adversity."

Gay Identity

Besides social support, friendship exerts a strong influence on gay men's identity development and maintenance. Consider Aristotle's notion that "all friendly feelings toward others are an extension of the friendly feelings a person has for himself."[24] A less psychologized interpretation would sound more like Charles Cooley's "looking-glass self" concept, that is, one comes to know oneself as reflected by close friends, by other selves.

To be part of a gay community of friends becomes something of a necessity in cultural contexts that do not provide other sources of emotional and identity support. Friendship among gay men is a means toward learning more about one's gay identity and a source of freedom from the limitations imposed by the culture on being able to live a gay life. As R. W. Connell notes, "Gay sexuality and friendship networks . . . are experienced as a realm of freedom and pleasure outside the severe constraints" of the other parts of one's life.[25] Especially for many gay men just coming out, finding a group or clique of gay friends with whom they are free to test out, explore, and develop a sense of being gay has been likened to a rite of passage: "Coming out to natal family, coworkers, or other straight people is optional, but to accept being gay (at least simulating pride and rejecting shame) in the company of other gay men is as much a sign of adulthood as paternity is in other cultures."[26] "Coming out" is not just declaring to heterosexuals that one is gay; it has historically also been about joining a network of friends and acquaintances, that is, of gay people like oneself.

Gay men in my study regularly emphasized how similar they were to their friends and how important this homophily of shared values, status, and interests was for their identity and self-esteem (see Table 7.1). Kath Weston found in her research that gays and lesbians stressed the importance of similar identities in their relationships while implicitly linking the language of differences to heterosexual couples.[27] Interestingly, this interpersonal identity congruence is emphasized at the same time as larger political discourse takes on a more postmodern tone, highlighting differences and diversities. Thus friendships serve a dual purpose of connecting individuals, at the micro level of interpersonal relationships, to others who are perceived to be— and who often are—similar to themselves, while simultaneously linking people, at the macro level, to the larger communities of other gay men and lesbians who potentially reflect more racial, class, age, and gender diversity than most people's friendship networks do.

Friendships, in other words, are a structure of relationships at the intersection of the micro and the macro, at the point where individual social psychological identity development and maintenance occurs and where community building and political strategies are forged (as chapter 8 argues). Friendship provides a haven in which gay men can deal with the constraints and threats of hegemonic masculinity. Connell phrases it this way: "Wariness, controlled disclosure, and turning inward to a gay network are familiar responses" to heterosexual masculinity and its undercurrent of threat.[28] And Charles stated, "My relationship with Everard has immeasurably enriched my life. He has been a vital connection, a haven, a reflection, a challenge, and evidence that I have more to me in relation to a larger world than I could ever know. He is where I go to know I'm not crazy."

Friends give gay men a cultural separation and time out from compulsory masculinity, while at the same time allowing some forms of it to be reproduced in creative combination with gay masculinities. An identity is created, and social support is provided to bolster it and give it legitimacy. As Table 7.2 shows, almost all the gay men in the survey reported that they felt truly themselves, open, and trusting to a very or extremely strong degree when they were with their best friend, and nearly as many said the same about their close friends. Given that many casual friends are acquaintances at work and are less likely to be other gay men, the percentages saying that they felt this way when they were with casual friends were significantly lower.

It is in the company of other gay men, then, that gender and sexual orientation identities get shaped; people find other selves and learn about (and often reproduce and reconfigure) gay cultural images, histories, and styles. Harry told me that "if it weren't for my friendships, I would not have been able to establish roots after I decided to move here." And when these identities are organized and mobilized, political movements can take shape. Dan said that if he lived in a world of heterosexuals only "my life would be pretty flat. So what do these [gay] friendships mean? A different and vastly larger view of the world. A world of activism."

Friendships sometimes link Aristotelian ideas of a friend as the "other self" to a politics of identity through the use of dominant cultural images of the family, as chapter 3 demonstrates. Because kinship metaphors appear to be more commonly used by writers and observers of gay life than by individual gay men talking about their own personal histories, such appropriation of traditional cultural institutions can serve as a political strategy: "In extending homosexuality beyond the sexual, the notion of identity-based community opened new possibilities for using kinship terminology to imagine lesbians and gay men as members of a unified totality. Identity provided the linking concept that lent power to analogies between gay and consanguineal relations. Wasn't this what families in the United States were all about: identity and likeness mediated by the symbolism of blood ties?"[29]

In attempting to create a culture of gay identity and likeness, despite actual variations and diversities, gay men have been able to simultaneously contest and reproduce hegemonic masculinity. The collective practices in society's institutions and symbolic culture give dominant masculinity "a social authority that shapes perceptions of gayness" for both gay and heterosexual men.[30] Hence, while gay men's friends might provide a refuge and a social psychological distancing from the practices of masculinity, these practices cannot be fully erased; in these networks of friends compulsory masculinity often gets reproduced. As Connell observes, the erotic image and object choice of many gay men is not a flamboyant, effeminate gay man, but "a very straight gay"—"the choice of embodied masculinity."[31]

The kinds of social support, tangible advice and information, and identity growth that gay friends provide other gay friends are captured by Henning Bech, who concisely summarizes many of the key points about the role of friendship in gay men's lives. He says: "Being together with other homosexuals allows one to mirror oneself in them and find self-affirmation. It allows one to share and interpret one's experiences. It allows one to learn in more detail what it means to be homosexual: how to act, what to think, thus lending substance to one's proclaimed identity, as well as assimilating certain techniques that may help bridge the gap between the identity and one's actual experiences and conduct."[32]

It's just that for many, though, what is learned in detail is how to incorporate the dominant culture's definitions about gender with what a community of friends reconstructs. Some are willing, even eager, to contest the dominant norms and constraints of the society's gendered order, while many, as I have shown, assimilate and synthesize the dialectics of competing masculinities. Some gay men find that they cannot readily participate, either politically or interpersonally, in gay culture, communities, and networks. For them, gay identity and gay subcultures become just another set of constraints, another world requiring conformity, that must be resisted. Fred often reflected this view by invoking a set of gay standards that friends use to judge each other; he felt that "my friendships are always under scrutiny by other gay men, to see if I'd do the wrong thing."

Some respond by withdrawing from gay friends and seeking the company of a more diverse network; others find themselves becoming more selective about who their friends are and choosing themselves into networks that more and more closely mimic their own particular styles, values, and interests. Many working-class gay men and people of color complain about the dominance of middle-class white male images as constitutive of "the gay community" or of "a gay man." For them, and for some other gay men, friendships may provide identity and social support when they first discover their own sexual orientation, but later they find it necessary to pare down their friendships and select those who are essential for their particular needs, identities, and interests. How some gay men end a friendship is the focus of the next section.

Fading Friendships

Aaron spoke about how he "can't recall a time" when he and his close friends were mad at each other: "This is an important point. More often than I would care to admit, I have fallen out with friends about one thing or another. And there has seldom been a rapprochement. It's as if they have died. I'm not so eccentric that I write off friends after one or two disagreements, but I hardly hesitate to zero out a friendship that seems 'toxic.' "

Obviously, not all friends provide social support, identity development and maintenance, or cultural diversity. Indeed, some friendships may overtly threaten these and may create situations that force people to alter their networks and daily associations. For many gay men, the process of coming out once entailed leaving behind straight friends and secretly participating in a more underground network of gay friends; today it's easier for many to incorporate both sets of friends as they openly acknowledge their gay identity. But this doesn't mean that there still aren't situations in which gay men find it necessary to end a friendship, modify its terms, confront a friend about some unpleasant situation or failed reciprocity, or give up on seeking social support from someone. Aristotle, of course, had some thoughts on this topic: "There is nothing strange about breaking friendships based on what is useful or pleasant when the partners no longer have the qualities of being useful or pleasant."[33]

The circumstances under which someone becomes "no longer pleasant" are varied, but consider this series of E-mail exchanges between two gay students at a university in New England that one of them forwarded to me. Within their messages, multiple masculinities are enacted, from the macho posturings of putting someone down, competing for another's boyfriend, or being more intelligent than the other, to the sharing of thoughts, emotions, vulnerabilities, and personal feelings about the nature of their friendship. Perhaps confronting each other by E-mail eliminates the intimacy of face-to-face contact and makes it easier for these men to open up. But in any case, the combination of the stereotypically masculine language of competition and the gay masculinity of disclosing emotionally about their friendship is ever-present.

Andy, a nineteen-year-old undergraduate, wrote the following message to a recently made friend, Ken, a twenty-four-year-old graduate student:

> I've been bothered increasingly lately by what may be misperceptions on my part. It has seemed to me for quite some time that you find me irritating, and often go out of your way to avoid or exclude me. What bothers me is having this uncertainty about

where I stand with you. Are we friends? Were we ever? Will we be in the future? I can't tell. Look, I like you, Ken, and I want to be your friend. If I'm being obnoxious, and I'm not aware of it, feel free to tell me. Write me a letter. Indicate in international flag language. Whatever. Just let me know. And, if you'd rather not stay (?) friends, that's okay too. P.S. I pretend to have a remarkably thick skin, but the truth is, it's all a facade. A lot of what you say hurts more than I demonstrate.

Ken responded within an hour:

I appreciated your letter. First, we are friends. Second, yes, you do annoy me at times, let me explain. When I first met you I thought we could be the best of friends (and perhaps still can); as we spent more time together I got the impression that you felt you had to constantly compete with me intellectually—take me down a peg, something I don't particularly take as friendly. Why is this? It seems we are both bright. (I hope you realize I always recognized this; I remember writing to my friends back home about you shortly after we first met and telling them about how intelligent, fun, and interesting you were—the brightest person I've met in college) and we are both very insecure (understand that about me, if nothing else Andy—I am one of the most thin skinned people you'll ever meet, if I feel that someone's trying to hurt me I will hold grudges, but I'm also incredibly loving and giving to my friends if I feel they care and love me). So our relationship began its descent as a result of that feeling: that I was more of a game than a friend of yours. It hit rock bottom when I found out last semester that you had a crush on Howard (don't ask me how I know this, it's not fair to drag them into this). I found it out actually only days after we went to that play and you made me look bad in front of Lee (whether or not you were intentionally doing that, that was my impression) and I pieced those two bits of information together and came up with a nemesis. Why I'm telling you all this now I don't know; perhaps because I no longer care what Howard thinks about me (he's damaged himself in my eyes enough that I'm no longer in love with him, although I do still care about him). Let's put all of that behind us, shall we. I welcome a close friendship with you again if you're willing to be a little more gentle on me (a decade from now you'll understand we are contemporaries and that the age difference is meaningless—just because I'm older, I'm not required because of age to be more mature or confident than you.) I really do appreciate your writing that letter and let this be a new beginning for us.

Finally, about twenty-four hours later Andy sent a reply that, in all its masculine finery, stated that Ken's perceptions of him trying to outdo Ken by displaying his intelligence were understandable, but incorrect. Andy's intention was not to put Ken down, he said, but to keep up with him, since he felt "a need to constantly validate my presence by demonstrating my intelligence." Andy also responded to the issue of Howard and their mutual crushes:

> I want you to know that I had absolutely NO INTENTION of acting on that crush, even though it WAS older than your crush. I had a crush on Howard from the first time I saw him at the gay students meeting. My heart nearly imploded when I heard how YOU felt about him. But, since you had spoken first, I thought I had an obligation to ignore/hide how I felt about him. This changed considerably, however, as our relationship changed. The more aggravated I felt you were towards me (even without knowing the reason, mind you!) the more frustrated I became. Here I was making this sacrifice for you, and this was how I was to be repaid? I suppose you can see how this led to my brief tryst with Howard. I will try to be more gentle with you. But if I take things too far, TELL ME!!! Can't think of anything more to add. Love, Andy

Andy rhetorically asked me, "Could straight friends reconcile like that? Would straight friends be so forgiving if one had trysted with the crushee of the other? This would NEVER have happened with straight friends, I think. In my experience, straight men are much less comfortable openly discussing their feelings with their friends." Research backs Andy on this one, but here those feelings also include a very culturally masculine competitiveness not only over intelligence but also over someone else's sexual attractions. Furthermore, it illustrates how precarious friendships can be in the early stages of formation and the kinds of issues that can very often lead to their dissolution.

Arguments with friends do not always end a relationship, but not every friendship eventually works out. People come into our lives, move on, and sometimes return. Often, they disappear, never to be heard from again, and are replaced by newer relationships. David said that he has never ended a friendship; "however, I have let friendships drift apart usually because our interests, opinions, lifestyles, hobbies drift over time such that we no longer find each other interesting." Because close friends are chosen, they can be unchosen as well. Just as beginning points of friendship formation are not marked by official ceremonies, endings are not defined by explicit rituals, either. When people are asked how their friendships have ended, rarely is the explanation linked to a specific incident; most simply reply that the friendship "just faded away." But I want to argue that "just fading away"—like the phrase "just friends"—conceals a much more complex process of behaviors, meanings, and choices than people readily admit. "Fading away" is, typically, the end result of a series of decisions that have been made, within and outside the friendship, by one or both of the friends themselves. It is often a way of saving face and of not having to confront someone directly.

By the time a friendship has become a close or best friendship, many of the differences between the two friends have already been reduced, or tolerated by the friends.[34] There may be less conflict in friendship than with any other close interpersonal relationship (kinship, romantic attachment) because of the self-selection and the choices that have been made along the way. But negative comments among friends often have a greater impact on well-being than positive comments do.[35] After all, we expect friends to support us and say nice things, so when they do the effect isn't as powerful as it is when they don't. We don't expect critical comments or disapproval about our behavior. However, not all arguments, jealousies, and status changes result in ended friendships; sometimes they only serve to strengthen and bond the friendship.

The tension between Ken and Andy, if it persists, will probably doom the friendship before it can become a more committed, closer one than it is now. By the time friends have become close, many issues have been resolved, shared values have been magnified, and "hot buttons" are being tastefully ignored in everyday interactions. Besides, those whose values or actions diverge too much are usually eliminated from the friendship circle, if the values haven't already been modified to achieve congruence with those of others in the group.[36] When friends change or create conflict, there is a tendency to start pulling back, not return calls, not initiate activities or conversations, and not share experiences and feelings. These choices become the reasons that the friends drift apart, and they cause the impression that the friendship "just faded away."

While the E-mail messages reprinted above describe the threats to a friendship in formation, the issues raised by these college students are relevant to the dissolution of more solid close and best friendships. Sources of tension in friendships and changes in the nature of the relationships tend to revolve around competition or envy, money and other favors, independence-dependence pulls, not making enough time for the relationship, seeing someone in a new way, and betrayal.[37] Some relationships end because people move and fail to keep in touch with one another; they grow older and change interests and identities; and they become involved in committed romantic relationships that alter the demands made on them in terms of time, space, and loyalties, as some of the gay men's comments presented in chapter 4 suggest.

Friends also go through economic and occupational transitions that affect the way they relate to others. Clyde Franklin offers a provocative argument about the diminution of friendship and its changing nature among African American men as they became more upwardly mobile.[38] For working-class black men race provides a source from which to construct their friendships as intimate; for middle-class black men class negatively constructs their friendships as less nurturing: "While working-class black men's same-sex friendships are warm, intimate, and holistic, upwardly mobile black men's same-sex friendships are cool, non-intimate, and segmented. Black men's friendships appear to change as they move up the social ladder."[39]

In other words, changes in environmental factors (loss of proximity and geographic mobility), individual factors (the emergence of possessiveness or jealousy or betrayal over time), situational factors (changes in marital or dating status, occupation or social class shifts, life-cycle transitions, and not spending enough time together), and dyadic factors (loss of value and status similarity; reductions in intimacy, disclosure, and liking; boredom) contribute to the dissolution of friendships.[40]

Which factors dominate in the dissolution depends on the stage of the friendship: "Casual friendships were more likely to end because of reduced proximity, whereas close and best friendships were more likely to end because of decreased interaction or interference."[41] Sometimes a close friendship becomes a more casual one, as Ed described: "I tend to hold onto friends, so I can't recall many specific incidents of termination, but I do recall times when I've consciously downgraded someone from friend to acquaintance." Also, limitations on the possibility of ending a friendship can be related to social forces outside the relationship; people embedded in highly interdependent and dense networks may find that attempts to terminate a friendship are "likely to be met with opposition from the network constituency."[42]

Another sociological explanation for friendship dissolution focuses on the issue of structural inequality in the relationship. Short-term assistance or reciprocity in a friendship is rarely an issue, but "the situation becomes more complicated when the support required is more onerous, time-consuming and long lasting," since this typically signals "a major change in people's circumstances which may, in any case, make it hard for them to service and sustain their friendships as before."[43] Not only might providing this kind of long-term support be difficult for some, as I mention earlier in the chapter, but the recipients may not want to accept their friends' support for fear of never being able to reciprocate or of becoming too dependent on the other.

People signal that a friendship is coming to an end by providing cues that the other is no longer liked or by excluding the other by saying they lack time to get together (according to published research, these indirect strategies of avoidance and withdrawal were used more for casual friendships), rather than by making some dramatic or public statement.[44] In general, most people just let friendships fade away, or allow them to have what Letty Cottin Pogrebin calls a "romantic ending." She classifies three styles of termination of friendship: baroque, classical, and romantic. Baroque endings are "bombastic, high-flown, and cannot be missed"; they involve confrontations, accusations, manipulation, exit speeches, and slammed doors. Classical endings entail controlled, rational discussions; attempts at reconciliations; and clean, tasteful breaks that are characterized by the friends' concern for one another. Romantic endings are formless fadeouts that make use of avoidance and withdrawal, the breaks whose causes are unknown and that are "shrouded in euphemism and understatement."[45]

Of the gay men I interviewed, eight told me about ending a friendship; everyone else talked only about friendships that had faded out. The formal endings of friendships had to do with disagreements over values, problems or jealousies over a romantic relationship, and behaviors that tested the basic meanings of friendship, as I now discuss.

Arguments and Conflicts

Every relationship has moments of disagreement. Sometimes they are fatal to the relationship, as Will described: His very close friendship with a straight woman ended after a big fight over her "constantly complaining. In the context of people with AIDS who had real complaints, I told her that hers seemed less serious. Besides, she didn't reciprocate when I had problems to talk about." But more often there are minor disagreements, or at most major arguments focused around topics of minimal importance to the relationship itself. Carl, for example, said, "Usually I argue about beliefs, and it's more of a discussion of viewpoints rather than an argument."

Given that many friends are similar in terms of their values and beliefs, arguments of this nature are rarely severe enough to ruin a friendship. Frank said that he doesn't tend to argue with friends "because we agree about everything." It is also possible that many people avoid confrontation; knowing their friends as well as they do, they simply ignore hot issues or conflicts. David stated, "I don't argue often with friends; we respect each other's attitudes and opinions. We may debate and discuss and inquire, but not argue."

The overwhelming majority of the respondents to the survey of gay men (see Table 7.3), said that they rarely or never have any *major* disagreements or conflicts with their *best* friend, and about half rarely or never have *minor* arguments with their best friend. Kevin said his arguments "occur when I feel I have

Table 7.3   Major and Minor Conflicts between Survey Respondents and Best Friend

	Major	Minor
How conflicts are experienced:		
How often do you experience disagreements? (percent never or rarely)	91.1	47.7
How bothered, disappointed, or hurt are you by them? (percent very or extremely)	62.5	13.1
How important is it to resolve them? (percent very or extremely)	94.3	63.9
How a conflict is handled:°		
Talk about it immediately	32.7	34.7
Talk about it later	29.2	27.4
Express emotions	26.3	22.4
Ignore it but behave differently	6.4	6.8
Avoid friend until conflict is over	3.5	2.3
Ignore it as if nothing happened	1.8	6.4

° These figures are percentages of the *responses,* since respondents were allowed to select multiple ways of resolving conflicts. Of the *respondents,* 58.9 percent selected "talk about it immediately" for major problems, 52.6 percent selected "talk about it later," and 47.4 percent selected "express emotions." For minor problems, the percentages were 59.4, 46.9, and 38.3, respectively. Less than 12 percent of the respondents selected other choices.

been judged or treated unfairly." George felt that he really hadn't argued with any of his friends: "The closest I've had to an argument with a close friend have been some tense emotional discussions about negotiating expectations with friends I'm in love with where our feelings are unsymmetrical." Frank responded, "We don't tend to argue because we generally agree about everything. I've never ended a friendship by arguing."

When they did argue, most of the gay men completing the survey said that they were very hurt or extremely bothered by major disagreements, much less so for minor ones. In addition, almost all felt that it was very or extremely important to resolve major problems, and most said the same about minor disagreements (see Table 7.3). And the most often-selected way of dealing with a major or minor conflict was talking about it immediately, followed closely by talking about it later and by expressing feelings about the argument; very few indicated that they would ignore the disagreement. Although age and duration of the friendship did not have an impact on ways of resolving conflict, younger men tended to express their emotions more readily, especially with friends of longer duration, and older men with best friends of longer standing were more likely to talk out a major problem immediately.[46] John said, "Arguments tend to be over misunderstandings or miscommunications. They get patched up fairly quickly."

These responses differ from research conclusions reached among samples of heterosexual friendships, which demonstrated that, in general, "when anger and conflict occur in friendships, it appears that the most common response is to bury one's head in the sand."[47] The gay men in my study like to talk, and they like to talk about personal feelings, as I have shown in the tables of data that focus on questions about what they do with friends, what they expect of friends, and what they talk over with friends.

However, research also shows that the closer the friendship, the more likely people are to talk problems out; indirect methods and avoidance are more typical of casual friendships. This is partly due to the fact that closer friends are often better integrated in larger networks, and avoidance is thus more difficult.

Mike told the story of his best friend, a lesbian, and of how they "had a public falling out over the direction of a gay/lesbian organization we were members in. At the time Theresa was very closeted. Three years ago, she and her partner made an attempt to re-establish the friendship, and we quickly grew to trust each other. This was in part facilitated by the fact that both she and her lover had grown in the coming-out process and were clearly less rigid. She is now my best friend."

But some people change after they get to know each other, as Vince found out: "I have ended a friendship recently. My friend Robert has become a miser. I don't like him anymore, he annoys me." Leo realized something about one of his friends that went to the core of the reciprocity dimension of friendship: "I ended it because I felt used, that I was expected to do something or be something in order to prove my friendship. And now we just don't call each other. If we see each other in public, we are polite, but there is no reason to maintain a conversation."

Boyfriends and Other Sexual-Romantic Relationships

People often lose friends when they become involved in a romantic relationship with someone else. Beverley Fehr concludes that "there is evidence that development of a romantic relationship reduces the number of friends and truncates interactions with retained friends."[48] Time limitations, jealousy, competition, betrayal, and dislike of the new partner can each contribute to a friendship's dissolving. It is especially difficult when a best friend gets involved with someone else, since a best friendship, Lillian Rubin writes, "stimulates the wish for exclusivity. Even the name we give it—*best* friend—facilitates the fantasy that the wish can become reality, or at the very least, that first place will be forever ours."[49] Hence, feelings of betrayal and abandonment can emerge when a best friend gets romantically involved and begins to transfer the sense of exclusivity.

Changes in friendship networks may be more related to life-cycle transitions, that is, "immersion in marriage and parent-hood does affect the quality of friendship ties, but not in any simple 'privatizing' or 'isolating' manner. Although there is considerable turnover in best friends during the early adult years, men in the middle stages of life are able to build and sustain enduring ties."[50] There are more strains on the friendship during the early adult years (when one is between the ages of eighteen and thirty) when new jobs, new romantic relationships, and mobility are more likely to come into play; durable relationships are established after this early-adult period even if the person is in a committed romantic relationship. Almost half (47.4 percent) of the over fifty-five-year-old men in my survey had a best friend of at least eleven years duration, compared to 15.4 percent of those under thirty and 26.7 percent of those between thirty-one and forty.

As Ann Stueve and Kathleen Gerson found among their heterosexual male sample, "older men were more likely to form and maintain long-lasting friendships. There was much turnover among 'best friends' in the early adult years but relatively little in the later stages of life."[51] This is supported by Theodore Cohen's findings that marriage and fatherhood lead men to restrict and limit their emotional life and time devoted to their peers, resulting in their friendships fading, although "in their transition to marriage, men made more gradual reductions in their friendship ties than occurred within the transitions to fatherhood," in part because marriage took place earlier in their life cycle.[52]

But getting involved in a relationship or becoming a parent does not necessarily end friendships; doing so also creates new friendships. Not only is another set of friends introduced into a person's life, but coupling and parenthood create couple friendships. While finding four compatible people can be difficult, many couples report the initiation of friendship with other couples. This is partly related to social class; middle-class couples are more likely to have couple friends because they pull away from old neighborhood ties, develop newer sets of friends after high school, and enter other social and work worlds away from kin and childhood friends, whereas young, working-class couples in the first few months of marriage "severed the old peer ties" and turned "to parents and siblings for company."[53]

Couple friendships also serve to reinforce the couple-ness

of relationships, reproducing the institution of marriage and other coupled selves. Rubin states that "couple friendships are an important part of the social cement in a marriage, providing support not just for each other's marriages but for the institution itself. Our relations with others like ourselves validate the choices we make in our lives."[54] But friendships between single people and couples often create power imbalances with "the needs and rhythms of the married couple almost always given first consideration" and where the couples "define both the limits and possibilities of the friendship."[55] Sometimes married people feel used by single people who call on them only when they are not romantically involved, and singles feel like a third wheel when around the couples. In other words, both "sides" are involved in the dynamics of maintaining or ending the friendship.

But how do these issues relate to gay men who are more likely than heterosexuals to exist in communities that combine coupled and single people? Among the gay men in my study, twice as many of those who were coupled, as compared to those who were single, had a best friend who was living with a romantic partner (48.6 percent to 24.7 percent). In addition, single gay men were almost twice as likely to have a long-term best friend (with whom they had been friends for eleven years or more) than were coupled men (35.6 percent to 19.0 percent, not including lover as best friend).

Sometimes tensions between friends can emerge when one of the friends gets involved with someone. Martin Levine reports that gay men's friendships are "remarkably stable":

> They typically lasted as long as the men remained romantically uninvolved. Lovers and boyfriends usually compromise friendships because they drew time and affection away from friends. These relationships made the neglected sister or best friend feel hurt, angry, and rejected, and they often provoked bitter fights and the dissolution of the friendship. The emotional fallout accompanying these breakups was similar to that occurring when "lovers" separated.[56]

This was the case for some of the gay men I interviewed. Will talked about how a friendship of his ended "when I got into a relationship and he didn't. We didn't speak for years. He tried to undermine the relationship; he didn't want the best for me. He felt abandoned; in his loneliness, he wanted me for his companionship." Kevin said, "I have ended one friendship in my life. It was because that friend judged my lover's character in a way that I considered to be unfair. We simply did not agree, and the communication ceased completely. Sometimes selfishness and inconsiderateness spoil friendship." For Fred, the ending of a friendship made him realize that his friend had always been patronizing and that the relationship may not have been so strong in the first place:

> I ended one close friendship because the other person developed an intense personal and sexual relationship that I felt preempted our already somewhat fragile and conditional friendship. I felt perhaps somewhat jealous, out of place, and thought my friend had become preoccupied, arrogant, and overbearing. It was difficult and somewhat painful at the time, but I think it was the right decision. . . . I liked his new friend, thought the relationship was good for him, but felt that our relationship had become extraneous, and that, in his good fortune, he had become patronizing—a quality that had always been evident, but that became intolerable to me in the new circumstances.

Sometimes, though, the outcome isn't so bleak. John said in his interview that "my friends resented my partner coming between us. Things have gotten a lot better and they now are his friends too, but I must confess, the tenor of their friendship with him is different from what it is with me. Our friendship is much closer." Frank also expressed the fact that his friend was "jealous of the time I spent with my lover at first. We stopped getting together so much, but my partner and I made sure that we included him in some of our activities so that he would be comfortable with both of us. Now, he will freely call my lover and vice versa, just to chat."

Other times, it's the partners who resent the best friend

and create potential problems, as Greg reported: "All my part-ners have hated Allan because they all knew he is number one." Adjustments are often made, and old friends and new lovers become friends, or each is simply accommodated by the other, as Eugene stated: "My best friend is the person I tell everything, and I share almost everything with my lover. But my lover has not knocked my friend off that particular pedestal. Indeed, they each have their respective and appropriate pedestals in my life and neither has given me any indication that the other's pedestal is in anybody's way."

More often, friends and their friends' lovers do get along. Aaron said, "I've never dated anyone who didn't get along with my closest friends," and Ben similarly reported that "sometimes you feel left out or excluded when a new lover appears, but no problem with this so far with my closest friend. I have met most of Rod's boyfriends, and there has been no problems." What can happen is that gay couples make friends with other couples, and single people become less involved in their lives. This is what David explained: "Most of our new friends have been with other couples. Some less close friendships with uncoupled indi-viduals have drifted apart because of changing interests." Will reiterated, "It's hard to be friends with single people when cou-pled. But we each need our own friend; we each have four or five on our own. Over time, more of my friends are coupled friends with us as a couple."

Just Fade Away

And then there were none. Some people are much better at it—they call regularly, schedule social events, deliver gifts at appropriate times, offer assistance sometimes when it has not even been asked for, and continue contact with cards, calls, and E-mails when someone moves away. Others get wrapped up in the move; they put effort into developing new connections and networks, slowly forgetting former friends and replacing them with equally committed friends who may more and more pro-vide the support, trust, and reciprocity that was already starting to fade or becoming routine with the former friends. If the former friendships really were deep and close, emotional and cognitive dynamics would mitigate distance in this age of communications, and friends would make time for each other. Or, as Robert Bell phrases it, "Friendships can be ended by external forces that drive the friends apart. But whatever the causal origins, friendships are ultimately broken from inside the relationship, not from outside it."[57]

Almost all of the gay men I interviewed said that they never actively ended a friendship, but just let it fade away. Ben commented, "In general, friendships just peter out. It is a great loss, but in most cases we drifted apart." Frank said, "I've never ended a friendship by arguing, but a few have just faded away over the years as I've grown up." As Andy put it, "Never ended one. I do tend to drift away from people, but I've never actively ended a friendship—well, once in the third grade, but I don't think it's relevant."

Not trying to keep in touch and using lack of time or a new job or a new relationship as the reasons for letting a friendship slowly fade only demonstrate that the friendship might never have been as solid as it once was thought to be. After all, according to Rubin, the amount of time one has available is not as salient as the relevancy of the friendship in one's life: "Women *make* time for such friendships because they value them so highly. . . . But given the wariness with which men approach each other, given their fear of displaying vulnerability or dependency to another man, there's not much incentive to find time for friends who are more than playmates."[58]

Leo said, "Friendships simply grow apart, no fight or anything, just people changing in different ways and less and less reason to call or get together." Carl said he "usually ends friendships by drifting apart. It happens a lot because of changes in viewpoints and no longer similar interests can be shared." No wonder friends look a lot alike in terms of interests and values; those who differ are cooled out. Ending friendships directly would seem too drastic, so these other excuses become the more "painless and graceful way to become less involved and end the friendship."[59] Using indirect methods to signal the end also leaves open the option of future friendly interactions should the people meet somewhere again. In short, "this reliance on indirect strategies may account for the perception that friendships just 'fade away.' If one gradually reduces the number of phone calls and invitations to socialize, and generally avoids contact, the friendship may simply wither on the vine."[60]

Maintaining friendships, as I discuss in chapter 6, requires perseverance, disclosure, and frequent contact. For those with whom connections are already casual, or for those who are close but who go through changes in their life without sharing these events and feelings, keeping up a friendship is not easy. The novelist John Barth writes, "That's how much of life works: our friends float past; we become involved with them; they float on, and we must rely on hearsay or lose track of them completely; they float back again, and we must either renew our friendship—catch up to date—or find that they and we don't comprehend each other any more." Charles captured many of these ideas and the ones I have been talking about—the failure to keep in touch, the drifting apart, the significant changes that occur when people mature, and the final fading away. His is perhaps the most common story people tell about their lost friendships:

> There is only one closest friendship which has ended. Others have faded in importance as I and they fell out of contact. In fact, that's the common theme in the end of the friendships. Once, a friend and I lost touch with each other and found that so much time had passed we were different people, having discovered more of ourselves, different from the ones who the other knew. Somehow we couldn't get back into the rhythm of the relationship and it just faded away from lack of interest.

Death

"Death is friendship's final closure." Pogrebin writes, "It devastates us at any age but more so when it strikes in the prime of life, adding existential terror to our loss."[61] No words better describe what many gay men have confronted as we near the end of almost two decades with AIDS. The late Paul Monette wrote poetically of his friends: "It's hard to keep the memory at full dazzle, with so much loss to mock it. Roger gone, Craig gone, César gone, Stevie gone. And this feeling that I'm the last one left, in a world where only the ghosts still laugh. But at least they're the ghosts of full-grown men, proof that all of us got that far, free of the traps and the lies."[62]

The importance of friendship in the lives of gay men, and the intensity and depth of feeling that gay men invest in their friendships, quickly becomes evident when a friend is tragically lost while still young. In June 1992 historian John D'Emilio gave a eulogy at a memorial service for his friend Ken Dawson, one of New York's leading activists and the director of Senior Action in a Gay Environment (SAGE). It is filled with the intensity of loss and with all the key words that characterize gay men's friendships: trust, strength, disclosing emotions, crying, bonding, opening up, loneliness, and struggle. Its power is in its sensitivity and in the way it embodies the complexities of heteronormative and gay masculinities:

> Each one of us here has had to find our own way of dealing with the mountains of grief that this epidemic has thrown our way. For myself, as acquaintances, and movement buddies, and close friends have died, I have managed my grief by collectivizing it. . . . With Ken's death I can't pretend any longer that the loss is someone else's. We knew each other for too many years and in too many ways. We played and worked and traveled together. We fought in the way that only very special friends can fight, and we knew the places where each of us had had to struggle. . . . I trusted him, I asked him for advice, and I gained enormous strength from his example. . . . I cared for Ken, I cherished him, because he opened himself to me, and let me see the struggles that were the source of his strength. . . . [One night], a bunch of us were sitting around talking about what was going on in our lives. When Ken's turn to talk came, he barely started when he began to cry. . . . And what he was crying about that night was my leaving New York. He didn't want me to go. We had known each other at that point for about seven years, and I certainly counted him among my friends. But I had no idea that I meant so much to him. We

bonded that night in a way that was permanent and, though I couldn't excise that core of loneliness, I could let Ken know that he wasn't alone.[63]

In addition to the personal losses gay men have experienced of friends in their friendship networks, for many gay men the loss of other same-aged gay men—even those they didn't know—has created a collective loss of friendship. More than half of the men in Levine's "clone" friendship cliques died from AIDS, including eventually Marty Levine himself; most of the rest were HIV positive, and only a few remained negative. The intensity of the loss and the amount of caregiving needed led to the dissolution of many of the friendship cliques and crowds: "AIDS-related diseases and fatalities caused clone structural entities either to collapse or to vanish. In most cases, the deaths of members broke cliques. . . . In some cases, the burden of continuous sickness, caregiving, and dying split cliques. That is, emotional strains and pressures caused men to abandon the group."[64]

In his infamous 1983 call to arms Larry Kramer cries out, "My sleep is tormented by nightmares and visions of lost friends, and my days are flooded by the tears of funerals and memorial services and seeing my sick friends. How many of us must die before *all* of us living fight back?"[65] He not only captures the personal pain of loss but also uses it to bully people into action, thereby illustrating the power and the potential of a political civic dimension to networks of friends.

AIDS has taken an incredible toll on most gay men's friendship networks while also opening up the possibilities of newer friends being made through grief and support. In his usual overstated style, Kramer exclaims, "Over the past seven years I have lost some five hundred acquaintances and friends to AIDS. . . . And also—because AIDS has brought gay men much closer, so that friendships that would ordinarily take years to develop are now quickly made and cemented—those of us fighting this epidemic find ourselves with many new friends very quickly indeed. . . . I believe most gay men now know more dead gay men than they realize, or allow themselves to think about."[66]

Using the deaths of large numbers of gay men, and emphasizing the importance of networks of support, many gays and lesbians have mobilized others into a collective sense of identity and political purpose. The way friendships can be harnessed into use for political action and community building, and the way they give modern meaning to Aristotle's notion of a civic friendship, are the topics of the final chapter.

"A VICARIOUS SENSE
OF BELONGING"

The Politics of Friendship
and Gay Social Movements,
Communities, and Neighborhoods

[F]riendship and its virtues are not merely private: they are public, even political, for a civic order, a "city," is above all a network of friends. Without
civic friendship, a city will degenerate into a struggle of contending interest
groups unmediated by any public solidarity.
— *Robert Bellah et al.,* Habits of the Heart

Friendship provides more than psychological well-being and social support. It also contains an element of community building,
mobilizing, and effecting social change. There is what Hannah
Arendt calls, "the political relevance of friendship."[1] Dan said
that "most of my friends are those who will show up at the next
[political rally]. This is not a deeply thought-out choice; I'm just
more interested in those who are active."

Friendship has the potential to develop and maintain unconventional values and styles of behavior through shared
choice and to transform social and political life.[2] How gay people develop an identity by building communities of choice, organize a political presence and transform social life, and structure
space (residential, commercial, sexual, global) is related, in part,
to friendship networks. The personal can become the political.
There are, in other words, social and political consequences to
the formation of friendships in gay men's lives, not the least of
which is the idea of civil society, as Aristotle explained when he
wrote that "friendship consists in community" and that "friendship also seems to hold states together."[3]

For Aristotle, political friendships are connected to familial   189 and personal relationships. Michael Pakaluk interprets Aristotle's idea of "community friendships" as dependent on household friendships, which are then extended to mediating institutions, such as a tribe or fraternal association, and finally to the state: "It is in a family that one can acquire love for oneself as someone whose nature is to be in relation to others, and it is this sort of self-love which is extended to the political communities."[4] From the micro to the macro, from interpersonal relationships that begin in families of choice to gay neighborhoods and organizations, friendships are a powerful social force.

There is little to suggest that the political power of friendships is on the wane in modern societies. Contrary to prevailing notions about market society and personal relations conflicting with each other, sociologist Allan Silver proposes that commercial society promotes friendship patterns that "connect, not some who are allied in struggle against others, but potentially all, through forms of association that cumulatively contribute to a moralized civil society."[5] Such eighteenth-century Scottish Enlightenment writers as Adam Smith and David Hume understood friendship in precommercial society as an instrumental, calculated, competitive, and necessary relationship, the purpose of which was to "help friends and hurt enemies" (as is evidenced in the classical heroic forms of friendship).

In commercial society, however, as Silver puts it, by "limiting instrumental exchange to the newly distinct domain of the market," a voluntary, "morally superior form of friendship" can be founded on sympathy and affection. Such a friendship is "unconstrained by necessity," which enhances the "moral quality of personal relationships," integrating "individuals into the larger society, linking them to successively more inclusive groupings," and resulting in a "civil society free of exclusivistic relationships hostile or suspicious toward others."[6] This overly romanticized view of capitalism, however, may understate the competitive individualism that often emerges among men. Solidary networks do occur where traditional ties break down, suggesting a dialectical rather than a causal process between commerce and friendship.[7]

In a civil society that sets up relationships of hostility, especially based on sexual orientation, linking gay men into exclusive groupings is a necessity. Hence, contemporary gay men's friendships have a potential sociopolitical impact in the ways they can challenge the heteronormativity of the dominant culture, not only through mobilization of social movements but also in the possible subversion of hegemonic definitions of masculinity. For example, Robert Martin writes that "For Whitman such a love [male love] has consequences for the organization of society; it challenges the very order of male power. . . . [I]t was a reordering of affective arrangements that could no longer be contained. Taking its origin in the discourses of male power, it nonetheless sought to explode them."[8]

R. W. Connell argues that gay men's sexual and friendship relationships have a political potential when he says that the relative equality in gay men's sexuality and their formation of more friendly interpersonal relationships, especially with women, disrupt the social relations of gender: "A more reciprocal sexuality and pacific everyday interactions are necessary if relations between men and women are to move beyond the current state of inequality, violence, and misogyny."[9] I want to consider this idea of subverting the hegemonic order by looking at gay men's friendships' potential for facilitating the formation of communities of identity and the development of neighborhoods and spaces that, in turn, can contribute to a civil society and to the mobilization of new social movements—all of which become politicized as they challenge, yet sometimes reproduce, the societal arrangements of male power.

Identity Communities and Friendships

Fred said that his friendships give him "a vicarious sense of belonging to a gay movement or community, in the larger sense." According to Aristotle's philosophy, communities constitute friendships.[10] And for contemporary gay people, according to Kath Weston, "the historical development of friendship ties among persons whose shared 'sexual' identity was initially defined solely through their sexuality turned out to be merely an

introductory episode in a more lengthy tale of community formation."[11] Community concepts (which were especially dominant in the 1970s and the 1980s) have to be understood as cultural constructs that signify ideas of togetherness, solidarity, and
face-to-face relationships, in opposition to the larger culture's
emphasis on individuality. Because gays and lesbians tend to
grow up outside of and sometimes fearing the very identity
group they later become part of, they must create their own
communities of belongingness, communities that are unlike
those of race and ethnicity, in which family provides the images
and identities.

Friendship networks, thus, become the primary site where
the daily lives of gay men and lesbians are carried out and
shaped. Jeffrey Weeks calls the relationship, whether marital or
nonmarital, "the defining element of the sphere of the intimate
that provides the framework for everyday life. . . . [I]t is the
focus of personal identity, in which the personal narrative is
constructed and reconstructed to provide the provisional sense
of unity of the self that is necessary in the world of postmod-
ernity."[12] From there, the potential for identity-based cultural
communities to develop emerges. Networks of friendships, often reconceptualized as kinships of choice, become the source
for developing communities of identity and equality. Unlike being born into a community of kin, an individual can choose a
community of identity that provides norms and relationships
that "stimulate and develop her identity and self-understanding
more adequately than her unchosen community of origin, her
original community of place."[13]

However, as became evident, a politics of difference
emerged, and concepts of community as a single, homogeneous,
and egalitarian category collapsed, especially since sexual orientation is distributed through a variety of class, racial, and gender
groups: "Gay community can best be understood not as a unified subculture, but rather as a category implicated in the ways
lesbians and gay men have developed collective identities, organized urban space, and conceptualized their significant relationships."[14] Differentiation within the gay male community, for example, emphasized class and racial identities and a rejection of

belonging to "the" gay community. Perhaps this led in part to the shift from a discourse centered around a "family of friends" that was meant to be inclusive of all gays and lesbians, to a language of family/marriage focused on dyadic, interpersonal relationships that often did not include networks of friends. Conceptualizing gay relationships more in kinship terms and less in community language may be one result of the postmodernization of identity and is perhaps nothing more than a relabeling of structures and interactions that did not significantly change.

Yet friendships continue to be the nexus between personal identity and membership into a larger community, whether that be "the" gay community for some, or a specialized subcultural one for others. This is amply illustrated by John D'Emilio's account of Harry Hay, who cofounded the Mattachine Society in the early 1950s: "He discovered gay male friendship circles in San Francisco among the city's actors, musicians, artists, and writers. When Hay returned to Los Angeles, friends from San Francisco provided introductions that gave him entree to homosexual networks in southern California."[15] As philosopher Marilyn Friedman writes, there is "the additional need for communities of choice to counter oppressive and abusive relational structures in those nonvoluntary communities by providing models of alternative social relationships and standpoints for critical reflection on self and community."[16]

Linking personal tastes, politics, and sexual styles to subgroups of others who share these dimensions is a process of becoming a member in a community. Claude Fischer makes clear in his work on urban networks that homophily—the sharing of similar values, characteristics, and opinions—is promoted by the complexities and differentiations brought on by the heterogeneity of urban living.[17] Despite the notion that the diversity of cities will result in networks of people who reflect that diversity, the facts point to the importance of both personal preference and structural constraints in the development of subcultures of shared interests and characteristics, as I report in chapter 5 about the gay men in my study.

Modernization, Fischer argues, has brought with it an increase in the number of age-graded institutions, resulting in people—especially younger single people—coming together in critical masses in urban areas with others of the same age. Fischer found that the average difference in age between friends was six years and that in more than half the cases it was five years or less. Also important, according to his study, is marital status: married people are much more likely to name other married people as friends, and never-marrieds to name never-marrieds. But these processes of homophily in urban residences vary selectively; for members of majority groups, the possibility of meeting more heterogeneous people is greater, but minority members have fewer choices and are more likely to select fellow minority members as friends. Fischer concludes, "Thus urbanism can have an asymmetric effect—increasing heterogeneity with respect to those characteristics an individual shares with many people and increasing homogeneity with respect to those he or she shares with few."[18] This supports many of the findings about gay men and their friendships presented in the last few chapters.

In short, urbanism promotes the emergence of communities or subcultures "formed of people who are minorities in the wider society" and who "are at least as involved in their social worlds as small-town residents are in theirs, but . . . their worlds are more specialized and uncommon."[19] Of course, not all networks of friends become communities. These subcultures or communities develop as a result of selective migration, accumulation of a critical mass, and intergroup friction. Urban centers attract people from a wide range of places who then form specific social, political, and economic institutions to meet the demands brought on by increasing numbers of differentiated people, and develop an in-group identity in contrast to other groups that conflict with them ideologically and/or compete with them for space, power, and other resources.[20]

The emergence of gay communities and subcultures in the large urban centers of North America during the 1970s verifies that these processes occur. Stephen Murray writes of the institutional completeness of a Toronto gay community in comparison to ethnic communities and argues that the former met the criteria set by sociologists for the definition of a

community. Furthermore, he later made a convincing argument that gay people are more than the "lifestyle enclaves"
described by Robert Bellah et al. in *Habits of the Heart;* gay
men and lesbians do indeed constitute a community that has
a collective history and memory, that can reproduce the complexities of institutional society, and that gets involved in public
life beyond its own private interests. He concludes, "The gay
community is at least as much as one as any other urban community."[21]

But what constitutes membership in a gay community: gay
identity, same-sex sexual behavior, gay friendship networks,
and/or living in a gay neighborhood? Having a gay identity is
almost sufficient, according to the overwhelming majority of
Murray's white respondents (Asian Americans felt that same-
sex sexual behavior and gay identity were necessary in order for
someone to be considered a member, and about half of the
Latino and African American gay men said either would do).
Having gay friends in the absence of a gay identity or a gay
neighborhood was not enough to make someone part of a gay
community.[22] In short, a network of gay friends does not constitute community unless one also has a gay identity.

But how likely is someone to have a gay identity without
having gay friends? Murray states that "Acceptance of being gay
is not just the most important criterion for establishing membership in the category *gay community,* . . . but is the central
moral imperative within it," and it takes place in the company
of other gay men.[23] For Ken Plummer, telling coming-out stories—which highlight how a "sense of identity or self is achieved
as gay or lesbian, along with a sense of community"—implies
that communities of people exist to hear the narratives and that
communities have a set of stories that "weave together their
history, their identity, their politics."[24] Participation in the gay
communities' institutions (bars, baths, restaurants, book stores,
media, political and social organizations, etc.) contributes to gay
identity achievement, and gay identity leads to the creation and
maintenance of gay communities which, in an ongoing dialectic,
provide a context for reproducing identity in a newer generation
of people searching for meaning and friendship. These gay net-

works of friends and acquaintances, manifested through the institutions and organizations, assist people in making the transition to gay identity, into gay neighborhoods, and into gay political and social communities. As Aaron, one of my respondents, said about getting to know one of his close friends, whom he met at a meeting of gay professional men, "I was new in town. . . . He made a real effort to get me into his network of friends, and I remain grateful for that."

This is not just a recent phenomenon, as George Chauncey makes clear in his study of early twentieth-century New York. He describes how migration of single men to the city from small towns in the 1920s "was encouraged and facilitated by gay friends who had gone before them, who sent them word about the gay life to be found there, and who assisted them in making the move by providing them initial accommodations and, in some cases, contacts that might lead to employment."[25] Once in the cities, many of these men developed extensive gay social networks "and created a distinctive culture that enabled them to resist, on an everyday basis, their social marginalization."[26] Through these communal ties newcomers were integrated into gay worlds and were given the space and skills to enact their gay identities, which were only one of many identities they managed in their lives.

Older gay men served as mentors to the younger ones, providing them with not only sexual encounters and romance, but also with the skills and information valued by the gay world. Furthermore, "Perhaps most important, mentors introduced men new to the gay world to their circle of friends," and soon the "small circle of new acquaintances came and brought their friends, who brought their friends."[27] Private parties in people's apartments and houses in the 1930s and 1940s were often the most important venue for gay men to meet others and to become incorporated into a circle of gay friends. And the drag balls of the 1920s and 1930s, which often attracted hundreds and thousands of gay men and connected different gay friendship circles with each other, "simply could not have been organized without the existence of the elaborate social networks that constituted the gay subculture."[28]

Social Movements and Friendships

But it's important to remember that not all gay men participate in gay culture, communities, institutions, and movements:
"Communities are *potential bases* for collective action. . . . Actual participation is characteristic of only a minority of any class,
ethnic group, or community."[29] Aaron spoke about the way
friendships could be political, but only at certain points in one's
development:

> My experience is that there is a lot of potential for gay friendships
> to have a political undercurrent when they involve people who are
> just coming out and/or people who are politically active around a
> particular issue or set of issues. Being about a dozen years re-
> moved from my principal coming-out experiences, and perhaps
> ten years removed from my most ardent political activism, I don't
> see as much potential for my gay friendships to be political. . . .
> Most of my friendships now do not have much of a political bent.

Yet the rise of gay and lesbian movements that mobilized to
effect changes in the larger cultural climate is one of the dramatic stories of the 1970s and 1980s, and one that is interconnected with the emergence of gay identities, communities, and
friendship networks. Fred argued this perspective when he said
there "is a kind of dialectical process between gay friendships
and gay social action. Each promotes and begets the other." He
likes to have friends with a "moderate degree of activism."

Friedman states that friendship has "disruptive possibilities" because it can create "shared perspectives that generate
disloyalties to existing social institutions," which can lead to
"beneficial social change."[30] The development of new collective
movements characterized by open, decentralized, and partici-
patory organizational structures and focused on postmaterial
ideologies and values is well documented.[31] Many of these theorists argue that earlier explanations of social movements—
such as the relative deprivation model, rational choice perspectives, or resource mobilization theory—have been supplanted
by newer ones that emphasize movements based on cultural
politics and quality-of-life issues, depend more on middle-class

constituents, and challenge the larger economic and political structures of a society.[32]

The questions of how these new social movement theories apply to the gay and lesbian movement has, however, been subject to some debate. Barry Adam says that "New social movements theory offers only partial applicability to gay and lesbian mobilization," since gay and lesbian organizations represent more than a middle-class movement, take on various structural forms in different societies, do more than protect existing living arrangements by innovating newer ones in a much wider range of arenas (such as those of the workplace, housing, religion, media, and health services), and engage with the state more to modify moral regulations.[33]

Changes in the way gay people saw themselves, migrated to large urban centers, and formed residential and commercial areas with greater concentrations of gays contributed to the emergence of collective identity and social movements. Shared gay identity and collective consciousness have been facilitated by the development of residential concentrations of homosexuals which, in turn, has depended on "the impersonal (bureaucratic) provision of economic opportunity and security."[34]

Geographic mobility, a critical mass of people in delimited urban spaces, the mobilization of symbolic resources such as the media, voluntary relationships less dependent on family of origin, and evidence that social change is possible are other factors involved in the development of a politics of gay identity and a potential social movement.[35] In fact, for new social movements to become mobilized and continue, personal networks of communication, mass media, and "high interpersonal interaction density" among members of a value community must play central roles.[36] Political scientist Dennis Chong concludes that "Preexisting social networks play a central role in the emergence of collective action."[37] His words lend credence to Larry Kramer's 1985 call to organize and do something about AIDS: "And who among us does not have friends? Friends to join our first small organization?"[38]

This interpersonal interaction in networks of people with "culturally derived identities," and the "emotional warmth that

derives from the network element of the movement" make social movements attractive to individuals.[39] Friedman writes that
"Friendship among women has been the cement . . . of the
various historical waves of the feminist movement"; it has also
been so for many communities of unconventional women, as is
documented by Janice Raymond in *A Passion for Friends*.[40] We
know that some of the earliest demonstrations against police
raids occurred among patrons of gay bars, the kinds of spots that
served as the community gathering place for friends.[41] Political
organizations, from the earliest 1950s Mattachine Society to the
liberation organizations that dramatically increased in number
following the Stonewall rebellion, were often born in someone's
living room, where a group of friends had gathered.[42] Mobilizing
others to join depended on friends calling friends, a method
identical to the snowball sampling techniques used by survey
researchers when attempting to reach hard-to-find samples.

A decision-theoretic model of social movements proposes
that invisible groups (such as gays) cannot depend on support
from nonmembers if they are to organize politically. Rather,
they must rely on generating commitment from individuals who
first have to identify with the group.[43] The story of the founding
of the Mattachine Society illustrates this point: Harry Hay's
"professional heterosexual acquaintances . . . convinced him
that a campaign on behalf of homosexuals would have to be
initiated by the oppressed themselves."[44] From that set of people who identify with the invisible group, some, but not most,
will contribute to the collective political effort.

Political theorists have developed a variety of models to
explain collective action and why people would participate in
such action when the public good that accrues from it would
benefit even "free riders" who do not contribute to the movement.[45] Often some sort of material "selective incentive" must
be offered—inducements that can only be enjoyed by those
who participate. However, "direct tangible selective benefits"
are rarely available for "public-spirited collective action"; most
people participate in political activities "out of a sense of obligation to their families, friends, and associates; they go along
to get along," that is, for social and psychological incentives.[46]

Chong argues that by caring for the interests of others, self-interest and genuine sympathy for others results; therefore collective actions need to be understood less for their material incentives and more for the social psychological benefits they offer. Ongoing social relationships and encounters with other members of a community create pressures to cooperate: "The desires to gain or sustain friendships, to maintain one's social standing, and to avoid ridicule and ostracism are all social goals that constitute selective incentives for individuals to participate in collective action" or to "inhibit people from participating in a cause that is considered unpopular in their community."[47]

While these pressures are stronger in smaller groups, large communities can make use of preexisting interpersonal relationships in mobilizing commitments to collective actions by working through networks of smaller organizational units in which "friendship and familial, religious, and professional relationships create an array of *ongoing* exchanges, obligations, and expectations that individual members have considerable incentive to uphold."[48] Again, the story of the founding of the Mattachine Society in 1950 demonstrates the role of friendship networks and identity development:

> Early on, [the founders] had recognized the value of their private meetings as a means of cementing relations among themselves and discarding many conventional attitudes about homosexuality. Consequently, even before they had formalized their structure or their goals, they began inviting selected gay friends and acquaintances to a biweekly discussion group on homosexuality.[49]

Although few returned for other meetings in the beginning, the gatherings became semipublic and eventually took off. And out of these meetings, "friendships formed, and the meetings took on the character of intimate gatherings."[50] For many of those who get involved in collective actions, gay identity acceptance and friendships precede mobilization; for others gay identity and friendship networks are developed, reproduced, and maintained through participation in the institutions of a

gay community, including organizations, bars, and social movements. As the data in chapter 5 show, clubs and organizations
and, to a lesser degree, bars are a major source of friendships
in this more middle-class sample.

Friendship networks continue to play an important role as
a medium of communications, especially in attempts to mobilize
groups of people. Witness the increasing use of E-mail distribution lists to solicit support for a petition, boycott, or other action.
Several years ago, when California Governor Pete Wilson ve-
toed Assembly Bill 101, which would have prohibited discrimination in the workplace and housing based on sexual orientation, people in and around Los Angeles hurriedly organized a
march and rally by calling one another on the telephone with
information about the time and place. I received a call and was
asked to contact at least two or three other friends and spread
the word. I was part of an organized phone tree, although many
of the people I called were not. In any case, the appearance of
several hundred people later that evening was mostly due to
friends calling on friends to show up. And for nearly ten un-
precedented days, marches throughout the streets continued
thanks to word of mouth among friendship networks and to
growing media attention.

In order for things as diverse as street rallies and grassroots
organizing and formal fund-raising events and benefits to take
place, networks of friends and acquaintances who can contact
each other is essential. Many gay and lesbian organizations depend on people (usually middle- or upper-class people, with
money to donate) to sponsor tables at a fund-raising event and
to call nine other people they know to ask them to purchase a
ticket at their table for the benefit. People are much more likely
to donate money or time if a friend phones; such informal solici-
tations are much more effective than is attempting to generate
financial or volunteer time commitment through ads or mailings
initiated by some unknown person or group. Participation in
social actions and movements, from checkbook activism to
grassroots mobilizing, has depended on the links people have
in their interpersonal networks of friends.

Friendship and Space

Dan told me how he found his house in a gay neighborhood thanks to a friend: "Best move I ever made. Nice to be in a place where you're presumed gay, where no one pays notice you're reading the gay magazines waiting in the checkout line." But Fred had "somewhat mixed feelings about living in a predominantly gay community. Somehow I dislike the 'enclave,' barrio, ghetto aspect of it. On the other hand . . . there is a liberating aspect of being part of [a gay neighborhood]."

Letty Cottin Pogrebin points out that "Sexual orientation also can affect where people choose to live and, hence, their friendship patterns."[51] Gay people's friends, and especially their casual acquaintances, are often the fellow gay residents of the district in which they live.[52] There are many gay public spaces, particularly in large urban areas, that provide gay men opportunities to form social circles, cliques, and new friendships. In general men control public space; gay men—and especially white middle-class gay men with their relative economic and political power—have been at the forefront in controlling gay public space.

The arrangement of space within a neighborhood increases the likelihood of getting to know and becoming friends with one's neighbors, simply through the process of passive social contact: "Those with whom one has the greatest amount of contact are most likely to become one's friends."[53] And these casual interactions in shared social space contribute to a sense of community and identity, as Henning Bech argues: "In order for a homosexual neighbourhood to actualize, the individuals will in any case have to leave their dwellings and enter the city or other people's places. But living close to others also has a significance for one's awareness of the potentialities of community and opportunity."[54]

As I mention earlier, gay men seeking refuge with others like themselves were evident in the late nineteenth and early twentieth centuries, when single men migrated from small towns in America and from Europe to New York, and to particular neighborhoods that provided housing and commercial services oriented toward single men. And since many of these single men were homosexuals, Chauncey argues, the beginnings of a gay community were set in motion: "The existence of an urban bachelor subculture facilitated the development of a gay world. . . . Rooming houses and cafeterias served as meeting grounds for gay men, facilitating the constant interaction that made possible the development of a distinctive subculture."[55]

In the first half of the century in New York, gay worlds developed in many of the hotels, apartment houses, restaurants, and speakeasies as the gay men sought security and understanding from like-minded others. Chauncey describes how an apartment building slowly became more and more gay as flats opened up and one of the gay residents "invited other friends to move in. Several friends did, and some of the newcomers encouraged their own friends to join them."[56] In addition, various YMCAs developed gay reputations, and many newcomers to the city built "a network of gay friends" through contacts there.[57]

Throughout the early part of the twentieth century, gay men would occupy other public spaces and convert them into havens for their socializing. And in many of these spaces gay social networks played key roles, contributing to the Harlem Literary Renaissance and to the development of Greenwich Village as a gay enclave. Besides the rooming houses and apartment buildings, gay men "turned many restaurants into places where they could gather with gay friends, gossip, ridicule the dominant culture that ridiculed them, and construct an alternative culture."[58] Like the political organizations, these commercial institutions served the needs of both those already part of the gay world and those just entering it:

> Particular restaurants served as the locus of particular gay social networks; overlapping groups of friends would meet regularly for dinner and camaraderie. The role of restaurants as social centers meant they often functioned as a crucial point of entry into the gay world for men just beginning to identify themselves as gay; for men already deeply involved in the gay world, they were a vital source of information about the gay scene, police activity, cultural events, and the like.[59]

Similar spaces provide sources of sexual, romantic, and friendship relationships for gay men today. Although urban centers are much more likely to have developed neighborhoods with economic, residential, and social support resources, even in small towns there are ways for people to meet one another.[60] However, gays and lesbians in rural areas tend to "rely on social networks with people they have little in common with but their sexual preferences," often leading to loneliness and isolation and sometimes the formation of incompatible romantic relationships.[61] But the power of friendships and networks of gay men to contribute to the development of a sense of self and a sense of community is evident in all these various guises, from early-twentieth-century restaurants to gay political organizations in contemporary urban centers to small-town bars. And the Internet, with its numerous World Wide Web bulletin boards and lists devoted to gay issues, has become the modern public space that links thousands, if not millions, to a larger community of people who become political friends—a global civic friendship—mobilizing in the struggle to find meaning and dignity in societies that continue to impose a hegemonic order that constrains and limits choices.

The Meaning of Friendship in Gay Men's Lives

In friendship, people can depart from the routine and display a portion of the self not affected by social control. That is, friendship allows people to go beyond the basic structures of their cultural institutions into an involuntary and uncontrollable disclosure of self—to violate the rules of public propriety, as Gerald Suttles phrases it.[62] Friendship is an escape from the dictates and pieties of social life. It's about identity: who one is rather than one's roles and statuses. And the idealism of friendship "lies in its detachment from these [roles and statuses], its creative and spiritual transcendence, its fundamental skepticism as a platform from which to survey the givens of society and culture."[63] For gay men these words illustrate the political potential friendship can have in their lives.

Through friends, gay men get to question the heteronormativity of the roles given to them by the culture. The heterosexual, nuclear family—or at least the ideology of the family—has been the dominant model structuring much of the legal, political, and social norms governing interpersonal relationships. But as the family becomes transformed into other arrangements, so too do the political and social institutions of the society that were originally organized to reproduce the normative structures. For example, the concept of "domestic partner" challenges insurance companies, public and private workplaces, religious institutions, and the legal system. But not all challenges are necessarily met with revolutionary alterations in the social system; many argue that the attempts to construct same-sex marriage rights and ceremonies merely replicate the dominant and oppressive structures of heterosexual society—something that would not occur if friendships were included in a model of domestic partner and family rather than being excluded from those concepts, which are usually limited to romantic dyadic relationships.

Friendship, perhaps in and of itself, may have the kinds of transforming power necessary to effect real, political changes. This may be even more the case for gay men's friendships, which challenge the social construction of heterosexual masculinity in the way it gets enacted, legitimated, and reproduced by gay people. Aaron stated it succinctly: "To the extent that being openly gay is political, then the friendships that I have with openly gay men are political." Michel Foucault said in a 1981 interview that gay culture can invent really new forms and values of relating between individuals and, if this is possible, then "gay culture will be not only a choice of homosexuals for homosexuals—it would create relations that are, at certain points, transferable to heterosexuals. . . . By proposing a new relational right, we will see that nonhomosexual people can enrich their lives by changing their own schema of relations."[64] In the myriad ways gay men deal with the contradictions of gay masculinity and hegemonic masculinity, friendship offers one model of successful liberation from the limits of dominant social life and its typically heterosexist institutions—a model that has the power not only to transform interpersonal relationships and psychological well-being, but also to create significant changes in the larger social system. As Graham Little writes:

> The larger formations of social life—kinship, the law, the economy—must be different where there is, in addition to solidarity and dutiful role-performance, a willingness and capacity for friendship's surprising one-to-one relations, and this difference may be enough to transform social and political life. . . . Perhaps, finally, it is true that progress in democracy depends on a new generation that will increasingly locate itself in identity-shaping, social, yet personally liberating friendships.[65]

Gay men's friendships might someday lead all men to a new, more modern, form of the heroic friendships of the past— one in which valor, bravery, and devotion are inextricably linked to intimacy, sharing, personal disclosure, vulnerability, and emotional support. To alter the dynamics of how gender gets enacted in everyday life would be a powerful and political outcome of gay men's friendships in today's globalized and interconnected world. For it is through friends that gay men "do" identity and community work. Through friends, a bridge between the micro and the macro aspects of quotidian life is constructed. Networks of friends and acquaintances become the interface between personal identity and membership in cultural and political communities.

And it is here in this network, especially for gay men, where issues of sexuality, masculinity, and social space get reified. Indeed, gay men's friendships may someday become the cornerstone of a new structure of social and personal relationships that has the power to transform everyone's lives and to create a new invincible community and culture of dignity and equality.

As Walt Whitman so eloquently stated in 1860,

> I Dream'd in a dream, I saw a city invincible to the
>   attacks of the whole of the rest of the earth;
> I dream'd that was the new City of Friends . . .

Research Methodology

Multiple objectives require multiple methods for achieving them. This holds true for my study. Similar to those used in other studies, the methodologies developed to achieve the goals of my project carry with them both strengths and weaknesses.

This study began in the late 1980s, when social psychologist Drury Sherrod and I wrote the questionnaire used in the research. It was constructed to gain information about the meaning of friendships in the lives of gay men and lesbians. As such, it was modeled after much of the psychological research of the time; it focused on how people feel about their friends, what they expect from friends, and how men and women differ in "doing" and "talking" friendship. Most of the questions reflect this psychological approach.

As a sociologist, I became more interested in the structural dimensions of friendship and the ways a society or subculture might affect friendship. Seeing friendship less as a voluntary choice and more as one linked to where people are located in the social system, I began to supplement the questionnaire data with interviews that delved into these issues. The data and information provided in the book are a result, then, of both sources and approaches. It truly is a social psychological study of gay men's friendships—of how gay men feel and think about their friendships and how these friendships are connected to other more structural components in their lives.

The Questionnaire Survey

About half the people contacted through gay organizations in the greater Los Angeles metropolitan area responded to the questionnaire study, resulting in 161 usable questionnaires. Unlike most research on friendships, this study does not depend on college student samples; it is composed primarily of white, educated, middle-class gay men who participate in urban gay organizations. Thus the results may not be generalizable to gay men who are nonwhite, nonurban, working class, or not openly gay, and who are not members of gay clubs. Table 5.2 presents some of the key demographics of the sample.

Sherrod and I obtained respondents by contacting gay and lesbian political, religious, social, and professional organizations. Since research on friendship might be compromised by the use of the snowball sampling techniques frequently employed with people difficult to reach—this method depends on people getting others they know (their friends) to participate—we decided that our method would be less biased for the research topic being addressed. The built-in bias of sampling friends of friends with snowball methods might have produced a distorted picture of friendship patterns.

The nineteen-page questionnaire was pilot-tested on a small sample of gay men, and the revised version took approximately thirty minutes to complete. Questionnaires were preaddressed and stamped for return. The questionnaire asked respondents to provide information on casual, close, and best friends, categories used in most research on friendship and classifications that readily emerge in most people's descriptions of their friends.[1] *Casual* friend is defined as "someone who is more than an acquaintance, but not a close friend; your commitment to the friendship would probably not extend beyond the circumstances that brought you together." A *close* friend is "someone to whom you feel a sense of mutual commitment and continuing closeness; a person with whom you talk fairly openly and feel comfortable spending time." A *best* friend is "the friend to whom you feel the greatest commitment and closeness; the one who accepts you 'as you are,' with whom you talk the most openly and feel the most comfortable spending time." We asked the respondents to exclude a lover or partner as a best friend and to select just one best friend when responding to the questions about a best friendship.

Questions were developed to measure four types of *social support:* tangible, belonging, appraisal, and self-esteem. In order to avoid a gender bias in the phrasing of items, both traditionally masculine or instrumental items (e.g., competing at sports) and traditionally feminine or expressive items (e.g., talking about relationships) were included. Reliability for the sixteen items used in the social support measures was .878 (Cronbach's alpha). Twenty items measured *self-disclosure* (e.g., talking friendship) and included low-intimacy items (e.g., hobbies, interests) and high-intimacy topics (e.g., personal strengths and weaknesses). Reliability for these items was .935 (Cronbach's alpha). Items measuring *activities* (e.g., doing friendship) included traditionally masculine (e.g., watching sports) and traditionally feminine ones (e.g., calling just to chat). Most items, as is reported throughout the chapters and in the tables, were measured using five-point Likert scales, with five being the highest score. In almost every measure differences among the three types of friendship (casual, close, and best) were statistically significant, using multiple analysis of variance (MANOVA), thereby verifying that respondents successfully distinguished among the various types of friendship. For additional details about the methodology and other data analyses, please see the earlier publications from the study.[2]

The Interviews

While the questionnaire provides important data, it does not measure the depth and details of what gay men experience on a daily basis with their friends. To fill that gap I interviewed a more diverse set of thirty gay men from various parts of the United States. These men were located in several different ways, and several different methods were used to interview them.

I conducted two focus groups, each with ten gay men and lasting one hour. One group was an "over-fifty-five" group that met monthly at a gay center; the other was a gay men's group open to any age that met once a week at another gay center. Both centers are in the greater Los Angeles area. I used information from these focus groups to assist me in developing a set of issues, questions, and background information for the interviews. One member of each group is part of the final thirty interviews.

Twenty-seven of the interviews were obtained by and completed using E-mail. The role of computers in linking gays and lesbians around the world and in forming cyberspace communities of friendship is a topic yet to be fully explored.[3] And it has potential for generating national and diverse nonprobability samples of respondents for research. However, it is not possible to generalize beyond such a sample, because computer use tends to be greater among higher education and income groups.

For this study I sent a notice to several gay bulletin boards and lists asking for participants. I also received a few names through personal contacts. These men were all sent a set of questions, which were completed and returned. Where further information or clarification was needed, I E-mailed back and probed further. In four cases I called the respondent and continued the E-mail interview by phone, and with three respondents I conducted only a face-to-face interview. Seven of the E-mail respondents were selected because they were part of a friendship network. I asked two people to designate their closest three or four friends, and they in turn were included in the study. In this way I was able to verify information and check on the reliability of the answers, as well as to get more longitudinal narratives. By piecing together various stories I was able to glean processes of friendship formation and maintenance. In all cases respondents who knew each other gave enough similar information to confirm any details or information provided by others in the group.

Using E-mail, I was able to generate a nationally and racially diverse sample (eight men, or 27 percent of the sample, were people of color). In addition, people whose ages ranged from eighteen to eighty participated in the interviews. Their mean age was forty, which is identical to the mean age of the questionnaire survey respondents. As with the questionnaire, very few respondents were current college students, and most were in middle-income occupations. A list of the participants and some information about them appears below. Names have been changed and details modified to preserve confidentiality.

My decision to conduct most of these interviews by E-mail may, I realize, leave me open to criticism. But like any data-collection technique, mine has strengths and weaknesses. This is a new method of data collection that is only now being explored; I personally have received two questionnaires that were sent by E-mail. The advantages include getting a more diverse sample from around the world (although I limited my sample to the United States). E-mail allows for interaction and probing, as any interview might. I can easily ask for clarifying information and more details, and in most cases people responded promptly. Furthermore, the relative anonymity (E-mail return names and addresses are often coded and can be deleted by the sender) allows respondents to open up in ways they might not in a face-to-face interaction.

The disadvantages are obvious: interpersonal signals, such as body and facial gestures, and voice intonations and tone, like sarcasm or irony, may be lost. Although many communicated emphasis and laughter using various cyber codes (happy faces, capital letters, etc.), this method precludes almost all the nuances that come from face-to-face dialogue. Also, the person completing the interview may not be who he says he is. Can I really be sure that a gay man who claims to be Latino and thirty-five is telling the truth? But the same uncertainty applies to questionnaire demographic items.

In short, E-mail interviews are somewhere between a questionnaire and a face-to-face interview. They allow for probing, clarification, and elaboration, although perhaps not as quickly as happens in a face-to-face interaction. But with a questionnaire it is almost impossible to probe for any clarifying information. At the same time E-mail interviews ensure greater anonymity or confidentiality than face-to-face interviews might, even if using them means missing the opportunity to get information nonverbally or through voice signals. As with all methodologies, there are trade-offs. But based on the ways I was able to verify information (follow-up phone calls, confirming information using several people in the same network, and conducting several interviews), I am confident that the information I received from the E-mail interviews is at least as good as the data collected using the questionnaires. And in almost all cases it was better in terms of details, depth, and quality. These were narratives, not just checkpoints on a five-point Likert scale. Gauging validity and reliability of data collected using E-mail and Web sites is something that some enterprising researcher might consider attempting to do. Data collection via E-mail is a technique I predict will become more widespread, and I am willing to take the chance of contributing to that debate.

Profiles of Interview Respondents

1. Andy: eighteen, white, college student, urban East Coast[4]

2. Bill: twenty-two, Asian, college student, rural Midwest

3. Carl: twenty-four, Latino/Asian, computer company, urban West Coast

4. David: twenty-nine, white, manager, suburban Midwest

5. Eugene: thirty-one, white, business, urban South

6. Frank: thirty-one, white, city government, urban East

7. George: thirty-four, white, engineer, suburban West Coast

8. Harry: thirty-four, Native American, computers, suburban Southwest

9. John: thirty-five, African American, librarian, urban

10. Kevin: thirty-six, white, computers, urban West Coast

11. Leo: thirty-six, white, secretary, urban

12. Mike: thirty-seven, white, professor, urban East

13. Nick: thirty-eight, white, electrical engineer, suburban South

14. Paul: forty, white, politics, urban East Coast

15. Rick: forty-one, white, social worker, urban South

16. Steve: forty-two, white, semiprofessional, urban South

17. Tim: forty-two, Asian/Native American, health care, urban
18. Vince: forty-four, white, lawyer, urban
19. Will: forty-four, white, lawyer, urban West Coast
20. Aaron: thirty-three, African American, teacher, urban East
21. Ben: thirty-five, white, business, urban East
22. Charles: thirty-two, African American, education, urban East
23. Dan: eighty, white, retired, urban West Coast
24. Ed: forty, Asian Pacific, computer analyst, suburban West Coast
25. Fred: sixty-two, white, retired educator, suburban East Coast
26. Greg: forty-five, white, media, urban West Coast
27. Harve: fifty-seven, white, health care, urban West Coast
28. Jim: sixty-seven, white, retired, urban West Coast
29. Louis: fifty-nine, African American, retired, urban West Coast
30. Mark: thirty-one, white, writer, urban Midwest

Notes

Introduction

1. Altman 1982, 189–90.
2. Fehr's otherwise comprehensive book, *Friendship Processes* (1996), makes no reference to gay and lesbian friendships.
3. Aristotle (trans. Martin Ostwald) 1156a10–12.
4. Aristotle 1156a34–37.
5. Aristotle 1156b6–7.
6. Aristotle 1156b34–35.
7. Stern-Gillet 1995, 172.
8. Aristotle 1168b6–7.
9. Stern-Gillet 1995, 172.
10. Stern-Gillet 1995.
11. Aristotle 1166a30–33.
12. Aristotle 1155a22.
13. Aristotle 1159b30–33.
14. Schwarzenbach 1996, 7.
15. Schollmeier 1994, 83.
16. Stern-Gillet 1995, 4.
17. Pakaluk 1994.
18. Schwarzenbach 1996, 114.
19. Schwarzenbach 1996, 101n.12.
20. Schwarzenbach 1996, 102n.12.
21. Names are fictitious. Brief descriptions of the thirty respondents in the interview portion of the study are presented in the Research Methodology appendix.
22. Cooper 1980, 332.
23. The Research Methodology appendix provides details about the data collection and about questionnaires. Also, see Nardi and Sherrod (1994) for summaries of the findings on lesbians and their friendships. Books by Raymond (1986) and Weinstock and Rothblum (1996) are good resources for information about lesbians' friendships.
24. Fehr 1996; Blieszner and Adams 1992.

25. From Whitman's "I Hear It Was Charged Against Me" (1860), in *Leaves of Grass.*

Chapter One

1. Friedman 1993, 187.
2. Reprinted in Welty and Sharp 1991, 78, 82.
3. Parekh 1994.
4. Simmel, in Wolff 1950, 325.
5. Barth 1966.
6. Names are fictitious. Brief descriptions of the thirty respondents in the interview portion of the study are presented in the Research Methodology appendix. All but three of the interviews were conducted by E-mail. For a discussion of the limitations and strengths of this methodology, please see the appendix.
7. Fehr 1996.
8. Rubin 1985.
9. Rubin 1985, 173.
10. Pogrebin 1987.
11. At least three other nonacademic books emphasizing the friendships between gay men and heterosexual women have been published over the past decades: Nahas and Turley 1979; Malone 1980; and Whitney 1990.
12. Friedman 1993, 219.
13. Mordden 1986, 175.
14. White 1980, 286.
15. White 1980, 287.
16. Altman 1982, 190.
17. See Leznoff and Westley 1956; Hooker 1965.
18. Bell and Weinberg 1978, 247.
19. Weinberg and Williams 1974.
20. Weinberg and Williams 1974, 286.
21. Warren 1974, 90–91.
22. Warren 1974, 91.
23. Berger 1982, 173.
24. Levine 1998.
25. Levine 1992, 79.
26. See also Kayal's (1993) work on volunteerism during the AIDS crisis.
27. Herdt and Boxer 1996, 189.
28. Herdt and Boxer 1996.
29. Weston 1991, 118.
30. Weston 1991.
31. D'Emilio and Freedman 1988.
32. Chauncey 1994.
33. Murray 1996.
34. The role of friendship in the lives of gays and lesbians living in

suburban and rural areas is not the primary focus of my study, although some of the respondents do live in those areas. See the work of Lynch (1992), Kramer (1995), Miller (1989), and Rist (1992) for discussions and descriptions of suburban and rural gay life.

35. Fischer 1982, 92, 118.

36. Fischer 1982, 114, 115.

37. Fischer 1982.

38. Fischer 1982, 120.

39. From "Sexual Choice, Sexual Act," an interview originally published in the fall 1982–winter 1983 special homosexuality issue of *Salmagundi* and reprinted in Foucault (1997, 153).

40. From "Sex, Power, and The Politics of Identity," an interview conducted in 1982, originally published in the August 7, 1984, issue of *The Advocate,* and reprinted in Foucault (1997, 163).

41. From "The Social Triumph of the Sexual Will," an interview conducted in 1981, originally published in the May 1982 issue of *Christopher Street,* and reprinted in Foucault (1997, 158).

42. "Social Triumph," (reprinted in Foucault 1997, 159).

43. "Sex, Power," (reprinted in Foucault 1997, 171, 170).

44. "Sex, Power," (reprinted in Foucault 1997, 171).

45. See Hammond and Jablow (1987) and Richards (1987) for related ideas on historical depictions of friendship and masculinity.

46. Homer 1951 (trans. Lattimore) 18.80–82.

47. Halperin 1990.

48. Halperin 1990, 77, 78.

49. Quoted in Selden 1947, 111.

50. Halperin 1990, 85.

51. Boswell 1994, 76.

52. Boswell 1994, 183.

53. Boswell 1994, 24, 27.

54. Rocke 1996, 191.

55. Rocke 1996, 183.

56. Rocke 1996, 191.

57. Richards 1987.

58. Katz 1992, 450.

59. Katz 1992.

60. Katz 1992, 450.

61. Martin 1989, 182.

62. See Katz 1983.

63. Rotundo 1993, 79.

64. Quoted in Rotundo 1993, 80–81.

65. Katz 1983, 1992.

66. Faderman 1981, 20.

67. Hansen 1992, 54.

68. Rotundo 1993.

69. Rotundo 1993.

70. From *Of Friendship,* reprinted in Welty and Sharp 1991, 81–82.

71. From "Friendship as a Way of Life," an interview published in the April 1981 issue of *Gai Pied* and reprinted in Foucault (1997, 136).

72. "Sex, Power" (reprinted in Foucault 1997); Katz 1995.

73. D'Emilio and Freedman 1988, 130.

74. Chauncey 1994, 120–121.

75. Connell 1992, 736.

Chapter Two

1. Katz 1983.

2. Chauncey 1994.

3. Bech 1997, 73.

4. Paine 1974a, 119.

5. Du Bois 1974, 30.

6. Allan 1989.

7. See Leyton (1974) for numerous studies focusing on cross-cultural aspects of friendship and kinship.

8. See Connell (1995) for ideas about the changing nature of masculinity and Gilmore (1990) for cross-cultural comparisons of masculinity and how it is achieved.

9. Du Bois 1974.

10. Schwimmer 1974, 49.

11. Brain 1976, 76.

12. Brain 1976, 85.

13. Driberg 1935.

14. Driberg 1935, 102.

15. Driberg 1935, 102.

16. Brain 1976, 62.

17. Brain 1976.

18. Brain 1976, 130.

19. Parekh 1994, 111.

20. Eisenstadt 1974, 139.

21. Schwimmer 1974, 52.

22. Schwimmer 1974, 57.

23. Paine 1974b, 10.

24. Paine 1974a, 128, 122.

25. Gladwell 1997, 55.

26. Wright 1982.

27. Caldwell and Peplau 1982; Sherrod 1989.

28. Tiger 1974, 47.

29. Tiger 1974, 46, 48.

30. Giddens 1992, 126.

31. For fuller descriptions of the studies from which these summaries are derived, see Blieszner and Adams (1992), Fehr (1996), and Winstead (1986).

32. See Duck and Wright 1993.
33. Davidson and Duberman 1982.
34. Fehr 1996.
35. Fehr 1996, 140–141.
36. Wellman 1992, 75.
37. Friedman 1993, 226.
38. Fehr 1996, 142
39. See Connell (1995) for an excellent critique of sex role theory.
40. Walker 1994a.
41. Walker 1994b, 54.
42. Allan 1989, 66.
43. Jackson 1977, 59.
44. Schwartz 1974, 84. See also Duck 1973.
45. Jackson 1977, 60.
46. Jackson 1977.
47. Jackson 1977.
48. Jackson 1977, 77.
49. Allan 1996, 87.
50. Allan 1996, 90.
51. Fischer 1982, 121.
52. Messner 1992.
53. Messner 1992, 91.
54. Franklin 1992, 212.
55. Duneier 1994.

Chapter Three

1. Rubin 1985; Lindsey 1981.
2. Weston 1991.
3. See Eskridge and Hunter 1997.
4. Hunt 1994, 171.
5. Lindsey 1981, 10.
6. Lindsey 1981, 63.
7. Hawkeswood 1997, 63.
8. Duneier 1992, 20.
9. Chauncey 1994, 291.
10. Hooker 1965, 101.
11. Warren 1974, 109–110.
12. Rodgers 1972, 181.
13. Crowley 1968, 134.
14. Sonenschein 1968.
15. Weston 1991, 120.
16. Rodgers 1972, 191.
17. Taylor 1989.
18. Reisman 1979.
19. Lindsey 1981, 105.

20. Fehr 1996.
21. Fischer 1982.
22. Fine 1986, 202.
23. Fine 1986, 199.
24. Schneider 1987; Levine 1979b.
25. Woods 1993, 166.
26. Barnhart 1975, 92.
27. Lindsey 1981.
28. Lindsey 1981, 153.
29. Lindsey 1981, 109.
30. Lindsey 1981, 226.
31. Rubin 1985, 18.
32. Rubin 1985, 22, 31.
33. See articles in Leyton (1974).
34. Eisenstadt 1974, 141.
35. For Bell (1981, 11), "the more traditional the kinship values, the more hostile the views toward friendship," whereas Du Bois (1974, 30) says that some people believe "friendships are a reaction against the engrossing demands of kinship ties."
36. Du Bois 1974, 31.
37. Schwartz 1974, 76.
38. Portions of this section appeared in Nardi (1997).
39. From "The AIDS network letter to Mayor Koch," originally written on March 3, 1983, and published for the first time in Kramer (1989, 56).
40. McWhirter and Mattison 1984.
41. McWhirter and Mattison 1984, 79.
42. Levine 1998.
43. Weston 1991, 34.
44. Weston 1991.
45. Weston 1991, 109.
46. Goldsby 1989, 35.
47. Prieur 1998.
48. See Shernoff 1984; Stein 1988.
49. Nardi 1982.
50. Hall 1978, 380.
51. Alexander 1997, 189, 198.
52. Bech 1997, 117.
53. Bech 1997.
54. Kramer 1989, 271.
55. Diaz 1997.
56. Weston 1991, 186.
57. Nardi 1990.
58. Eskridge and Hunter 1997.
59. Eskridge and Hunter 1997.
60. Nonas 1992, 52.
61. Clunis and Green 1988, 106.

62. Weston 1991, 209.
63. Bech 1997, 117.
64. Halperin 1990.
65. Halperin 1990, 85.

Chapter Four

1. Lee 1976.
2. See Nardi (1997) for a review and critique of this assumption.
3. Crowley 1968.
4. Fehr 1996.
5. Connell 1992, 735.
6. Rose 1985; O'Meara 1989.
7. Sapadin 1988, 401.
8. Fehr 1996.
9. Bell 1981.
10. Bell 1981, 105.
11. Blumstein and Schwartz 1983; Connell 1992; and "Paradise Found," an article published in the June 1983 issue of *Vanity Fair,* and "Sexual Culture," an article originally published in a 1983 issue of *Mother Jones,* both reprinted in White (1994). See also the controversial books by Rotello (1997) and Signorile (1997) calling for a change in those cultural norms.
12. Bell 1981.
13. Rubin 1985.
14. Swain 1992, 167.
15. Sonenschein 1968.
16. Sonenschein 1968, 72.
17. Weston 1991, 120.
18. Eighty percent of the questionnaire respondents and almost 65 percent of those interviewed said their best friend was a gay man (see Table 5.1). Respondents were asked to select one best friend who was not their current romantic partner, if any, in answering questions about a best friend.
19. Rubin 1985.
20. Weston 1991.
21. Compare these figures to those generated by a 1990 survey of readers of *Out/Look,* a lesbian/gay magazine no longer in publication, conducted by Nardi and Sherrod (1990, 86): Around 72 percent of the respondents to that survey had been attracted to their best gay male friend in the past, and 52 percent were currently attracted to him; of those who had been attracted to their friend in the past, 77 percent had been "very or extremely" attracted to their best friend, compared with 23 percent who were so at the time of the survey.
22. Fehr 1996; Feingold 1988.
23. Hall and Ames 1994, 81.
24. Meilaender 1994, 187.

25. Interestingly, male friendship dyads are more matched in terms of physical attractiveness than are pairs of female friends, according to a meta-analysis of studies in social psychology conducted by Feingold (1988). However, these are not measures of how attracted one person is to the other, and information about the sexual orientation of the subjects was not collected in these studies.

26. Bérubé 1990, 38.

27. Seiden and Bart 1975, 220.

28. Connell 1992, 748.

29. Connell 1992; Sonenschein 1968.

30. In the Nardi and Sherrod (1990, 86) gay magazine survey, 43 percent of the gay male respondents had had sex with their best gay male friend in the past, and 5 percent were involved in a sexual relationship with him at the time of the survey. On average, they had sex with four of their casual or close male friends (out of a mean number of twenty-four casual male friends and six close male friends).

31. Chi-square significance level was $p > .05$.

32. Levine 1998, 44.

33. As I discuss in chapter 6, the reasons for ending a friendship were more often things such as betrayals, changes in residence or jobs, failure to keep up communications, and other nonsexual matters.

34. Levine 1998, 105.

35. See McWilliams and Howard (1993) for a discussion of solidarity and hierarchy in cross-sex friendships.

36. As an interesting comparison, 34 percent of the lesbians who were also sampled as part of the larger study said their best friend was an ex-lover (Nardi and Sherrod 1994). In the gay magazine reader survey (Nardi and Sherrod 1990, 86), 11 percent of the gay men surveyed said their best gay male friend was a former lover and that they were together for an average of seventy-two months.

37. Chi-square significance level was $p > .05$.

38. This, by the way, is a similar figure to that generated by data collected in thirty years of surveys of gay men (see Nardi 1997). Around 41 percent of the gay men in the gay magazine survey (Nardi and Sherrod 1990) were in a relationship.

39. Chi-square significance level was $p > .05$.

40. Fehr 1996, 191.

41. Chi-square significance levels were $p < .02$ for numbers of casual friends and $p < .01$ for sex with casual friends.

42. Using stepwise multiple regression to predict number of friends and having sex with friends, only coupled status entered the equations for casual friends.

43. Fehr 1996, 12–16.

44. Bloom 1993, 547.

45. Fehr 1996, 20.

46. From "On the Genealogy of Ethics: An Overview of Work in

Progress," an interview conducted in 1983 by Paul Rabinow and Hubert Dreyfus and printed for the first time in Foucault (1997, 257).

47. Connell 1992, 749.

48. Connell 1992, 748.

49. I risk saying this in light of psychoanalytic attempts to pathologize homosexuality as a form of narcissism and do not mean to suggest a narcissistic relationship.

50. Connell 1992, 748.

51. See Pleck, Sonenstein, and Ku 1993.

52. Connell 1992, 747.

53. Connell 1992.

Chapter Five

1. Homophily is defined by Lazarsfeld and Merton (1954, 23) as "a tendency for friendships to form between those who are alike in some designated respect"—usually in terms of status (group-affiliations positions within a group) and values.

2. Duck 1973; Fehr 1996.

3. Jackson 1977, 6; see also Blieszner and Adams 1992; Fehr 1996.

4. Lazarsfeld and Merton 1954, 33, 35.

5. Jackson 1977.

6. Allan 1989, 23.

7. Blieszner and Adams 1992.

8. Pogrebin 1987.

9. Franklin 1992.

10. See Almaguer 1991; Carrier 1992; Hemphill 1991.

11. Achilles 1967.

12. Connell 1992, 748.

13. Fehr 1996.

14. Respondents were asked to select one best friend other than a lover or romantic partner about whom to answer questions about a best friend.

15. Bell 1981; Fischer 1982.

16. These figures were quite similar to the mean number of close male friends (six) and casual male friends (twenty-four) reported by gay men in a volunteer sample of readers conducted for a gay magazine survey by Nardi and Sherrod (1990, 86). That study was completed by gay men whose mean age was thirty-five. Eighty-two percent of the respondents were college graduates or had additional education, and 96 percent were white.

17. Pearson r correlations between number of *casual* friends and scores on a satisfaction with the quantity of casual friends scale (.33) and scores on a satisfaction with the quality scale (.46) were significant at $p < .001$; for *close* friends, it was less strong: .31 between number of close friends and satisfaction with quantity and .27 for satisfaction with quality. Chi-squares also were significant ($p < .05$) for these relationships.

18. Mean satisfaction scores on a 5-point scale with 5 = extremely satis-

fied were 3.3 (casual), 3.7 (close), and 4.2 (best). These were significantly different using MANOVA at p < .05.

19. Bell and Weinberg 1978.

20. Weinberg and Williams 1974; Saghir and Robins (1973) found that 56 percent of the gay men had four or more close friends, compared with 35 percent of the heterosexual men.

21. Warren 1974.

22. McWhirter and Mattison 1984.

23. McWhirther and Mattison 1984, 245.

24. Cohen 1992.

25. ANOVA and chi-square were significant for these variables at p < .05.

26. Jackson, Fischer, and Jones 1977.

27. Fischer 1982.

28. Since most of the surveys were obtained through gay organizations and clubs, the percentages for clubs and organizations are very likely higher than are those for other samples of gay men.

29. Pogrebin 1987, 211.

30. From "Straight Women, Gay Men," originally written in 1991 and published for the first time in White (1994, 315).

31. Schneider and Stoller 1995; Stoller 1997.

32. Bell and Weinberg 1978.

33. These data also include some male friends because the question was worded as "many friends are of the opposite sex." Therefore, the people who responded to it affirmatively may also have had male friends.

34. Warren 1974; Pogrebin 1987.

35. Rodgers 1972.

36. Pogrebin 1987, 213.

37. DiLallo and Krumholtz 1994, 240.

38. Hoffman 1968, 52.

39. Moon 1995.

40. Moon 1995, 492.

41. Moon 1995, 496.

42. Moon 1995, 500.

43. Hassett and Owen-Towle 1994.

44. Hassett and Owen-Towle 1994, 63.

45. Fee 1996, 234.

46. Fee 1996, 46–47.

47. Fee 1996, 251.

48. Connell 1992.

49. Fee 1996, 172.

50. Fee 1996, 189.

51. Pogrebin 1987.

52. Pogrebin 1987, 216.

53. Nestle and Preston 1994, 10.

54. Miles and Rofes 1998.

55. Stoller 1997, 177.

56. Paine (1974a, 119).

Chapter Six

1. Allan 1989, 47.

2. Milardo 1986, 162.

3. Fehr 1996. For more elegant descriptions of friendship, see such anthologies as *The Oxford Book of Friendship* (Enright and Rawlinson 1991) and *The Norton Book of Friendship* (Welty and Sharp 1991).

4. See Wright (1982) for arguments warning about overemphasizing the gender differences in friendship research.

5. Fehr 1996; Blieszner and Adams 1992.

6. Fehr 1996, 44.

7. Fischer 1982.

8. Fehr 1996.

9. Fehr 1996.

10. Fehr 1996, 58.

11. Hess 1972.

12. Allan 1989, 34.

13. Fehr 1996.

14. Bleiszner and Adams 1992, 62.

15. Milardo 1986.

16. Jackson 1977, 77.

17. Berg and Clark 1986.

18. Berg and Clark 1986.

19. Berg and Clark 1986, 117.

20. Chambliss 1965.

21. Milardo 1986, 163.

22. Goffman 1959.

23. Milardo 1986, 161.

24. Miell and Duck 1986.

25. See Fehr (1996) for gender-related differences in conversation among friends.

26. Miell and Duck 1986.

27. Miell and Duck 1986, 142.

28. Blieszner and Adams 1992, 95.

29. Rawlins 1992.

30. Rawlins 1992, 8.

31. Rawlins 1992, 14–15.

32. Rawlins 1992, 15.

33. Rawlins 1992.

34. Rawlins 1992, 21–22.

35. Rawlins 1992.

36. Milardo 1986, 161.

37. Although this finding is highly affected by the use of E-mail as a

sampling technique for this study, even those who were interviewed face-to-face mentioned E-mail as a way of keeping in touch.

38. Questions about E-mail were not on the questionnaire and might be much higher than these figures for other means of keeping in touch. Note, though, that the interview numbers themselves are probably inflated as a result of the methodology of obtaining E-mail interviews (see Research Methodology appendix).

39. Blieszner and Adams 1992; Rose and Serafica 1986.

40. Fehr 1996.

41. Fehr 1996, 185.

Chapter Seven

1. Fleming and Baum 1986.
2. Cohen et al. 1997.
3. Fleming and Baum 1986, 216.
4. Sherrod 1989; Fehr 1996.
5. Fischer 1982.
6. Fischer 1982.
7. Fischer 1982, 137.
8. Fischer 1982, 131.
9. Lynch 1992.
10. Fleming and Baum 1986.
11. Cohen and Wills 1985.
12. Differences among types of friendship (best, close, casual) on scale scores on various social support measures were significant using MANOVA ($p < .001$, Pillai's test).
13. Wellman 1992.
14. Allan 1989, 109.
15. Allan 1989, 105.
16. Allan 1989, 108.
17. Allan 1989, 109.
18. Smith and Brown 1997.
19. Turner, Catania, and Gagnon 1994, 1547.
20. LeBlanc, London, and Aneshensel 1997.
21. Allen LeBlanc, in a personal communication (July 1997), helped me clarify these data.
22. Cf. Turner et al. 1994.
23. Turner et al. 1994, 1550.
24. Aristotle 1168b5.
25. Connell 1992, 744.
26. Murray 1992, 123.
27. Weston 1991.
28. Connell 1992, 745.
29. Weston 1991, 127.
30. Connell 1992, 746.
31. Connell 1992, 746.

32. Bech 1997, 116.

33. Aristotle 1165b2.

34. See Lazarsfeld and Merton 1954.

35. Fehr 1996.

36. Lazarsfeld and Merton 1954; Fehr 1996.

37. Fehr 1996.

38. Franklin 1992.

39. Franklin 1992, 212.

40. Fehr 1996.

41. Fehr 1996, 196.

42. Milardo 1986, 160.

43. Allan 1989, 108.

44. Fehr 1996.

45. Pogrebin 1987, 93, 94.

46. Out of all the ways respondents under the age of forty resolved major conflicts with a best friend, these men choose expressing emotions 38.5 percent of the time. The responses of those over forty with a best friend of longer than eleven years indicate that these men choose talking the problem out immediately 39.1 percent of the time.

47. Fehr 1996, 165.

48. Fehr 1996, 191.

49. Rubin 1985, 187.

50. Stueve and Gerson 1977, 90.

51. Stueve and Gerson 1977, 87.

52. Cohen 1992, 120; Reid and Fine 1992.

53. Rubin 1985, 117.

54. Rubin 1985, 120.

55. Rubin 1985, 128, 129.

56. Levine 1998, 102–3.

57. Bell 1981, 24.

58. Rubin 1985, 66.

59. Bell 1981, 26.

60. Fehr 1996, 199.

61. Pogrebin 1987, 104.

62. Monette 1992, 278.

63. Used with permission of John D'Emilio (personal communication, July 1997).

64. Levine 1992, 79.

65. From "1,112 and Counting" originally published in the March 14, 1983, issue of *New York Native* and reprinted in Kramer (1989, 49).

66. Kramer 1989, 218, 220.

Chapter Eight

1. Arendt 1968.

2. Friedman 1993; Little 1989; Jerome 1984.

3. Aristotle 1159b33, 1155a22.

4. Pakaluk 1994, 209.

5. Silver 1990, 1494.

6. Silver 1990, 1481, 1494, 1484

7. Thanks to Barry Adam (personal communication, January 1998) for these ideas and words.

8. Martin 1989, 182.

9. Connell 1992, 749.

10. Pakaluk 1994.

11. Weston 1991, 122.

12. Weeks 1995, 37.

13. Friedman 1993, 252.

14. Weston 1991, 124.

15. D'Emilio 1983, 58.

16. Friedman 1993, 245.

17. Fischer 1982.

18. Fischer 1982, 190.

19. Fischer 1982, 194.

20. Fischer 1982.

21. Murray 1996, 195.

22. Murray 1996.

23. Murray 1996, 218–19.

24. Plummer 1995, 82, 87.

25. Chauncey 1994, 271.

26. Chauncey 1994, 272.

27. Chauncey 1994, 278.

28. Chauncey 1994, 298.

29. Murray 1979, 171.

30. Friedman 1993, 219.

31. See Melucci 1989; Morris and Mueller 1992.

32. Adam 1995.

33. Adam 1995, 178.

34. Murray 1992, 36.

35. Murray 1996.

36. Kaase 1990, 98.

37. Chong 1991, 35.

38. From "We Can Be Together: How to Organize the Gay Community," originally published in the July 17, 1985, issue of *Long Island Connection* and reprinted in Kramer (1989, 91).

39. Kaase 1990, 98.

40. Friedman 1993, 248; Raymond 1986.

41. Achilles 1967.

42. D'Emilio 1983.

43. Gartner and Segura 1997.

44. D'Emilio 1983, 60.

45. Chong 1991.

46. Chong 1991, 232.

47. Chong 1991, 34–35.

48. Chong 1991, 35.

49. D'Emilio 1983, 66.

50. D'Emilio 1983, 67.

51. Pogrebin 1987, 134.

52. Data presented in chapter 5 show that the neighborhood is a much better place to meet casual friends than it is to meet close or best friends. See also Levine 1998.

53. Fleming and Baum 1986.

54. Bech 1997, 116.

55. Chauncey 1994, 136.

56. Chauncey 1994, 151.

57. Chauncey 1994, 156.

58. Chauncey 1994, 163.

59. Chauncey 1994, 163–64.

60. Levine 1979a. See Schneider (1997), Smith (1997), and Miller (1989) regarding small towns and gay and lesbian lives.

61. Kramer 1995, 211.

62. Suttles 1970.

63. Little 1989, 145.

64. From "The Social Triumph of the Sexual Will," an interview conducted in October 1981, originally published in the May 1982 issue of *Christopher Street* and reprinted in Foucault (1997, 160).

65. Little 1989, 154–55.

Appendix

1. Wright 1982.

2. Nardi and Sherrod 1994; Nardi 1992.

3. Haag and Chang 1997.

4. Respondents were asked to indicate their occupation, but not everyone responded in a similar way. Hence, some answers reflect more general areas of employment or job roles rather than specific occupations.

Achilles, Nancy. 1967. The development of the homosexual bar as an institution. In *Sexual Deviance,* edited by John Gagnon and William Simon, 228–44. New York: Harper and Row.

Adam, Barry D. 1995. *The Rise of a Gay and Lesbian Movement.* Rev.
ed. New York: Twayne.

Alexander, Christopher J. 1997. *Growth and Intimacy for Gay Men:
A Workbook.* Binghamton, NY: Harrington Park Press.

Allan, Graham. 1989. *Friendship: Developing a Sociological Perspective.*
Boulder, CO: Westview.

———. 1996. *Kinship and Friendship in Modern Britain.* Oxford: Oxford University Press.

Almaguer, Tomás. 1991. Chicano men: A cartography of homosexual
identity and behavior. *Differences: A Journal of Feminist Cultural
Studies* 3(2):75–100.

Altman, Dennis. 1982. *The Homosexualization of America.* New York:
St. Martin's Press.

Arendt, Hannah. 1968. *Men in Dark Times.* New York: Harcourt, Brace.

Aristotle. 1962. *Nicomachean Ethics.* Translated by Martin Ostwald. Indi-
anapolis, IN: Bobbs-Merrill.

Barnhart, Elizabeth. 1975. Friends and lovers in a lesbian counter-
culture community. In *Old Family/New Family,* edited by Nona
Glazer-Malbin, 90–115. New York: Van Nostrand.

Barth, John. 1966. *The Floating Opera.* New York: Avon.

Bech, Henning. 1997. *When Men Meet: Homosexuality and Modernity.*
Chicago: University of Chicago Press.

Bell, Alan P., and Martin S. Weinberg. 1978. *Homosexualities: A Study
of Diversity Among Men and Women.* New York: Simon and
Schuster.

Bell, Robert R. 1981. *Worlds of Friendship.* Beverly Hills, CA: Sage.

Bellah, Robert N., Richard Madsen, William M. Sullivan, Ann Swidler, and Steven T. Tipton. 1985. *Habits of the Heart.* Berkeley: University of California Press.

Berg, John H., and Margaret S. Clark. 1986. Differences in social exchange between intimate and other relationships: Gradually evolving or quickly apparent? In *Friendship and Social Interaction,* edited by Valerian J. Derlega and Barbara A. Winstead, 101–28. New York: Springer-Verlag.

Berger, Raymond M. 1982. *Gay and Gray: The Older Homosexual Man.* Boston: Alyson.

Bérubé, Allan. 1990. *Coming Out Under Fire: The History of Gay Men and Women in World War Two.* New York: Free Press.

Blieszner, Rosemary, and Rebecca G. Adams. 1992. *Adult Friendship.* Newbury Park, CA: Sage.

Bloom, Allan. 1993. *Love and Friendship.* New York: Simon and Schuster.

Blumstein, Philip, and Pepper Schwartz. 1983. *American Couples: Money, Work, Sex.* New York: Morrow.

Boswell, John. 1994. *Same-Sex Unions in Premodern Europe.* New York: Villard.

Brain, Robert. 1976. *Friends and Lovers.* New York: Basic Books.

Caldwell, Mayta A., and Letitia Anne Peplau. 1982. Sex differences in same-sex friendship. *Sex Roles* 8(7):721–32.

Carrier, Joseph. 1992. Miguel: Sexual life history of a gay Mexican American. In *Gay Culture in America,* edited by Gilbert Herdt, 202–24. Boston: Beacon.

Chambliss, William J. 1965. The selection of friends. *Social Forces* 43(3):370–80.

Chauncey, George. 1994. *Gay New York.* New York: Basic Books.

Chong, Dennis. 1991. *Collective Action and the Civil Rights Movement.* Chicago: University of Chicago Press.

Clunis, D. Merilee, and G. Dorsey Green. 1988. *Lesbian Couples: Creating Healthy Relationships for the 90s.* Seattle: Seal Press.

Cohen, Theodore F. 1992. Men's families, men's friends: A structural analysis of constraints on men's social ties. In *Men's Friendships,* edited by Peter M. Nardi, 115–31. Newbury Park, CA: Sage.

Cohen, Sheldon, William J. Doyle, David P. Skoner, Bruce S. Rabin, and Jack M. Gwaltney Jr. 1997. Social ties and susceptibility to the common cold. *Journal of the American Medical Association* 277(24): 1940–44.

Cohen, Sheldon, and T. A. Wills. 1985. Stress, social support, and the buffering hypothesis. *Psychological Bulletin* 98:310–57.

Connell, R. W. 1992. A very straight gay: Masculinity, homosexual experience, and the dynamics of gender. *American Sociological Review* 57:735–51.

———. 1995. *Masculinities*. Berkeley: University of California Press.

Cooper, John. 1980. Aristotle on friendship. In *Essays on Aristotle's Ethics,* edited by Amelie Oksenberg Rorty. Berkeley: University of California Press.

Crowley, Mart. 1968. *The Boys in the Band.* New York: Dell.

Davidson, L., and Duberman, L. 1982. Friendship: Communication and interactional patterns in same-sex dyads. *Sex Roles* 8:809–22.

D'Emilio, John. 1983. *Sexual Politics, Sexual Communities.* Chicago: University of Chicago Press.

D'Emilio, John, and Estelle Freedman. 1988. *Intimate Matters: A History of Sexuality in America.* New York: Harper & Row.

Diaz, Rafael Miguel. 1997. Latino gay men and the psycho-cultural barriers to AIDS prevention. In *In Changing Times: Gay Men and Lesbians Encounter HIV/AIDS,* edited by Martin P. Levine, Peter M. Nardi, and John H. Gagnon, 221–44. Chicago: University of Chicago Press.

DiLallo, Kevin, and Jack Krumholtz. 1994. *The Unofficial Gay Manual: Living the Lifestyle.* New York: Doubleday Main Street Books.

Driberg, J. H. 1935. The "best friend" among the Didinga. *Man* 35: 101–2.

Du Bois, Cora. 1974. The gratuitous act: An introduction to the comparative study of friendship patterns. In *The Compact: Selected Dimensions of Friendship,* edited by Elliott Leyton, 15–32. Newfoundland Social and Economic Papers No. 3, Institute of Social and Economic Research, Memorial University of Newfoundland.

Duck, Steven. 1973. *Personal Relationships and Personal Constructs: A Study of Friendship Formation.* London: John Wiley.

Duck, Steven, and Paul H. Wright. 1993. Reexamining gender differences in same-gender friendships: A close look at two kinds of data. *Sex Roles* 28:709–27.

Duneier, Mitchell. 1992. *Slim's Table: Race, Respectability, and Masculinity.* Chicago: University of Chicago Press.

Eisenstadt, S. N. 1974. Friendship and the structure of trust and solidarity in society. In *The Compact: Selected Dimensions of Friendship,* edited by Elliott Leyton, 138–45. Newfoundland Social and Economic Papers No. 3, Institute of Social and Economic Research, Memorial University of Newfoundland.

Enright, D. J., and David Rawlinson, eds. 1991. *The Oxford Book of Friendship.* New York: Oxford University Press.

Eskridge Jr., William N., and Nan D. Hunter. 1997. *Sexuality, Gender, and the Law.* Westbury, NY: Foundation Press.

Faderman, Lillian. 1981. *Surpassing the Love of Men: Romantic Friendship and Love Between Women from the Renaissance to the Present.* New York: Quill/William Morrow.

Fee, Dwight. 1996. Coming over: Friendship between straight and gay men. Ph.D. diss., Sociology Department, University of California, Santa Barbara.

Fehr, Beverley. 1996. *Friendship Processes.* Thousand Oaks, CA: Sage.

Feingold, Alan. 1988. Matching for attractiveness in romantic partners and same-sex friends: A meta-analysis and theoretical critique. *Psychological Bulletin* 104(2):226–35.

Fine, Gary Alan. 1986. Friendships in the work place. In *Friendship and Social Interaction,* edited by Valerian J. Derlega and Barbara A. Winstead, pp. 185–206. New York: Springer-Verlag.

Fischer, Claude S. 1982. *To Dwell Among Friends: Personal Networks in Town and City.* Chicago: University of Chicago Press.

Fischer, Claude S., Robert Max Jackson, C. Ann Stueve, Kathleen Gerson, Lynne McCallister Jones, with Mark Baldassare. 1977. *Networks and Places: Social Relations in the Urban Setting.* New York: Free Press.

Fleming, Raymond, and Andrew Baum. 1986. Social support and stress: The buffering effects of friendship. In *Friendship and Social Interaction,* edited by Valerian J. Derlega and Barbara A. Winstead, 207–26. New York: Springer-Verlag.

Foucault, Michel. 1997. *Ethics: Subjectivity and Truth. The Essential Works of Michel Foucault,* Vol. 1, edited by Paul Rabinow. New York: New Press.

Franklin, Clyde W. 1992. "Hey home—Yo, Bro": Friendship among black men. In *Men's Friendships,* edited by Peter M. Nardi, 201–14. Newbury Park, CA: Sage.

Friedman, Marilyn. 1993. *What Are Friends For? Feminist Perspectives on Personal Relationships and Moral Theory.* Ithaca, NY: Cornell University Press.

Gartner, Scott Sigmund, and Gary M. Segura. 1997. Appearances can be deceptive: Self-selection, social group identification, and political mobilization. *Rationality and Society* 9(2):131–61.

Giddens, Anthony. 1992. *The Transformation of Intimacy: Sexuality, Love & Eroticism in Modern Societies.* Stanford, CA: Stanford University Press.

Gilmore, David D. 1990. *Manhood in the Making: Cultural Concepts of Masculinity.* New Haven, CT: Yale University Press.

Gladwell, Malcolm. 1997. Listening to khakis. *The New Yorker,* July 28.

Goffman, Erving. 1959. *The Presentation of Self in Everyday Life.* New York: Doubleday.

Goldsby, Jackie. 1989. All about Yves. *Out/Look* 2:34–35.

Haag, Anthony, and Franklin Chang. 1997. The impact of electronic networking on the lesbian and gay community. *Journal of Gay and Lesbian Social Services* 7(3):83–94.

Hall, David, and Roger Ames. 1994. Confucian friendship: The road to religiousness. In *The Changing Face of Friendship,* edited by Leroy S. Rouner, 77–94. Notre Dame, IN: University of Notre Dame Press.

Hall, Marny. 1978. Lesbian families: Cultural and clinical issues. *Social Work* 23:380–85.

Halperin, David. 1990. *One Hundred Years of Homosexuality.* New York: Routledge.

Hammond, Dorothy, and Alta Jablow. 1987. Gilgamesh and the sundance kid: The myth of male friendship. In *The Making of Masculinities: The New Men's Studies,* edited by Harry Brod, 241–58. Boston: Allen & Unwin.

Hansen, Karen V. 1992. " 'Our eyes behold each other': Masculinity and intimate friendship in antebellum New England." In *Men's Friendships,* edited by Peter M. Nardi, 35–58. Newbury Park, CA: Sage.

Hassett, Chris, and Tom Owen-Towle. 1994. *Friendship Chronicles: Letters Between a Gay and a Straight Man.* San Diego: Bald Eagle Mountain Press.

Hawkeswood, William G. 1997. *One of the Children: Gay Black Men in Harlem.* Berkeley: University of California Press.

Hemphill, Essex, ed. 1991. *Brother to Brother: New Writings for Black Gay Men.* Boston: Alyson.

Herdt, Gilbert, and Andrew Boxer. 1996. *Children of Horizons.* Boston: Beacon.

Hess, Beth. 1972. Friendship. In *Aging and Society: A Sociology of Age Stratification.* Vol. 3, edited by Matilda Riley, Marilyn Johnson, and Anne Foner, 357–93. New York: Russell Sage Foundation.

Hoffman, Martin. 1968. *The Gay World.* New York: Basic Books.

Homer. 1951. *The Iliad.* Translated by Richard Lattimore. Chicago: University of Chicago Press.

Hooker, Evelyn. 1965. Male homosexuals and their worlds. In *Sexual Inversion,* edited by Judd Marmor, 83–107. New York: Basic Books.

Hunt, Mary E. 1994. Friends and family values: A new old song. In *The Changing Face of Friendship,* edited by Leroy S. Rouner, 169–82. Notre Dame, IN: University of Notre Dame Press.

Jackson, Robert Max. 1977. Social structure and process in friendship choice. In *Networks and Places: Social Relations in the Urban Setting,* by Claude S. Fischer et al., 59–78. New York: Free Press.

Jackson Robert Max, Claude S. Fischer, and Lynne McCallister Jones. 1977. The dimensions of social networks. In *Networks and Places: Social Relations in the Urban Setting,* by Claude S. Fischer et al., 39–58. New York: Free Press.

Jerome, Dorothy. 1984. Good company: The sociological implications of friendship. *Sociological Review* 32(4):696–718.

Kaase, Max. 1990. Social movements and political innovation. In *Challenging the Political Order: New Social and Political Movements in Western Democracies,* edited by Russell J. Dalton and Manfred Kuechler, 84–101. New York: Oxford University Press.

Katz, Jonathan Ned. 1983. *Gay American Almanac: A New Documentary.* New York: Harper Colophon.

———. 1992. *Gay American History: Lesbians and Gay Men in the U.S.A.* Rev. ed. New York: Meridian.

———. 1995. *The Invention of Heterosexuality.* New York: Dutton.

Kayal, Philip M. 1993. *Bearing Witness: Gay Men's Health Crisis and the Politics of AIDS.* Boulder, CO: Westview.

Kramer, Jerry Lee. 1995. Bachelor farmers and spinsters: Gay and lesbian identities and communities in rural North Dakota. In *Mapping Desire: Geographies of Sexualities,* edited by David Bell and Gill Valentine, 200–13. London: Routledge.

Kramer, Larry. 1989. *Reports from the Holocaust: The Making of an AIDS Activist.* New York: Penguin.

Lazarsfeld, Paul F., and Robert K. Merton. 1954. Friendship as social process: A substantive and methodological analysis. In *Freedom and Control in Modern Society,* edited by Morroe Berger, Theodore Abel, and Charles H. Page, 18–66. New York: Van Nostrand.

LeBlanc, Allen J., Andrew S. London, and Carol S. Aneshensel. 1997. The physical costs of AIDS caregiving. *Social Science and Medicine* 45(6):915–23.

Lee, John Alan. 1976. Forbidden colors of love: Patterns of gay love and gay liberation. *Journal of Homosexuality* 1:401–17.

Levine, Martin P. 1979a. Gay ghetto. In *Gay Men: The Sociology of Male Homosexuality,* edited by Martin P. Levine, 182–204. New York: Harper & Row.

———. 1979b. Employment discrimination against gay men. *International Review of Modern Sociology* 9:151–63.

————. 1992. The life and death of gay clones. In *Gay Culture in America*, edited by Gilbert Herdt, 68–86. Boston: Beacon.

————. 1998. *Gay Macho: The Life and Death of the Homosexual Clone*. New York: New York University Press.

Leyton, Elliott, ed. 1974. *The Compact: Selected Dimensions of Friendship*. Newfoundland Social and Economic Papers No. 3, Institute of Social and Economic Research, Memorial University of Newfoundland.

Leznoff, Maurice, and William A. Westley. 1956. The homosexual community. *Social Problems* 3:257–63.

Lindsey, Karen. 1981. *Friends as Family*. Boston: Beacon.

Little, Graham. 1989. Freud, friendship, and politics. In *The Dialectics of Friendship*, edited by Roy Porter and Sylvana Tomaselli, 143–158. London: Routledge.

Lynch, Frederick R. 1992. Nonghetto gays: An ethnography of suburban gays. In *Gay Culture in America*, edited by Gilbert Herdt, 165–201. Boston: Beacon.

Malone, John. 1980. *Straight Women/Gay Men: A Special Relationship*. New York: Dial.

Martin, Robert K. 1989. Knights-errant and gothic seducers: The representation of male friendship in mid-nineteenth-century America. In *Hidden From History: Reclaiming the Gay and Lesbian Past*, edited by Martin Duberman, Martha Vicinus, and George Chauncey, 169–82. New York: Meridian.

McWhirter, David, and Andrew Mattison. 1984. *The Male Couple*. Englewood Cliffs, NJ: Prentice-Hall.

McWilliams, Susan, and Judith A. Howard. 1993. Solidarity and hierarchy in cross-sex friendships. *Journal of Social Issues* 49(3):191–202.

Meilaender, Gilbert. 1994. When Harry and Sally read the Nicomachean Ethics: Friendship between men and women. In *The Changing Face of Friendship*, edited by Leroy S. Rouner, 183–96. Notre Dame, IN: University of Notre Dame Press.

Melucci, Alberto. 1989. *Nomads of the Present*. Philadelphia: Temple University Press.

Messner, Michael. 1992. *Power at Play: Sports and the Problem of Masculinity*. Boston: Beacon.

Mieli, Mario. 1977. *Homosexuality & Liberation: Elements of a Gay Critique*. London: Gay Men's Press.

Miell, Dorothy, and Andy Duck. 1986. Strategies in developing friendships. In *Friendship and Social Interaction*, edited by Valerian J. Derlega and Barbara A. Winstead, 129–43. New York: Springer-Verlag.

Milardo, Robert M. 1986. Personal choice and social constraint in close relationships: Applications of network analysis. In *Friendship and Social Interaction,* edited by Valerian J. Derlega and Barbara A. Winstead, 145–66. New York: Springer-Verlag.

Miles, Sara, and Eric Rofes, eds. 1998. *Opposite Sex: Gay Men on Lesbians, Lesbians on Gay Men.* New York: New York University Press.

Miller, Neil. 1989. *In Search of Gay America.* New York: Harper & Row.

Monette, Paul. 1992. *Becoming a Man: Half a Life Story.* New York: Harcourt Brace Jovanovich.

Moon, Dawne. 1995. Insult and inclusion: The term *fag hag* and gay male "community." *Social Forces* 74(2):487–510.

Mordden, Ethan. 1986. *Buddies.* New York: St. Martin's Press.

Morris, Aldon, and Carol McClurg Mueller, eds. 1992. *Frontiers in Social Movement Theory.* New Haven, CT: Yale University Press.

Murray, Stephen O. 1979. Institutional elaboration of a quasi-ethnic community. *International Review of Modern Sociology* 9:165–77.

———. 1992. Components of gay community in San Francisco. In *Gay Culture in America,* edited by Gilbert Herdt, 107–46. Boston: Beacon.

———. 1996. *American Gay.* Chicago: University of Chicago Press.

Nahas, Rebecca, and Myra Turley. 1979. *The New Couple: Women and Gay Men.* New York: Seaview.

Nardi, Peter M. 1982. Alcohol treatment and the non-traditional family structures of gays and lesbians. *Journal of Alcohol and Drug Education* 27: 83–89.

———. 1990. AIDS and obituaries: The perpetuation of stigma in the press. In *Culture and AIDS,* edited by Douglas Feldman, 159–68. New York: Praeger.

———. 1992a. Sex, friendship, and gender roles among gay men. In *Men's Friendships,* edited by Peter M. Nardi, 173–85, Newbury Park, CA: Sage.

———. 1992b. That's what friends are for: Friends as family in the gay and lesbian community. In *Modern Homosexualities: Fragments of Lesbian and Gay Experience,* edited by Ken Plummer, 108–120. London: Routledge.

———. 1997. Friends, lovers, and families: The impact of AIDS on gay and lesbian relationships. In *In Changing Times: Gay Men and Lesbians Encounter HIV/AIDS,* edited by Martin P. Levine, Peter M. Nardi, and John H. Gagnon, 55–82. Chicago: University of Chicago Press.

Nardi, Peter M., and Drury Sherrod. 1990. That's what friends are for: The results. *Out/Look* 8:86.

———. 1994. Friendship in the lives of gay men and lesbians. *Journal of Social and Personal Relationships* 11:185–99.

Nestle, Joan, and John Preston, eds. 1994. *Sister & Brother: Lesbians & Gay Men Write About Their Lives Together.* New York: HarperSanFrancisco.

Nonas, Elisabeth. 1992. All in the family. *The Advocate,* August 13, 49–52.

O'Meara, J. Donald. 1989. Cross-sex friendship: Four basic challenges of an ignored relationship. *Sex Roles* 21:525–43.

Paine, Robert. 1974a. Reprint. An exploratory analysis in "middle-class" culture. In *The Compact: Selected Dimensions of Friendship* edited by Elliot Leyton, 117–37. Newfoundland Social and Economic Papers No. 3, Institute of Social and Economic Research, Memorial University of Newfoundland. Originally published in 1969 in *Man* 4(4):505–24.

———. 1974b. Anthropological approaches to friendship. In *The Compact: Selected Dimensions of Friendship,* edited by Elliot Leyton, 1–14. Newfoundland Social and Economic Papers No. 3, Institute of Social and Economic Research, Memorial University of Newfoundland.

Pakaluk, Michael. 1994. Political friendship. In *The Changing Face of Friendship,* edited by Leroy S. Rouner, 197–213. Notre Dame, IN: University of Notre Dame Press.

Parekh, Bhikhu. 1994. An Indian view of friendship. In *The Changing Face of Friendship,* edited by Leroy S. Rounder, 95–113. Notre Dame, IN: University of Notre Dame Press.

Pleck, Joseph H., Freya L. Sonenstein, and Leighton C. Ku. 1993. Masculinity ideology: Its impact on adolescent males' heterosexual relationships. *Journal of Social Issues* 49(3):11–29.

Plummer, Ken. 1995. *Telling Sexual Stories: Power, Change and Social Worlds.* London: Routledge.

Pogrebin, Letty Cottin. 1987. *Among Friends.* New York: McGraw-Hill.

Prieur, Annick. 1998. *Mema's House, Mexico City.* Chicago: University of Chicago Press.

Rawlins, William K. 1992. *Friendship Matters: Communication, Dialectics, and the Life Course.* New York: Aldine de Gruyter.

Raymond, Janice. 1986. *A Passion for Friends.* Boston: Beacon.

Reid, Helen M., and Gary Alan Fine. 1992. Self-disclosure in men's friendships: Variations associated with intimate relations. In *Men's Friendships,* edited by Peter M. Nardi, 132–52. Newbury Park, CA: Sage.

Reisman, John M. 1979. *Anatomy of Friendship*. New York: Irvington Publishers.

Richards, Jeffrey. 1987. "Passing the love of women": Manly love and Victorian society. In *Manliness and Morality: Middle-Class Masculinity in Britain and America, 1800–1940,* edited by J. A. Mangan and James Walvin, 92–122. Manchester, England: Manchester University Press.

Rist, Darrell Yates. 1992. *Heartlands: A Gay Man's Odyssey Across America*. New York: Plume.

Rocke, Michael. 1996. *Forbidden Friendships*. New York: Oxford University Press.

Rodgers, Bruce. 1972. *Gay Talk [The Queens' Vernacular]*. New York: Paragon.

Rose, Suzanna. 1985. Same- and cross-sex friendships and the psychology of homosexuality. *Sex Roles* 12:63–74.

Rose, Suzanna, and F. C. Serafica. 1986. Keeping and ending casual, close, and best friendships. *Journal of Social and Personal Relationships* 3:275–88.

Rotello, Gabriel. 1997. *Sexual Ecology: AIDS and the Destiny of Gay Men*. New York: Dutton.

Rotundo, E. Anthony. 1993. *American Manhood: Transformations in Masculinity from the Revolution to the Modern Era*. New York: Basic Books.

Rubin, Lillian. 1985. *Just Friends*. New York: Harper & Row.

Saghir, Marcel T., and Eli Robins. 1973. *Male and Female Homosexuality*. Baltimore: Williams and Wilkins.

Sapadin, Linda. 1988. Friendship and gender: Perspectives of professional men and women. *Journal of Social and Personal Relationships* 5(4):387–403.

Schneider, Beth E. 1987. Coming out at work. *Work and Occupations* 13:463–87.

———. 1997. Owning an epidemic: The impact of AIDS on small-city lesbian and gay communities. In *In Changing Times: Gay Men and Lesbians Encounter HIV/AIDS,* edited by Martin P. Levine, Peter M. Nardi, and John H. Gagnon, 145–69. Chicago: University of Chicago Press.

Schneider, Beth E., and Nancy E. Stoller, eds. 1995. *Women Resisting AIDS: Feminist Strategies of Empowerment*. Philadelphia: Temple University Press.

Schollmeier, Paul. 1994. *Other Selves: Aristotle on Personal and Political Friendship*. Albany, NY: SUNY Press.

Schwartz, Ronald D. 1974. The crowd: Friendship groups in a Newfoundland outport. In *The Compact: Selected Dimensions of Friendship,* edited by Elliott Leyton, 71–92. Newfoundland Social and Economic Papers No. 3, Institute of Social and Economic Research, Memorial University of Newfoundland.

Schwarzenbach, Sibyl A. 1996. On civic friendship. *Ethics* 107:97–128.

Schwimmer, Erik. P. 1974. Friendship and kinship: An attempt to relate two anthropological concepts. In *The Compact: Selected Dimensions of Friendship,* edited by Elliott Leyton, 49–70. Newfoundland Social and Economic Papers No. 3, Institute of Social and Economic Research, Memorial University of Newfoundland.

Seiden, Anne, and Pauline Bart. 1975. Woman to woman: Is sisterhood powerful? In *Old Family/New Family,* edited by Nona Glazer-Malbin, 189–228. New York: Van Nostrand.

Selden, Elizabeth, ed. 1947. *The Book of Friendship: An International Anthology.* Boston: Houghton Mifflin.

Shernoff, Michael. 1984. Family therapy for lesbian and gay clients. *Social Work* 29:393–96.

Sherrod, Drury. 1987. The bonds of men: Problems and possibilities in close male relationships. In *The Making of Masculinities: The New Men's Studies,* edited by Harry Brod, 213–40. Boston: Allen & Unwin.

———. 1989. The influence of gender on same-sex friendships. In *Close Relationships,* edited by Clyde Hendrick, 164–86. Newbury Park, CA: Sage.

Signorile, Michelangelo. 1997. *Life Outside: The Signorile Report on Gay Men.* New York: HarperCollins.

Silver, Allan. 1990. Friendship in commercial society: Eighteenth-Century social theory and modern sociology. *American Journal of Sociology* 95(6):1474–1504.

Smith, James Donald. 1997. Working with larger systems: Rural lesbians and gays. *Journal of Gay & Lesbian Social Services* 7(3):13–21.

Smith, Richard B., and Robert A. Brown. 1997. The impact of social support on gay male couples. *Journal of Homosexuality* 33(2):39–61.

Sonenschein, David. 1968. The ethnography of male homosexual relationships. *Journal of Sex Research* 4:69–83.

Stein, Terry. 1988. Homosexuality and new family forms: Issues in psychotherapy. *Psychiatric Annals* 18:12–20.

Stern-Gillet, Suzanne. 1995. *Aristotle's Philosophy of Friendship.* Albany, NY: SUNY Press.

Stoller, Nancy E. 1997. From feminism to polymorphous activism: Lesbians in AIDS organizations. In *In Changing Times: Gay Men and Lesbians Encounter HIV/AIDS,* edited by Martin P. Levine, Peter

M. Nardi, and John H. Gagnon, 171–90. Chicago: University of Chicago Press.

Stueve, C. Ann, and Kathleen Gerson. 1977. Personal relations across the life-cycle. In *Networks and Places: Social Relations in the Urban Setting*, by Claude S. Fischer et al., 79–98. New York: Free Press.

Suttles, Gerald. 1970. Friendship as a social institution. In *Social Relationships*, edited by George McCall, Michael McCall, Norman Denzin, Gerald Suttles, and Suzanne Kurth, 95–135. Chicago: Aldine.

Swain, Scott O. 1992. Men's friendship with women: Intimacy, sexual boundaries, and the informant role. In *Men's Friendships*, edited by Peter M. Nardi, 153–171. Newbury Park, CA: Sage.

Taylor, Ella. 1989. *Prime Time Families*. Berkeley: University of California Press.

Tiger, Lionel. 1974. Sex-specific friendship. In *The Compact: Selected Dimensions of Friendship*, edited by Elliott Leyton, 42–48. Newfoundland Social and Economic Papers No. 3, Institute of Social and Economic Research, Memorial University of Newfoundland.

Turner, Heather A., Joseph A. Catania, and John Gagnon. 1994. The prevalence of informal caregiving to persons with AIDS in the United States: Caregiver characteristics and their implications. *Social Science and Medicine* 38(11):1543–52.

Walker, Karen. 1994a. Men, women, and friendship: What they say, what they do. *Gender & Society* 8(2):246–65.

———. 1994b. "I'm not friends the way she's friends": Ideological and behavioral constructions of masculinity in men's friendships. *Masculinities* 2(2):38–55.

Warren, Carol A. B. 1974. *Identity and Community in the Gay World*. New York: Wiley.

Weeks, Jeffrey. 1995. *Invented Moralities: Sexual Values in an Age of Uncertainty*. New York: Columbia University Press.

Weinberg, Martin S., and Colin J. Williams. 1974. *Male Homosexuals: Their Problems and Adaptations*. New York: Oxford University Press.

Weinstock, Jacqueline S., and Esther D. Rothblum, eds. 1996. *Lesbian Friendships: For Ourselves and Each Other*. New York: New York University Press.

Wellman, Barry. 1992. Men in networks: Private communities, domestic friendships. In *Men's Friendships*, edited by Peter M. Nardi, 74–114. Newbury Park, CA: Sage.

Welty, Eudora, and Ronald A. Sharp, eds. 1991. *The Norton Book of Friendship*. New York: Norton.

Weston, Kath. 1991. *Families We Choose: Lesbians, Gays, Kinship*. New York: Columbia University Press.

White, Edmund. 1980. *States of Desire: Travels in Gay America.* New York: Dutton.

———. 1994. *The Burning Library.* New York: Knopf.

Whitney, Catherine. 1990. *Uncommon Lives: Gay Men and Straight Women.* New York: Plume.

Whitman, Walt. 1900. *Leaves of Grass.* Philadelphia: David McKay.

Winstead, Barbara. 1986. Sex differences in same-sex friendships. In *Friendship and Social Interaction,* edited by Valerian J. Derlega and Barbara A. Winstead, 81–99. New York: Springer-Verlag.

Wolff, Kurt, ed. 1950. *The Sociology of Georg Simmel.* New York: Free Press.

Woods, James D. 1993. *The Corporate Closet: The Professional Lives of Gay Men in America.* New York: Free Press.

Wright, Paul. 1982. Men's friendships, women's friendships, and the alleged inferiority of the latter. *Sex Roles* 8(1):1–20.

246 Index

of friends, 111–13; major and
minor conflicts between respondent and best friend,
177–79; not spending more
time with best friends, 134–
35; profile of close and casual
friends, 108; profiles of best
friends and best gay male
friends, 107; research methodology, 207–13; sexual at-
traction to friends, 81–85; sexual orientation of best friends,
107; sources of female friends,
116–17; topics of discussion
with friends, 144–49
Suttles, Gerald, 204
Swain, Scott, 77

Tiger, Lionel, 38
Tim (respondent): definition of a
friend, 136–37; on having sex
with friend, 90
Trumbull, Henry Clay, 28
Trust, in development and maintenance of friendship, 148

Vince (respondent): definition of
a friend, 137; ending a friendship, 179; on fuck buddy as
friend, 92; spending holiday
time, 72; on time for friends,
134
von Kupffer, Elisàr, 28

Walker, Karen, 42
Warren, Carol, 18–19, 53
Weeks, Jeffrey, 192
Weinberg, Martin, 18, 109
Wellman, Barry, 41
Weston, Kath, 20, 53, 60–61, 65,
78, 166, 191–92
White, Edmund, 17, 74, 114
Whitman, Walt, 28, 206
Wilde, Oscar, 114
Will (respondent): disagreement
with straight woman friend,
176; discussions with close
friends, 146; on friends separate from family, 66; on gay
men as friends, 109; on loss of
a friendship, 153; need to
maintain some distance from
friends, 160–61; reason for
ending of a friendship, 182; relations of couples with single
people, 183
Williams, Colin, 18
Wills, T. A., 157, 159
Wilson, Pete, 201
Winthrop, Theodore, 28
Woods, James, 56
Workplace: friends as family in,
54–56; friends in, 104; gay
men in, 55–56; meeting people and developing friendships
in, 45, 55, 111; as source of
friends for gay men, 112–13